Enduring Modernity

This book brings together the work of the late Anders Petersen, presenting his exciting and innovative transdisciplinary paradigm that offers insights into anxiety, depression and grief, and the connection between these conditions and the failings of contemporary civilization that give rise to them. With attention to the ways in which neoliberal hegemony and its imperatives of 'performance', 'evaluation', 'self-realisation', 'resilience' and 'flexibility' lead to self-criticism on the part of those who do not measure up to the prevailing criteria, resulting in ailments of mental health, it challenges the paradigmatic diagnosis of such conditions in terms of individual diseases or neurological malfunctions, to be treated by medication and training in order to return the individual to work and life 'as normal'. An examination of the wrong-headed approach to what Petersen analysed as contemporary social pathologies, *Enduring Modernity: Depression, Anxiety and Grief in the Age of Voicelessness* will appeal to scholars of sociology and social theory, seeking new understandings aimed at emancipation from social suffering.

Anders Petersen was Associate Professor of Sociology at Aalborg University, Denmark, and former President of the Danish Sociological Association.

Bert van den Bergh teaches cultural philosophy in the Department of European Studies at The Hague University of Applied Sciences, The Netherlands.

Sabine Flick is Professor of Sociology at the Institute of Sociology at the University of Education, Freiburg, Germany.

Kieran Keohane is Professor in the Department of Sociology and Criminology and the School of Society, Politics and Ethics at University College Cork, Ireland.

Domonkos Sik is Associate Professor of Sociology at the Eötvös Lorand University, Budapest, Hungary.

The Social Pathologies of Contemporary Civilization
Series editors
Bert van den Bergh, Sabine Flick, Kieran Keohane, and Domonkos Sik

Breaking decisively with the often ideological and moralistic approach of treating problems of health and well-being as discrete and individual problems to be addressed in isolation both from one another and their broader social contexts, this series pursues the investigation of the ways in which contemporary malaises, diseases, illnesses and psychosomatic syndromes are related to cultural pathologies of the social body and disorders of the collective ésprit de corps of contemporary society.

It avoids reductive psychological and biomedical understandings of pathologies – including depression, stress-related illnesses, eating disorders, suicide and deliberate self-harm – to focus instead on the socio-cultural contexts in which they occur, examining the radical changes to social structures and institutions, and the deep crises in our civilization as a whole to which such conditions are connected.

The Social Pathologies of Contemporary Civilization thus welcomes manuscripts from a broad range of disciplinary perspectives across the humanities and social sciences – sociology, philosophy, psychology, anthropology, politics, economics and cultural studies, as well as from the fields of medicine social care, therapeutic practice and the healing arts – that explore the fruitfulness locating health and well-being not simply in the individual body or soul, but within a trans-disciplinary imagination that takes into account the integral human person's situatedness within collective social bodies, particular communities, entire societies, or even whole civilizations.

Titles in the series

Late Modern Subjectivity and its Discontents: Anxiety, Depression and Alzheimer's Disease
Kieran Keohane, Anders Petersen, Bert van den Bergh

States of Intoxication: The Place of Alcohol in Civilisation
John O'Brien

Healing Rites of Passage: Salutogenesis in Serious Fun Camps
Peter Kearney

Empty Suffering
A Social Phenomenology of Depression, Anxiety and Addiction
Domonkos Sik

Enduring Modernity
Depression, Anxiety and Grief in the Age of Voicelessness
Edited by Bert van den Bergh, Sabine Flick, Kieran Keohane, Domonkos Sik

For more information about this series, please visit: https://www.routledge.com/The-Social-Pathologies-of-Contemporary-Civilization/book-series/ASHSER1434

Enduring Modernity

Depression, Anxiety and Grief in the Age of Voicelessness

Anders Petersen

Edited by
Bert van den Bergh, Sabine Flick, Kieran Keohane, and Domonkos Sik

Routledge
Taylor & Francis Group
LONDON AND NEW YORK

First published 2025
by Routledge
4 Park Square, Milton Park, Abingdon, Oxon OX14 4RN

and by Routledge
605 Third Avenue, New York, NY 10158

Routledge is an imprint of the Taylor & Francis Group, an informa business

British Library Cataloguing-in-Publication Data
A catalogue record for this book is available from the British Library

ISBN: 9781032661001 (hbk)
ISBN: 9781032714387 (pbk)
ISBN: 9781032714356 (ebk)

DOI: 10.4324/9781032714356

Typeset in Times New Roman
by codeMantra

Contents

Acknowledgement

We would like to thank Carmen Kuhling, Søren Christian Krogh, Svend Brinkmann and Michael Hviid Jacobsen for their contribution to this book.

Also we would like to thank the publishers for letting us reuse Anders Petersen's text.

Anders Petersen – his life and memory

Anders Petersen (born July 30, 1973 in Silkeborg, Denmark, died May 20, 2022) was a Danish sociologist and associate professor at Aalborg University. In his research, he has examined the challenges and paradoxes of late modern existence. He contributed to the debates on social suffering, performance society and diagnostic culture, in both the academic and the public spheres. Anders ended his life at the age of 48. We miss our dear friend and inspired colleague badly. This volume is a first step in our endeavour to continue sharing the work that he so brilliantly and uniquely undertook.

The original publication of the chapters

Chapter 3. *International Sociology* 26 (1), 5–24. 2011.

Chapter 4. Kieran Keohane, Anders Petersen, Bert van den Bergh (eds.): *Late Modern Subjectivity and Its Discontents* (Routledge 2017), pp. 24–40.

Chapter 5. Nicholas Hill, Svend Brinkmann, Anders Petersen (eds.): *Critical Happiness Studies* (Routledge 2020), pp. 35–48.

Chapter 6. Michael Hviid Jacobsen (ed.): *Emotions in Culture and Everyday Life: Conceptual, Theoretical and Empirical Explorations* (Routledge 2023), pp. 116–132.

Chapter 8. *Distinktion: Scandinavian Journal of Social Theory*, 12:3, (2011): 343–362.

Chapter 9. *The Social Pathologies of Contemporary Civilization* (Routledge 2013), pp. 175–193.

Chapter 11. Michael Hviid Jacobsen (ed.): *Emotions, Everyday Life and Sociology* (Routledge 2018), pp. 191–209.

Chapter 12. Michael Hviid Jacobsen, Anders Petersen (eds.): *Exploring Grief: Towards a Sociology of Sorrow* (Routledge 2019), pp. 205–224.

Notes on Contributors

Svend Brinkmann is Professor of Psychology at the Department of Communication and Psychology, Aalborg University, Denmark.

Michael Hviid Jacobsen is Professor of Sociology at the Department of Sociology and Social Work, Aalborg University, Denmark.

Søren Christian Krogh is a Postdoctoral Researcher at Centre for Youth Studies, Aalborg University, Denmark.

Carmen Kuhling is a Sociologist at the University of Limerick, and a Psychotherapist.

Rasmus Willig is former Associate Professor of Sociology at the Department of Social Sciences and Business Economics, Roskilde University, Denmark, and presently is Representative of Andelsgaarde and Principal of Suhrs Højskole in Copenhagen, Denmark.

1 Introduction

The work of Anders Petersen

Bert van den Bergh, Sabine Flick, Kieran Keohane and Domonkos Sik

Anders Petersen's model, and Anders Petersen as a model

Walter Benjamin tells us that you can learn a lot about a person from the books that they have on their shelves. Visiting Anders Petersen's office at Aalborg University and browsing through his bookshelves while Anders went out to teach a class or to talk with a student, for whom Anders was first and foremost an inspirational and generous teacher, we see that most of the books lining Anders bookshelves were in Danish, naturally, and the titles were enigmatic and tantalizing. But many of the books were in English, and scanning forwards and backwards over Anders' shelves, feeling out for common ground and a shared horizon of ideas, somewhere between Adorno and Weber, Honneth and Sennett, above the bookshelves, overlooking Anders' desk, hung a large poster-portrait of the craggy, lived-in face of the Canadian philosopher Charles Taylor.

Charles Taylor was one of Anders' first and most important models. Taylor's (1989) *Sources of the Self* and *The Malaise of* Modernity (1991) had been two of the books that set Anders off on his path. To the modern subject the quest for personal, individual, authentic self-realization is a moral imperative. This imperative is amplified and intensified, and at the same time made all the more difficult and ever more elusive under conditions of late modernity and neoliberalism. This problem describes the field and the focus of Anders' work. We talked about *A Secular Age* (2007) and we shared the view that the book was Taylor's working over again, all over again, the same questions and issues that he'd addressed in the earlier books; and we felt that Taylor's big book was a little bit disappointing, in so far as while it raised and worked over the same questions, deepening and elaborating the themes, ultimately Taylor seemed to hold out on us, because in so far as he promised answers, they were at the level of a Deist theological horizon, whereas Anders [and we too] identified first and foremost as a secular Sociologist. And yet perhaps more than anyone else on his bookshelf, Charles Taylor had gripped Anders Petersen's sociological imagination.

"Charles Taylor asks the fundamental questions", Anders said. The deep questions Charles Taylor asks and the elusive answers that he seeks are the eternal questions concerning the meaning of life, and in relation to how we settle on the meaningfulness [or otherwise] of life, how do we live a good life? This was an

DOI: 10.4324/9781032714356-1

intellectual, and also a personal, existential practical and professional question for Anders Petersen, as all of those who knew him and worked with him and who find themselves within the covers of this book, and outside of it too, will attest. What one learns from a model, René Girard (1976) tells us, is what the model desires. This is complicated in the case of Charles Taylor as a model for Anders Petersen, because Charles Taylor's deep Roman Catholicism are the grounds from which his questions emerge, and the eschatological horizons where Charles Taylor seems to suggest that answers are to be found. All very alien to Anders Petersen's modern Danish secular-Lutheran rational sensibilities. But if what one learns from the model is what the model desires, one learns thereby what is desirable. Even if Charles Taylor's answers to the fundamental questions were ultimately disagreeable to him, Anders Petersen learned from Taylor's desire for their asking, and for their answering. And Anders Petersen learned from Taylor's desire that his belief be true – desire for faith; and, as a corollary, that faith would be rewarded: that the world would be saved. Anders Petersen's 'sociological faith' was that secular-rational sociology would disclose truths that would help to save us from the social pathologies of contemporary civilization.

Of course, such faith in emancipatory critical social sciences is inherently ambivalent. Unlike in the case of religion providing transcendental narratives of consolation, one can never be sure if there is a solution to pathologies like alienation, anomie or loss of meaning. As there is no secular framing that could restore the meaninglessness of these sufferings, the only way out is the transformation of the responsible distorted structures. However, it is hard to see hopeful tendencies in the contemporary era: the decades-long tendency of the 'exhaustion of utopic energies' (Habermas, 1986) does not seem to turn around. That is what transforms the role of a critical sociologist in late modernity into a burdensome existential challenge.

Anders Petersen was aware of this challenge. He learned from Charles Taylor, and so in turn Anders Petersen not only teaches us the right questions to ask but also shows us a method for answering those questions; a method distilled from ideas that have influenced the model, the model's models. Charles Taylor's models are numerous and various, ranging from Classical and Continental philosophers, from the Greeks, through Augustine, through Enlightenment rationalism, Romanticism, modernism, phenomenology, hermeneutics and philosophical anthropology; and Anders Petersen emulated Charles Taylor's method of cosmopolitan, transdisciplinary scholarship, folding in a rich mix of ideas from contemporary sociology, psychology and cultural analysis. But above all, the red thread that Anders Petersen followed into the Labyrinth was Charles Taylor's model, G.W.F. Hegel and Hegel's dialectical method.

Charles Taylor's and Anders Petersen's work on the human condition is situated in dialectical tension between metaphysics and phenomenology, mediated and manifested in the Hegelian struggle for recognition, and, more specifically, the irony and paradox of the dialectic – that the very thing that is at the heart of Enlightenment and Modernity, individual self-consciousness and the historical realization of *Geist*, achieved only by 'subjecting oneself to the infinity of the difference' in struggles for recognition with equal and opposite self-consciousnesses. But authentic self-realization as a secular religion in the service of realization of *Geist*, under conditions of social acceleration and de-symbolization, is at risk of degenerating, corrupting and becoming the very antithesis – the dialectical opposite inversion of what was initially posited: the promise of Enlightenment unfolds in new forms of tyranny and darkness so that, as in the words of Adorno and Horkheimer, "the fully enlightened earth radiates disaster triumphant" (1979: 3). In Charles Taylor's and Anders Petersen's dialectical diagnoses of 'the malaise of modernity' or 'social pathologies of contemporary civilization', respectively, centres on the paradox that the individual's quest for authentic self-realization, attenuated and appropriated, amplified and intensified under conditions of late modernity and neoliberalism, became the principle of the individual's self-destruction, even in the very name of authentic self-realization, so that, in Taylor's words, "the highest spiritual ideals threaten to lay the most crushing burdens on mankind" (Taylor, 1989: 519). Anders Petersen was a sociologist of that crushing burden.

When we read Anders Petersen's critical diagnostics of the social pathologies of contemporary civilization, we may feel the same burden that Anders felt, the burden that all modern people carry, the burden of individual authentic self-realization – the burden of responsibility for living [perhaps we should say what passes today for living?] a good life, while the horizons of meaningfulness within which such a life can be lived disintegrate and dissolve by processes of social acceleration and de-symbolization. But while reading these penetrating and illuminating diagnostic essays of the malaises of our time, we should in them read and redeem Anders Petersen's elective affinity with his model, Charles Taylor – a strange and unlikely affinity for sure, between Charles Taylor's avowed Catholic deism and Anders Petersen's commitments to authentic self-realization within an avowedly modern rational secularism; antitheses mediated by a Hegelian dialectical imagination that they both share.

In Anders Petersen's analyses, under the auspices of the neoliberal revolution, every turning towards the light becomes an ever more refined, ever more exquisite turning of the screw: psychoanalysis' emancipatory reflexive journey of self-discovery is eclipsed by reductive bio-psychiatric neuro-chemical diagnostics; humanistic psychotherapeutic dialogical empathic understanding is de-sublimated into commodified self-help guides and technologies of subjection; the pursuit of happiness is appropriated and assimilated as ideology and affirmative culture. Through his systematic and subtle studies of the deleterious, disorienting and depressing cascade effects of how the principles and processes of neoliberalism ramify into every corner of lives and our minds, Anders Petersen [perhaps too much] came to share Adorno's pessimism – that Enlightenment had given way to a negative dialectics, so much so that when times are as wrong as they are becoming, it becomes impossible to live a right life; a good life could no longer be lived.

But Anders Petersen's work is always dialectical. He is constantly seeking to build towards and find syntheses between the philosophical discourses of late modernity and grounded empirical social research. Anders relates to the Taylorian project in a negative dialectical way. Unlike Taylor (and Kierkegaard), Petersen cannot resolve the modern challenge of authenticity by (re)turning to God. However, he would not submit and submerge in a defeatist, nihilistic conclusion, so he steps out from the philosophical realm to the empirical-historical-sociological world and seeks the traces of actors navigating between impossible faith and devastating negative dialectics. However, what Anders found there was also problematic – to say the least! At this point, it is difficult to imagine further directions, yet Anders Petersen tried valiantly to do so.

The dialectical imagination is clearly evident in all of Anders Petersen's work, whether demonstrated in historical-genealogical synoptic-synthetic reviews of the existing literature, in sociology, history, psychology, literature and cultural anthropology (the masterful, rich review of 'grief' for example); or in new and original empirical research projects (for instance the focus group study with kindergarten teachers on their experiences of institutional pressures for 'flexibilization', where first hand data is analysed, formulated and worked up in terms of Axel Honneth's theory of recognition). In these, and in all of Anders Petersen's work, he shows us how mapping historical and empirical observations onto classical and contemporary sociological theories, always with an eye to bringing the background philosophical discourse into the foreground, and always seeking out and finding syntheses between ideas, theories and practices, and explicating their implications and applications for transformative praxes, whether in social work, pedagogy or psychology. The reconciliation of both general dialectical principles – thesis and antithesis, reason and imagination, objective facts and subjective meanings is the Hegelian synthesis that Anders Petersen's model of excellent scholarship constantly strives for, and achieves. Anders Petersen is an excellent model of sociological reason – working with both sides – deductive reason and inductive reason, seeking a reflective equilibrium between antithetical positions, carefully building a methodic argument towards a working consensus to settle at a point whereby we may, as Hegel says, "cancel the opposition while preserving the difference" (1977: 110–111).

Anders Petersen remains alive to Hegel's dialectical optimism – that even as darkness encroaches the quest for authenticity contains within itself seeds of self-transformation: individualism, for all of its affinities with meaninglessness, nihilism and tyranny, continues to be a powerful moral resource, containing simultaneous tendencies of degenerate narcissism but also vital energies seeking higher self-fulfilment. Taylor calls his excavation of the sources of the self a work of 'retrieval': as we slide towards instrumentality and nihilism, it is ever more important to articulate the sources of authenticity. Anders Petersen shares this mission, conducting Foucauldian 'archaeologies of the present' and genealogies of the unfortunate subject of late modernity. This kind of work resonates with Walter Benjamin's 'redemptive critique', and in a more contemporary key with Dany Robert Dufour's (2011) call for the scholar today as a *conservateur* – seeking to conserve those elements of the traditions of Modernity by means of which we might save ourselves from the fires of history. This is the work for which Anders Petersen is a model.

The dimensions of contemporary social pathologies

Depression, anxiety, grief, enduring Modernity in an age of voicelessness – the key themes Anders Petersen addressed in his work are closely interrelated. He was well aware of the dangers of the naturalizing methods of labelling which characterize positivist psy-sciences. And also, he was well aware of the importance of phenomenologically grounding the various patterns of social suffering manifesting as mental disorders. After overviewing Anders Petersen's philosophical inspirations, in the following two sections, his interrelated work on depression and anxiety is discussed.

Living in an age of depression

In *How Everyone Became Depressed*, psychiatry historian Edward Shorter (2013) takes pains to show that there was a strong and long European tradition in which depression and anxiety were closely connected, a tradition which was broken by *DSM-III*-chief Robert Spitzer when he decided that the group working on depression should be separated from the one working on anxiety. "They didn't know what they were doing", Shorter concludes bitterly (2013: 132). Well, didn't they indeed?

The first two editions of the *DSM* were strongly informed by psychoanalytic theory. In his famous essay 'Mourning and Melancholy', Sigmund Freud (1917) presented severe depression as unsuccessful grief. The melancholic can't get rid of the lost object. And that is because melancholia is in some way related to an object-loss which is withdrawn from consciousness, in contradiction to mourning, in which there is nothing about the loss that is unconscious. Mourning means hard work, *Trauerarbeit*, which the melancholic person can't accomplish: "all libido shall be withdrawn from its attachments to that object" (Freud 1917: 244f). The work of grief viewed as individual labour. But is it that and that only?

The performance society – also the title, in Danish, of the last solo book written by Anders[1] – thrives on flexibility on the one hand and controllability on the other hand. Purportedly limitless freedom of choice is connected with omnipresent monitoring and protocolization. The individualized subject is unleashed and at the same time enchained. The desired self-realization turns out to be a very difficult, competitive and confusing task. In a society where achievement has become the ideal for a good life, the normative underlying framework of what should entail a good life loses all meaning. It is not important what one is good at, but it is crucial to constantly achieve optimally in some area or another. The normative definition of what constitutes a good life loses significance in this context; it becomes empty. The late modern *Homo oeconomicus* has to manifest and empower him-/her-/xself in a highly insecure context. And this can be – and often proves to be – frightening or depressing; and not uncommonly, frightening and depressing at once. How can it be both at the same time?

Social pathologies as pathologies of the social. In all sorts of ways, Anders Petersen – in his modestly passionate way – defended the social sphere against the hyperindividualization of malaise and pleasure, and of life as such.

'Happiness', defined and institutionalized in a certain 'ideological' that is (neo)liberal way, is to be understood as the flexible antipode of the stasis of depression and the disempowerment of anxiety. The neglect in our late modern world of the social dimensions of phenomena like grief, as Anders evaluates with a typical Petersen twist, "seems almost outrageous".[2] Individualized grief appears predominantly as blocked autonomy. The new member of the *DSM*-family – 'prolonged grief disorder' – is defined as the other of anxiety disorder and especially depression. All three concern the anathema of (neo)liberal culture: the *Homo immobilis*, the immobile and unmobilizable subject.

Anders Petersen liked to agree-to-disagree. He wanted to investigate further, dig a little deeper, think a bit more nuanced. Modestly, but always passionately. Urging us to follow. Not so much wanting us to comply, probably more to disagree, but anyhow to 'think along if we feel like a room with a window', to use a variant of one of his chapter titles in this volume. See what the view entails. Look hard. Think through. Explore alternative possibilities. Like the ending of the anxiety chapter in this volume, in authentic Petersen style, underlines: "Perhaps!"

Perhaps a paradox makes life often unliveable in our times, for many people, for longer episodes. Probably! Late modernity is an epoch in which fixing meets liquidization in extreme ways. Disciplining has taken a new, two-faced form. The promise is freedom and self-realization, the demand is pliability and self-abnegation. In normal (work) life a monitoring culture dis-trusts people persistently. Such lack of trust or support – much more than work pressure as such, though that mostly is high too – could be counted as the main source or cause of the so-called burn-out syndrome or 'occupational burn-out': a pathology of the social, leading to an individual ailment. And whoever can no longer clap along in and with the ubiquitous monitoring drill will subsequently be embraced (or smothered) by the omni-vigilant diagnostic culture.

Apparent *Mündigkeit* [maturity/ autonomy/ responsible citizenship/ the right to have a say in determining the conditions of one's own life in general] turns into cloudy *Unmündigkeit* [dis-enfranschisement; voicelessness]: that is the constant confrontation the late modern subject has to deal with; the reversal (or perversion) of the liberation indicated in the famous Kantian definition of enlightenment, *Aufklärung*. Anders Petersen, being a true sociologist, combining prescription and description, that is to say critical analysis of the so-called good life and empirical studies of the vicissitudes of the people who are supposed to lead such a life, shows beautifully and painfully how this paradoxy or perversity entails processes of disenfranchisement, leading to the feeling of being voiceless, lacking agency, of being again and again in the hands of a puppeteer.[3] Isn't one tempted to urge people who feel like this to 'cry out loud if you feel like a mouth without a voice'? Sadly however, what this cry could entail or bring about is mostly as unclear as the course that is being set, and reset, and reset, and reset.

The novel idea of the Great Man that goes along with the 'new spirit of capitalism', as expounded by Luc Boltanski and Eve Chiapello, is 'depressogenic' in nature. Being 'authentic' has a very specific, contemporary meaning here, a meaning which is institutionalized in all sorts of ways.[4] It signifies all the traits that make the subject suitable for functioning smoothly within the context of this new capitalism, namely being "flexible, mobile, enterprising, creative, polyvalent, adaptable, tolerant, daring, social, innovative and malleable".[5] Being actively available and flexibly forwardish. Taking life as a series of projects. Having an entrepreneurial mindset, thereby pretending to be the leading company of oneself – 'Me Ltd.' – but making sure in the end always to act on behalf of the omnipresent almighty monster enterprise or enterprise monster called The Divine Market.

Living up to these demands will lead to 'happiness', so the enticement goes.[6] Not complying with them means being considered in-authentic. And especially the condition which since 1980 in the *DSM* is termed 'major depressive disorder' bundles all the opposites of the desired characteristics of the vaunted ideal-type subject of new capitalism. The depressed individual is in-active, in-accessible, in-flexible and future-less. Immobile and unmobilizable. And of course, this stagnated being then has to be re-activated via action techniques, especially cognitive behaviour therapy and antidepressants. The latter, as Alain Ehrenberg (1998: 203) states pointedly in *La Fatigue d'être soi – dépression et société*, should not be called 'happiness pills' but 'pills of initiative'.

Happycracy, as described by Eva Illouz (2020; 2018; 2008), who published in the first edition of what Anders wanted to promote as Critical Happiness Studies, derives from what was emerging in the late 1990s: positive psychology. It seeks to provide scientific legitimacy to a very simple idea: happiness can be constructed, taught and learnt. It suggests that all one needs to do is to desire it and listen to the experts in order to become happy. The happiness industry claims it can shape individuals into creatures capable of obstructing negative feelings, fully controlling unproductive desires and defeatist thoughts, and maximizing their own potential. The 'promise of happiness', as Sara Ahmed (2010) would phrase it, reveals the affective and moral work performed by the 'happiness duty' – the expectation that we will be made happy by participating in what is deemed good – being 'authentic' in late modern style – and that our own happiness will make others happy as well. But what follows when we make our desires and even our own happiness conditional on the happiness of others: "I just want you to be happy"; "I'm happy if you're happy"?

Anders Petersen liked to agree-to-disagree. He was a kind but not a compliant man. He followed, for instance, Ehrenberg and Allan Horwitz, but also questioned their thoughts. He tunes in with Ehrenberg's analysis of the discourse on depression as presenting the flipside of the late modern, new capitalist ideal of self-realization. This ideal is very hard – or impossible – to accomplish because of the competitive context in which it takes place and because of the absence in this context of clear guidelines for self-optimalization. Limit-less freedom. *Mer à boire*. "Depression portrays for all of us the style of the uncontrollable in the age of limitless possibilities", Ehrenberg wrote in *La Fatigue d'être soi*. And: "If, as Freud thought, 'a person becomes neurotic because he cannot tolerate the amount of frustration which society imposes on him', he becomes depressed because he must tolerate the illusion that everything is possible for him" (Ehrenberg, 1998: 249).

However, when Ehrenberg states that the position of the individual has changed but not worsened, Anders chooses to disagree: "I simply think he is off the mark in only considering the changed social status of psychic suffering when accounting for increased rates of mental illnesses".[7] He also rejects the antipode of Ehrenberg's view as represented in Dan Blazer's (2005) *The Age of Melancholy*, a perspective which Anders calls postmodern. Within such a perspective, today's societal situation is typified by overall disintegration and extreme hopelessness. Anders summarizes Blazer's angle nicely: "everything is sedimented, but nothing settles". And he continues: "While Blazer's view of transformation is rooted in a wide-ranging perception of disintegration, mine is linked to a perception of complexity".[8] So according to Anders, our situation is not simply hopeless, but neither does it involve just simply change. He wants to dig a little deeper into the complexities of contemporary social and individual life.

Anders Petersen also wanted to investigate matters a little further than Alan Horwitz and Jerome Wakefield (2007) did. There is more at stake than processes of pathologization of 'normal' feelings like sadness. Anders states:

> The process of pathologization per se, does not explain why these particular mental disorders are socially constituted as pathological. Or, to be more precise, it does not explain why these particular symptoms are understood as signifiers of mental illness in contemporary society.[9]

Being a sociologist, Anders wants to describe and prescribe, or more precisely, he intends to analyse the social conditions of these rising symptoms and then evaluate if these conditions need to be criticized. Are these symptoms and their rise signs of social pathology? Possibly!

Was the historical movement of the modern *psyche* one from the age of anxiety to the age of depression and back to an age of anxiety? Partly, possibly. But let us keep the interwovenness of Anders' themes close in mind. What happened around 1980 when depression and anxiety were divorced from one another? Was this indeed a catastrophe, like Shorter has suggested? Perhaps! But maybe not exactly for the reasons Shorter presented. Do depression and anxiety indeed belong with each other? What can be said about this from a phenomenological viewpoint? We will get back to this question.

After a rise of depression, there seems to be a rise of anxiety, as Anders concluded. This entails more than pathologization of the normal, he ascertains. It also implies more than collateral damage of performance culture. It involves internalization of ideologically generated norms; a rebound of the 'anti-authoritarian totalitarism' of late modern (neo)liberal disciplining (Dufour, 2011: 14). Self-assurance, self-confidence, turns into 'fear and trembling'. Anders refers to Christoph Dejours, who speaks of a structural self-doubt because of the presence of a culture of fear. People are constantly afraid of being guilty of incompetence and underperformance, which might and shall lead to misrecognition.[10] And there is more: the feeling of losing control. What do the symptoms in this so-called age of anxiety tell us, Anders asks.

> When invoking such a gaze on the definitions of general anxiety disorder, social phobia and panic disorder one rather obvious element of the symptoms arises. They evolve around individual loss of control of one's life, particularly concerning the individual mind (sense of self) and the body.

However, he continues, "loss of control is also a pertinent part of other mental disorders – for example, depression".[11] For example indeed! In what way do these two belong to each other?

Before finally turning to Anders' answer to this question, another thing should be mentioned which typified his quest: the issue of possible positive aspects of allegedly negative phenomena like anxiety, and this also in connection with the social sphere. "Instead of dealing with the social aspects of these pathologies", Anders writes in *Return of the Age of Anxiety*, speaking about a rise in anxieties among the young,

> the common reaction against this development is individualized treatment. That is, various forms of psychopharmacology and cognitive behavioural therapy are the most prescribed forms of treatment for these anxieties. The overall logic of these types of treatment is the individual removal of the symptoms connected with the pathological behaviour.[12]

Instead of this 'individual removal', we should have the heart for a collective recognition of the possible protective side of anxiety. Since "the [...] analysis of what it entails to be a human being – or a subject – in contemporary society", Anders writes, "is very much a story about blurring boundaries", we really should think through in what ways the apparent rise of anxieties is linked to "the quasi-anthropological human need for boundaries".[13] Maybe the same goes for the possible flipside of anxiety: depression? Does the latter 'disorder' maybe also involve – sometimes, or partly, or even sometimes mainly – a protective move, a (further) retreat from in-sane circumstances or/and demands?

So what might be – thinking phenomenologically – the bond between depression and anxiety? This is one of the questions addressed by Anders Petersen in terms of disconnection, inauthenticity and distunement.[14] In contemporary culture, depression is *understood* as in-authenticity, that is as the flipside of the traits of the wanted 'tuned-in' 'authentic' subject. However, when one zooms in on depression as it is *experienced*, one comes to see it at dis-tunement or de-tunement, that means as a disconnection at a very elementary level. The so-called depression epidemic is to be understood as an expression of a massive collision of the presently dominating form of subjectivity – the late modern version of *Homo oeconomicus*, the *Me Ltd*, the enterprising subject or the subject as enterprise – with *Homo resonans*, the human being in need of basic connection or attunement. This need is presently very much neglected, un-answered. The individual ailment of depression is – not always of course, but quite frequently – rooted in a pathology of the social or the relational. And for anyone who is detached at such an elementary level, who no longer is in-the-world so to speak, but beside-the-world, this world becomes an outlandish, more or less frightening and not uncommonly terrifying place.

So indeed, there is something rotten in the state of the Global Village. What is bothering us is not only change and transition (Ehrenberg), nor is it simply exaggeration or pathologization (Horwitz). But neither are we in a condition of overall disintegration and utter hopelessness (Blazer). There is hope. There is still the possibility of a radical turn. As Hartmut Rosa (2019: 459) has affirmed at the end of his *Resonance: A Sociology of Our Relationship to the World,* taking up again a hopeful thought from the beginning of the book: "*A better world is possible*", and it can be recognized by its central criterion, which is no longer domination and control, but listening and responding. If we could turn away from the false anthropology of (neo)liberalism, then we would stand a chance. *Homo resonans* presently is crushed by *Homo oeconomicus*. The *DSM* as a framework and as a way of thinking about (in)sanity is based on this anthropological error. Resistance against it marked the life and work of Anders Petersen.

It also marks the activities of psychiatrist and philosopher Thomas Fuchs, who works and thinks in the spirit of the phenomenological tradition. Our culture neglects what he calls 'the living body', in German our *Leiblichkeit*. The body, at this very basic level – in German *Leib* and not *Körper* – is not a thing but a sphere, a dynamic sphere, a sphere of affective attunement. *Leiblichkeit* (corporeality) in other words means *Interleiblichkeit* (intercorporeality), like Maurice Merleau-Ponty has explained in his way extensively as well. Because of the aforementioned anthropological error, we were, are and will be in need of a counter-anthropology. Fuchs (2021) has recently delivered one in his *In Defense of the Human Being: Foundational Questions of an Embodied Anthropology*. Our embodied, intercorpereal, interrelated existence is under threat and needs to be defended. Says Thomas Fuchs. Said Anders Petersen.

The style in which Anders said this can be typified as modestly furious. Modest, because that is what and how he was. Furious, because he was also passionate in his defence of the human being as *Homo resonans* against the aforementioned anthropological error. An error of which the 'success' not so much *seems* but simply *is* outrageous. So, using an outspoken variant of Anders' cautious expressions, one could say that it is hardly provocative to claim that we find ourselves in a culture of de-humanization.

Living in an age of anxiety

The negative dialectic of modernization produces various forms of social suffering, anxiety is one of them. Unlike depression perhaps, which seems to be a rather unambiguously negative experience (i.e. the deprivation from the chance of an authentic existence), anxiety is a complex phenomenon. As Kierkegaard (1980) and Heidegger (2012) have shown, it has existential functionality. Anxiety provides a special perspective on life, which is a prerequisite of self-transformation and ultimately a meaningful, authentic existence. By defining anxiety as a psychopathology, which needs to be eliminated, this existential stake is denied (Horwitz, 2013). In his dialectical analysis, Anders Petersen did not forget about this: he argued that one of the main social pathologies of the contemporary era is related to the proliferation of an overly biomedical concept of anxiety. The consequent 'diagnostic culture' sees only symptoms and pathologies to be eradicated, while it transforms non-medical forms of suffering (e.g. sorrow, guilt or shyness) into mental disorders. In this sense, the discursive psychologization is partly responsible for the emergence of an age of anxiety.

However, this dynamic is not the only one: the negative dialectic of modernization also occurs on a structural level, creating paradoxes that translate into experiences of suffering. Beside the over-medicalization of human existence, the increased level of anxiety can also be understood as a 'normal' reaction to the 'pathological' structural transformations. At this point, Anders engages not only with the well-known contemporary 'diagnosis of our times' explaining how risk, uncertainty, fragmentation and disembedding have become basic experiences, but he also reflects on the ambiguous concept of social pathology itself. The concept of social pathology might seem to have become outdated since Durkheim's time, which is indicated by the criticisms concerning the linking of individual diseases with social distortions (e.g. Honneth, 2014). However, according to Anders Petersen, the concept still has merit, if used in a careful and reflective manner.

For this purpose, Boltanski and Chiapello's (2005) analysis of the 'new spirit of capitalism' is called upon. Late modern subjects are shaped within the frames of the *projet cité*. They constantly face the expectations of flexibility, adaptability, mobility, relatability, openness, readiness, reflectivity and most importantly hyperactivity. Subjects exposed to the constraints of global network capitalism (being further accelerated by information technology) have no choice but to try to keep on adjusting. As we have learned from Foucault (1997), structures of power are also responsible for shaping subjects: they create a horizon of normalcy, along with the technologies of the self. In this sense, the attempts to become adequate in the world of project capitalism also reconfigure the subjects: independently from their success of becoming a 'project-self', the subjects internalize the expectations of hyper-flexibility and hyper-activity. Anxiety emerges due to these mechanisms: the inevitable failure of becoming an adequate project-self produces a backlash. There is no such thing as 'flexible or active enough': there is always space for further stretching the self. Thus, the subject aiming for more and more flexible agency inevitably reproduces its own inadequate version: that is the rigid, immobile, unrelatable, closed and most importantly paralyzed version of the failed project-self. In this sense, the success-driven subject of project capitalism inherently exists in the negative mirror of their own failed version, i.e. the anxious, depressed subject.

Based on this diagnosis, the horizon of social pathologies can be rephrased as well. It is the very structural constellation, which reproduces the phenomenological pattern of anxiety – in this sense anxiety as a psychopathology is the consequence of the negative dialectics of modernization itself. The subjects are nothing more but the 'symptom carriers' of a social world, which is characterized by paradox structures. As Anders Petersen explains, this paradox process is further aggravated by the collective responses. By medicalizing anxiety, it is essentialized and anchored on the level of the subject, despite the fact that its increasing prevalence is caused by distortive social structures. In this sense, project-capitalism not only reproduces anxiety but also veils its social origins by framing it as a subject's psychopathology instead of a social pathology. We could learn from Anders Petersen that anxiety is about drawing boundaries, which becomes particularly important in an era of blurring boundaries. In this sense, instead of its complete elimination, a more differentiated concept of anxiety is needed: it should be understood both as a social pathology (and treated as such) and as an existential phenomenon (and cultivated as such).[15]

These diagnoses are not only elaborated on a theoretical level but also examined in empirical research. For this purpose, the abstract concepts need to be translated into falsifiable research questions. At this point, Anders Petersen focuses on a 'phenomenology of disenfranchisement'. He and his colleagues chose an interesting field for the analysis of the expansion of the 'new spirit of capitalism': by examining kindergartens, which are located as far from the realm of market transactions as possible, they demonstrate how deeply the culture of performance has perverted late modern social structures. Few spaces exist which are consensually considered to be driven by the logic of 'care' instead of rationales of profit or bureaucracy – the kindergarten certainly belong to them. If even these lifeworld places are 'colonized' by the system's culture of performance, that is an indicator of profound paradoxes – which would have been probably even difficult to imaginae for Habermas or Boltanski. Yet, the lived experience of the (Danish) kindergarten teachers seems to be burdened in many ways: they feel that their recognition is becoming more dependent on their performance, which is measured by their flexibility. Furthermore, this moral economic order is so deeply embedded in their horizon, that they do not even dare to criticize the *status quo*. In this sense, they feel equally stressed by the permanent expectation of performance and also deprived of the chance to voice any criticism of the system rationalities to which they have become subject. Overall, this experience is translated into the sense of disenfranchisement – powerlessness, voicelessness, on the manifest level: they become subordinated to unbearable structural constraints. The secondary consequence of such social suffering is the potential combination of anxiety (due to the constant pressure) and depression (due to the sense of finality and helplessness).[16]

To understand how the structures of project capitalism pervert the lifeworld, the analysis of the technologies of power are called upon. Among the micro-mechanisms of governance, those are particularly important, which seem to be beyond suspicion. In other words, which seem to represent no particular interest, i.e. express neutrality or 'disinterestedness' (Bourdieu, 1998). 'Evaluations' are prime examples for such mechanisms: they inevitably include the possibility of standardization and based on these standards, the criticism of performance. At this point, as indicated above, Anders Petersen refers to Dejours (1998): by implying constant self-evaluation and comparison with the others' performance, workplace evaluations are responsible for a culture of fear. Since the logic of quantification enables personal and interpersonal comparison, from the perspective of evaluations, there is no such thing as 'good enough', only 'momentarily good'. Accordingly, the technologies of evaluation, which has spread to every social sphere due to triumphant managerialism, are also becoming the technologies of an anxious self. They shape subjectivities in such a way that a negative horizon of impossible adequacy is incorporated: under the constant pressure of evaluations, the actors do not have a chance of catching up with themselves, they are destined to lag behind themselves, while ceaselessly worrying. These empirical analyses not only illustrate the micro-level consequences of a culture of performance but also show the stakes of the negative dialectics of modernization. Contemporary actors to inhabit a negative horizon, without a prospect of critique or relief. Mental disorders such as depression and anxiety are only the tip of the iceberg: they represent the extreme cases, which are amplified by the biomedical gaze. However, as the empirical research shows, even at the everyday level, that is late modern 'normalcy' is tainted by distortive structures. Accordingly, no one is safe from the related social suffering, which affects everyone, even if not drastically.[17]

Beyond depression, grief and anxiety – continuing Anders Petersen's work

The thematic focus points of depression, anxiety, disenfranchisement and grief all circulate around the same negative dialectic. The structural transformations of modernization result in a constellation wherein authentic existence is expected, but hindered at the same time. The existential paradox of late modern subject is constituted in several layers. While the liquified structures of project capitalism seemingly create space for autonomy, they also dissolve those social ties which are necessary for meaningful existence (that is a potential cause of depression). While the much vaunted flexibility promises a new horizon of possibilities for self-fulfilment, but as a never-fulfillable expectation, it also becomes a source of constant mental pressure (that is the potential cause of anxiety). While individuals are considered to have been given previously unseen freedom and agency, in fact this means that they are left on their own with the hardships and they are expected to deal with suffering alone. Due to these tendencies of late modern moral economy, solidarity ties are undermined: the burdening of structural constraints of global capitalism – such as the demands of acceleration and flexibility – on the subject is naturalized, while dumping the responsibility for well-being onto the atomized actors is also justified. From this perspective, the result of the negative dialectic in late modernity is an existential trap: not only the subjects suffer from the structural paradoxes, but the cause of their suffering is also veiled to them, which makes the horizon of change inaccessible. The subjects being stuck in an unbearable, yet unchangeable constellation have no other choice but to mourn and to inhabit the narrow space provided to them.

Besides further deepening the diagnoses of the times of contemporary civilization, the structural and phenomenological exploration of this existential paradox is one of the most important legacies of Anders Petersen. There is an important tradition of critical theory which comes to similar conclusions about the consequences of negative dialectics: Benjamin, Virilio and Lash all refer to our coming to face the dead-end of modernization, which implies mourning (Lash, 1999). In this sense, grief becomes a fundamental component of contemporary existence: as there seems to be no way back to meaningful horizons of expectation, the praxes of critique are complemented – or even replaced – by the praxes of mourning.[18] Anders Petersen's work can also be read from this perspective: he provides a theoretical framework for circumscribing a fundamentally negative space of possibility. In this sense, his work can be located in the context of several recent works in the same vein: Berlant's (2011) book *Cruel Optimism* explores why actors pursue tracks which actually hinder their flourishing; Scott (2019) explores the 'social life of nothing' expressing the inhabiting of negative structures; Allen (2020) attempts to renew critique on the basis of subjects characterized by the experience of 'loss, negativity, ambivalence, and mourning'. Along with these authors, Anders Petersen too provides a way to contemplate the potential continuation of the negative dialectics.

The question might be raised: What kind of social structures are reproduced by the subjects embedded in a lifeworld characterized by depression, anxiety and grief? No matter how burdensome they are, not even these existential traps are permanent – accordingly, the contemporary phase of negative dialectic is far from being the final one. For those who seek a way out from the deadlock of the culture of performance (resulting in the combination of intensifying depression and anxiety), detecting the systematic cracks in the structures of project capitalism and acceleration society is a central task. As the negative consequences of the culture of performance come to be experienced by more and more people, the fragmented yet general reflection on those negative consequences and their underlying causes intensifies. Based on these reflections, new strategies for dealing with them emerge. Despite not being able to provide substantive alternatives, the persistence and intensification of critical reflection still indicates the possibility of reconfiguring the *status quo*. Anders Petersen opened paths for exploring these structural cracks: the culture of performance and the interrelatedness of recognition and evaluation are central fields for contemporary critical theory. By tracking the consequences of long-term exposure to these constraints, we might also explore those hybrid existential patterns, which balance at the verge of depression and anxiety, while also seeking a way out from their dead-end. We cannot be sure how and when the present structures of negative dialectics can be overcome, but we can be sure that such processes will be initiated by those actors who are suffering from their consequences but are not paralysed by them. Accordingly, the exploration of these existential positions, by authors like Anders Petersen, is indispensable for future critical theory.

These analyses could prove to be particularly important when it comes to not simply diagnosing current social pathologies, but also imagining alternative futures. By revealing the structural constraints of global project capitalism and the related culture of performance as the ultimate causes of depressed and anxious social suffering, utopic – or at least non-dystopic – horizons can be elaborated.

Project capitalism is all about internalizing the flexibility requirement of global markets, which results in atomizing individualization: that is the aim of the discourses of meritocratic justification, biopolitical technologies of the self and selfish moral economies. Beside their distinctive impact, a common feature of these components is that they point to a negative version of solidarity. They do not simply erode or dissolve solidarity, but rather they banish the concept of solidarity from the realm of possibility. The sense of infinity characterizing anxious or depressed social suffering originates from a horizon where social support is unimaginable. The hyper-individualized, atomized subjects are not simply deprived of care, but as they naturalize project capitalism's discourses, they cannot perceive themselves or the others anymore as worthy of solidarity. The same structural reasons are responsible for this distortion, which causes the suffering in the first place: within the context of project capitalism, there is no space for 'caring', only for endless evaluations. That is why we may argue that in accordance with the diagnoses of Anders Petersen, reconfiguring solidarity is just as important in the contemporary context as reframing the various forms of social suffering manifesting as mental disorders in a non-individual way.

Notes

1 See Chapter 7.
2 See Chapter 12.
3 See Chapter 8.
4 See Chapter 5.
5 See Chapter 3.
6 See Chapter 3.
7 See Chapter 4.
8 See Chapter 2.
9 See Chapter 4.
10 See Chapter 9.
11 See Chapter 4.
12 See Chapter 4.
13 *Ibid.*
14 See Chapter 6.
15 See Chapter 4.
16 See Chapter 7.
17 See Chapter 8.
18 See Chapter 10.

References

Adorno, T and Horkheimer, M (1979) *Dialectic of Enlightenment*. London: Verso.
Ahmed, S (2010) *The Promise of Happiness*. Durham, NC and London: Duke University Press.
Allen, A (2020) *Critique on the Couch: Why Critical Theory Needs Psychoanalysis*. New York: Columbia University Press.
Berlant, L (2011) *Cruel Optimism*. Durham, NC: Duke University Press.
Blazer, D (2005) *The Age of Melancholy: 'Major Depression' and Its Social Origin*. London: Routledge.

Boltanski, L and Chiapello, E (2005) *The New Spirit of Capitalism*. London: Verso.
Bourdieu, P. (1998) *Practical Reason: On the Theory of Action*. Redwood City: Stanford University Press.
Dejours, C (1998) *Souffrance en France. La Banalisation de l'Injustice Sociale*. Paris: Éditions du Seuil.
Dufour, DR (2011) *L'individu qui vient ... après le libéralisme*. Parijs: Éditions Denoël.
Ehrenberg, A (1998) *La Fatigue d'être soi – dépression et société*. Paris: Odile Jacob.
Foucault, M (1997) Society Must Be Defended: Lectures at the Collège de France. 1975–1976. New York: St. Martin's Press.
Freud, S (1917/1959) Mourning and melancholy. In: Strachey, J (ed.) Sigmund Freud Collected Papers, 152–170. New York: Basic Books.
Fuchs, T (2021) *In Defence of the Human Being: Foundational Questions of an Embodied Anthropology*. Oxford: Oxford University Press.
Girard, R (1976) *Deceit, Desire and the Novel: Self and Other in Literary Structure*. Baltimore, MD: Johns Hopkins University Press.
Habermas, J (1986) The new obscurity: the crisis of the welfare state and the exhaustion of utopian energies. *Philosophy & Social Criticism*, 11(2), 1–18.
Hegel, GWF (1977) *Phenomenology of Spirit*. Oxford: Oxford University Press.
Heidegger, M (2012) *Being and Time*. Cambridge: Cambridge University Press.
Honneth, A (2014) The diseases of society. Approaching a nearly impossible concept. *Social Research: An International Quarterly*, 81(3), 683–703.
Horwitz, AV (2013) *Anxiety. A Short History*. Baltimore, MD: Johns Hopkins University Press.
Horowitz, A and Wakefield, J (2007) *The Loss of Sadness: How Psychiatry Transformed Normal Sorrow into Depressive Disorder*. Oxford: Oxford University Press.
Illouz, E (2008) *Saving the Modern Soul: Therapy, Emotions, and the Culture of Self-help*. Berkeley: University of California Press.
Illouz, E and Cabanas, E (2018) *Happycratie. Comment l'industrie du bonheur a pris le contrôle de nos vies,*67-82 Paris: Premier Parallèl.
Illouz, E and Cabanas, E (2020) Hijacking the language of functionality? In praise of 'negative' emotions against happiness. In: Hill, N, Brinkmann, S and Petersen, A (eds) *Critical Happiness Studies*. London: Routledge, pp 67–82.
Kierkegaard, S (1980) *The Concept of Anxiety*. Princeton, NJ: Princeton University Press.
Lash, S (1999) *Another Modernity, A Different Rationality*. Oxford: Blackwell.
Rosa, H (2019) *Resonance: A Sociology of our Relationship to the World.* Cambridge: Polity Press.
Scott, S (2019) *The Social Life of Nothing: Silence, Invisibility and Emptiness in Tales of Lost Experience*. London: Routledge.
Shorter, E (2013) *How Everyone Became Depressed*. Oxford: Oxford University Press.
Taylor, C (1989) *Sources of the Self: The Making of the Modern Identity*. Cambridge, MA: Harvard University Press.
Taylor, C (1991) *The Malaise of Modernity.* Toronto, ON: House of Anansi Press [*The Ethics of Authenticity.* Cambridge, MA: Harvard University Press].
Taylor, C (2007) *A Secular Age*. Cambridge, MA: Harvard University Press.

Part 1

Depression, anxiety and happiness

2 Introduction to part 1

Carmen Kuhling

Anders Petersen's various single and co-authored papers on depression and anxiety, and their purported antithesis, 'happiness', provide an excellent counterpoint to the narrow and reductionistic individualistic and bio-psychiatric accounts of these conditions that tend to dominate in most contexts. A red thread running through all of Anders Petersen's work is the idea that depression and anxiety cannot be understood without understanding macro-level social, economic and cultural transformations associated with modernity, capitalism and neoliberalism that have reconfigured our understanding of the self, created distorted subjectivities and impoverished social relations. Meanwhile, the unhappy conditions of life in late modernity and neoliberalism that give rise to new epidemics of depression and anxiety are accompanied by a pervasive ideological injunction to 'be happy!'. Influenced by many sources in classical and contemporary social and political thought, especially critical theory, Anders Petersen shows us that, since the publication of the *Diagnostic & Statistical Manual – DSM-III* in the early 1980s, depression and anxiety have increasingly come to be understood as undesirable individual psychiatric diseases that must be medicated away, rather than as conditions that could be the basis for self-reflection and social critique. In 'Authentic Self-Realization and Depression', Anders Petersen looks at how 'the new spirit of capitalism' (Boltanski and Chiapello, 2005) constructs the individual as an active, self-realizing, projective self whose value is limited to what they can actively contribute to the economic order so that we are under constant pressure to 'self-actualize', to fully 'realize our potential' and to become the most active, most 'successful' versions of ourselves. And not alone are we pressurized to become flexible, polyvalent, multi-tasking entrepreneurs of ourselves, we are interpellated and admonished to be happy in our servitude and to 'clap along' to neoliberalism's relentless, wearying, never-ending apocalyptic carnival of competitive individualism. While several contemporary authors influenced by Foucault (1991) have advanced critiques of how we become subjects under modern and more recently late-modern neoliberal orders, Anders Petersen gives us an original, stronger and clearer perspective by bringing the Foucauldian general thesis of 'subjectivization' into dialectical conversation with Ehrenberg's (2010) particular analysis of depression as 'weariness of the self', thereby giving us a synthetic formulation of the unhappy plight of the

DOI: 10.4324/9781032714356-3

contemporary subject in the context of broader societal demands associated with changes in the nature of work and the neo-liberal social order.

Anders Petersen's work on anxiety gives us an anthropological and historical-genealogical approach to show us how anxiety defined as a diagnosable disease in the *DSM-III* came to displace earlier, richer understandings of anxiety within philosophical, anthropological and historical accounts, and as an experience belonging to the human condition that as such was central to modern understandings of the self. In the *DSM-III* the definition of anxiety entirely eradicated any reference to social context or complex formulations of the self in favour of a medicalized, individualized and biochemically based understanding of anxiety as a discrete disease entity. In 'Return of the Age of Anxiety: The Embedding of a Late Modern Social Pathology', Anders Petersen's critical historical genealogy recovers and redeems anxiety from its having been reduced to an individual disease, and helps to restore anxiety to its proper place as belonging to the spectrum of experiences of the human condition, and as a valuable socio-cultural signifier of, and as a historically conditioned psycho-sociological response to social tensions and traumas of the 20th century such as the Holocaust, Hiroshima and the Cold War, and by doing so, Anders Petersen gives back to us Anxiety as a prism and a lamp to illuminate our contemporary late modern and 21st-century social-pathogenic conditions.

Anders Petersen's essays on 'Self-realization and Depression', 'Return of the Age of Anxiety' and the 'Pursuit of Happiness as Ideology' considered individually, severally and collectively are an exemplary demonstration of what C. Wright Mills (1959) famously calls the 'sociological imagination' as a quality of mind that is able to grasp and express and thereby show us how such conditions as depression and anxiety and the injunction to be happy while they may be experienced as individual persons 'private troubles' are very often – and more often than not – inextricably bound up with 'public issues' of historical socio-economic and socio-cultural structures, so much so that 'neither the life of an individual nor the history of a society can be understood without understanding both'. Anders Petersen is thus a model sociologist, one who helps to establish a new field of inquiry that he has described in terms of the 'social pathologies of contemporary civilization'. Anders Petersen's approach to mental and emotional distress argues that what we have become accustomed to thinking of as diseases experienced and suffered at the level of individual people's bodies are really symptoms of historical and cultural pathologies of social and bodies politic, but the sources of pathologies as belonging to the institutional and discursive orders of contemporary civilization are made invisible because of the embedding of the hegemony of bio-psychiatric-neuro-chemical thinking, a paradigm that itself is a part of a much larger ideological configuration of neo-scientism, neo-social-Darwinist evolutionism and political-economic neoliberalism. In contrast to the dominant reductive, myopic and deeply ideological perspectives, Anders Petersen's sociological imagination offers us an expansive and generous view of a whole historical social field that the disease paradigm masks and causes us to overlook: how a person's life always and everywhere exists within a matrix of social and cultural contexts, and the role that such webs of significance play in individual mental health and wellbeing.

Scholars have been critiquing the reductive bio-psychiatric-neurochemical model from a range of perspectives for the past 60 years (Rogers and Pilgrim, 2014) yet this model remains hegemonic in policy and practice in most international contexts. In my own professional life as a sociologist and as a practising psychotherapist, I have found that Anders Petersen's work resonates powerfully and profoundly with both my undergraduate students in the social sciences and the people who I meet with in my psychotherapy practice. Whether in the lecture theatre or in the therapy room Anders Petersen speaks to my students and to my clients, and he has helped me, my students, and people in therapy to see how broad social and cultural transformations are affecting people's individual psychic and emotional lives and impacting on their health and wellbeing in complex and multifaceted ways. Anders Petersen's humanistic understanding of depression, anxiety and (un)happiness gives us the ground on which we may find relief from individual suffering, and his powerful critique of the prevailing late-modern neoliberal institutional and ideological order gives us a hopeful horizon for collective redemption.

References

Boltanski, L and Chiapello, E (2005) [1999] *The New Spirit of Capitalism*. London: Verso Books.

Ehrenberg, A (2010) *The Weariness of the Self: Diagnosing the History of Depression in the Contemporary Age*. Montreal and Kingston: McGill-Queen's University Press.

Foucault, M (1991) *Discipline and Punish*. London: Penguin.

Mills, CW (1959) *The Sociological Imagination*. Oxford: Oxford University Press.

Rogers, A and Pilgrim, D (2014) *A Sociology of Mental Health and Illness*. London: McGraw-Hill.

3 Authentic self-realization and depression

Anders Petersen

Introduction

There can scarcely be many fiction writers as stringent in their merciless dissection of society's normative developmental tendencies as Michel Houellebecq. Sour, tough, cynical, sarcastic and with a chilly ruthlessness that practically freezes the blood – this is Houellebecq's narrative style in his novels depicting the state of modern society. Wielding an incisive pen, Houellebecq cuts to the bone of what he regards as the western normative value set which creates growth in individual suffering rather than the possibility of achieving the good life. From his perspective, the structure of society is such as to inevitably rebound on the individual in the form of psychological disorders. In Houellebecq's universe, the symptoms of such disorders pile up on each other: powerlessness, languor, despair, mania and lassitude are just a few of the more diffuse kinds of disorder that haunt Houellebecq's characters. However, careful study of Houellebecq's novels reveals that depression is the pathology he most often utilizes to describe the dark side of society's nature. In Houellebecq's first novel, *Extension du domaine de la lutte* (1994; trans. as 'Whatever' by Paul Hammond, 1998), for example, the principal character, Michel, describes a visit to the doctor as follows:

> At the end of an hour he pronounces a few phrases of general import on periods of blankness, extends my leave of absence and increases my dosage of medication. He also reveals that my condition has a name: it's a depression. Officially, then, I'm in a depression. The formula seems a happy one to me. It's not that I feel tremendously low; it's rather that the world around me appears high.
>
> (Houellebecq, 2002 [1994]; my translation)

Besides the opportunity to enjoy Houellebecq's eloquence, the reader is also presented with considerable latitude for interpretation when the principal character declares that the world is 'high'. Or to put it another way: he communicates no plausible analytical interpretation of the nature of the phenomenon. From a sociological perspective, his contemporary diagnosis functions as a kind of inadequate illustration of the manner in which modern society displays a considerable degree of

DOI: 10.4324/9781032714356-4

acceptance of depression. But this does not mean that Houellebecq is sociologically wide of the mark by choosing to assign Michel a depression as a characteristic expression of the form of the pathology from which he suffers. Depression would appear to have a firm hold on the societal arena. But why does depression shine so brightly in society's firmament, and why has so much attention been devoted to the phenomenon?

In this chapter, I attempt to defend the following thesis: depression is the social pathology which most starkly reveals the dark side of today's social demands for authentic self-realization. In this way, I present a spectrum of interpretation in which the prominent societal role played by depression will be subjected to analysis in relation to the pressure exerted on the psyche of the individual by today's demands for self-realization. It is not by chance that the works of French sociologist Alain Ehrenberg, and especially the ideas expressed in his best-known work, *La Fatigue d'être soi – dépression et société* (2000 [1998]), provide the article's principal source of inspiration. When this book first appeared, it attracted enormous attention because of the manner in which it linked the modern view of depression with the development of society's norms of self-realization. However, I do not follow Ehrenberg to the letter, and neither do I provide any exhaustive theoretical interpretation of his sociological universe. Instead, I utilize selected tools from his theoretical toolbox, and draw upon supplementary theories to the extent I find it necessary.

The work of substantiating the thesis is advanced in four steps. First, I focus attention on alternative perspectives on depression to the one for which I am arguing. The stimulating aspect of these perspectives is that they offer a different link between contemporary analysis and the prominent role of depression in our day. On the basis of this explanatory model, it is possible in step two to begin to sketch out the demarcation lines for the perspective of this article. Here I focus on how society's demand for lasting and authentic self-realization may be regarded as a chronic stress factor which risks rebounding in the form of depression. In the next step, I attempt to show how the contemporary view of depression is in clear contradiction with the normative demands of present-day society. These steps lead me to focus attention on the normative role played by the consumption of antidepressants in relation to today's view of depression.

The increase in depression

In *The Loss of Sadness*, Allan V. Horwitz and Jerome Wakefield offer their explanation of how the burgeoning rates of depression in contemporary western societies can be understood. Their main claim is that "the 'Age of Depression' results from a faulty definition of depressive disorder" (Horwitz and Wakefield, 2007: 6). What they argue is that the explosion of putative depressive disorder does not stem from a real rise in this condition but has been made possible by a faulty definition of depression in the *DSM-IV* in which the categories of depression and sadness have been conflated. In their perspective, the rise of depression is thus primarily a product of methodology and not the result of social factors per se. Although very enlightening, their perspective is not convincing as far as I am concerned. Instead, I argue that the expansion of the diagnosis, and hence the increased rates of depression, is first and foremost caused by a change in the way in which the concepts of mental health and sociality are defined to match a society imbued with values of autonomy and self-realization. To further elucidate this perspective, I compare it to the work of Dan G. Blazer (2005). Like me, Blazer is interested in the social origins of depression: but as we shall see, his perspective is quite different from mine.

In *The Age of Melancholy* (Blazer, 2005), Blazer makes use of a relatively radical postmodern perspective in which the keyword for today's societal situation is disintegration. The heading of Chapter 8 in Blazer's work is thus: "Things Fall Apart: Society and Depression in the 21st Century" (Blazer, 2005: 135). Society's processes of social transformation have altered the structure of western society beyond all recognition, and no process of social re-entrenchment seems to have taken place. Consequently, the most noticeable consequences are crisis, chaos, instability and individual isolation; or to use a geographical metaphor: everything is sedimented, but nothing settles. To further illuminate the correlation, Blazer utilizes a terminology of loss, in which the rapidly increasing frequency of depression is explained with the help of no fewer than eight different loss categories, including loss of self, loss of unity, loss of meaning and the creeping nihilism that permeates modern western society (Blazer, 2005: 152–159). From an overall perspective, these rank beneath the greatest loss of all, namely loss of hope. Hopelessness seems to haunt contemporary western society. This causes Blazer to speculate on whether "the swelling prevalence of depression in Western society perhaps reflects an increasingly dominant hopelessness within society" (Blazer, 2005: 152). Blazer's approach may appear rather esoteric, but his point is crystal clear: the inherent hopelessness, lack of meaning, nihilism etc. of postmodern society reinforces and amplifies the symptoms which underlie the modern view of depression. To sum up, Blazer claims that the social role of depression may be ascribed to the social and cultural forces which define the postmodern condition.

From my point of view, Blazer's investigation into the social origins of depression is below the mark. Late modern society – to use Giddens' (1991) terminology – is not characterized by hopelessness as such. In my opinion, the hopelessness of the late modern era – to return to Blazer's terminology – is the exclusive characteristic of those who have been unlucky in their self-realization. In this respect, Blazer does not appear to draw an accurate picture of contemporary western society; he seems rather to be trapped in his postmodern viewpoint, which leads him to use an oversimplified argument. He quite simply overestimates the explanatory power of the analysis of loss, and thereby also the relationship between loss and the incidence of depression. The divergence between his position and my own may thus be said to be grounded in different approaches to the diagnosis of contemporary society. While Blazer's view of transformation is rooted in a wide-ranging perception of disintegration, mine is linked to a perception of complexity. The latter perspective implies that the shift to the late modern society is not synonymous with a general erosion of society's norms, but rather with a sweeping upheaval in these. This implies that everything cannot merely be said to be falling apart, as Blazer asserts. New norms have taken root in society's overall nexus, as a result of which the introduction of a new social logic can be demonstrated, as evidenced by the establishment of the era of authenticity. However, this approach does not in any way imply that conformity with the normative demands of contemporary society is bound up with a ready-made cloak of realization which can merely be donned. On the contrary, the demands are woven from an enormously multifaceted and complex material.

The point is that the norms which apply in society today are relatively comprehensible (and thereby seductive), at any rate with regard to their immediate *form*. However, the *content* of such realization is multifarious and so loosely defined that the actual act of conformity is more than usually strenuous. This differentiation between form and content is of central importance, for while the form of contemporary norms is relatively evident, the guidelines for how their content is to be fulfilled are somewhat blurred, and the risk thereby arises of these norms generating anomie. This differentiation plays an important role in the analysis of the causes of the rapid rise in the incidence of depression in our day. Rather than focusing on the correlation between an absence of norms and depression, I therefore prefer to focus on the relationship between depression and norm complexity.

Depression and authentic self-realization as a chronic stress factor

Alessandro Ferrara has termed our time the era of authenticity, by which he means that "the notion of authentic subjectivity is to contemporary modernity as the notion of autonomous subjectivity is to early modernity" (Ferrara, 1998: 5). As a consequence of this change, a special culture of authenticity has arisen, as well as a special ethic and view of subjectivity. As Charles Taylor writes, authentic self-realization relies upon the capacity of individuals to construct, create, define and position themselves in relation to others: "Defining myself means finding what is significant in my difference from others" (Taylor, 1991: 35–36). In this view, what is important is to be true to yourself and to your own unique inner voice: "If I am not [true to myself], I miss the point of my life; I miss what being human is for *me*" (Taylor, 1994: 30). Authentic self-realization thus becomes a powerful moral ideal which is conditioned by the introspective cultivation of the individual's core. In our day, the authentic self is thus subject to the essentialist premise that there is an inner impulse which will blossom if it is merely given a helping hand. The individual defines his or her uniqueness solely by cultivating this inner impulse. But authentic self-realization is also what controls the sociality of the individual; only through authentic self-realization can the individual live up to society's normative socialization demands.

In this sense, the self is a malleable raw material which, under favourable conditions, can be shaped to meet the relevant requirements. At the same time, this implies that the individual's core is portrayed as the primary energy source, supplying all of the fuel for the motors of performance. In brief, this means that the criterion for the success of authentic self-realization is located in the psyche, as the seat of the individual's personal performance resources. Seen in this light, it is hardly surprising that our era celebrates the possibility of continual manipulation of the core. The core of the individual is regarded as a kind of investment object, from which the personal added value of the individual must be derived. But in what sense can today's authentic self-realization demands be described as a chronic stress factor which calls forth depression? First of all, we must understand what a chronic stress factor is. According to Blair Wheaton, one of the leading sociological scholars on stress research, a chronic stress factor is first and foremost defined as persistent stress, the presence of which has the potential to negatively affect an individual's mental health. The essential aspect of a chronic stress factor is thus that the individual can only with difficulty withdraw from the source of the stress. The definition therefore requires that the chronic stress factor cannot easily be dismissed, eliminated or dissolved. Chronic stress factors thus imply a lack of control over their immediate nature (Wheaton, 1999: 177). If we relate this to the fact that authentic self-realization has become an organized practical technique and institutional demand, we can approach an answer to the above question (Honneth, 2004: 471). The individual is quite simply under extreme pressure to meet this demand, and consequently also under enormous social pressure to live up to the norms that the demand implies. In this way, the institutional pressure of expectations may be said to comprise the foundation of authentic self-realization as a chronic stress factor. However, if we are to truly comprehend the complexity of this problem, we must also understand what it is that individuals expose in their authentic self-realization, and consequently, what is subjected to stress in the process of self-realization. In the following, I show that the decisive factor in this connection is the use of the core of the individual as the primary fuel in self-realization.

The significance of the inner self

According to Alain Ehrenberg, clear parallels may be drawn in this context with the world of sport. The competitive aspect is particularly interesting, as sport, more than any other domain, draws a clear distinction between winners and losers. Competition in the world of sport constitutes a simple application of the laws of meritocracy. If you are better than someone else and win in a fair contest, the court is so to speak on your side. It becomes even simpler when we try to explain why some people win and others lose (Ehrenberg, 1986: 49). Besides talent, skill and training, sports enthusiasts speak of the need to 'have in it you', referring to an individual's winner mentality and winner instinct. Both of these concepts relate to the ability of individuals to psychologically motivate and simulate themselves to deliver excellent performance. In this sense, winners are honoured, besides their actual victories, for their ability to maximize their psychological performance and realize this in a specific area of action. Ehrenberg's main point is that the view of competition which dominates in sport has now infiltrated almost every area of society (Ehrenberg, 1995: 39). Translated into practical terms, if individuals are to strengthen their chances of winning on an ongoing basis, they must continuously stimulate and encourage their psychological powers in order to drive forward the process of authentic self-realization. Only in this way can the individual harmonize his or her innermost performance cylinders with the self-realization demands presented by society. Authentic self-realization has thus become a demanding performance which must be continuously staged if it is to retain its validity. Continuous performance activities, logically enough, allow little opportunity for rest, so there is no time to rest on one's laurels. In fact, rest is regard as stagnation, which incurs a penalty – and a harsh one. The penalty for stagnation may be regarded as the symbolic death of the individual: if someone is not developing, they are disintegrating. Ergo, stagnation is the quicksand in which the individual's authentic self-realization drowns. It is therefore hardly surprising that the realization of our authentic selves is regarded as a lifelong process, in which the continual pursuit of personal winning opportunities demands a constantly rising performance graph.

The self in the roulette game of self-realization

To apply a metaphor to the perspective outlined above, the contemporary individual might be regarded as the ball in a game of self-realization roulette, in which all the red and black fields represent demands for the incessant optimization of the psyche. The inner grammar of the roulette game requires quite simply that the individual follows the development of the demands for authenticity. It is in this connection that the demand for authentic self-realization maximizes its effect as a chronic stress factor. The loose definition of the content of authentic self-realization results in the psyche of the individual being exposed to considerable stress. The stress factor here is clear, as the demand for self-realization is unaccompanied by any guide or dictionary that can translate the norms to actual content. Individuals must in other words themselves undertake the realization of these difficult-to-translate norms and thereby dissect their complex semantic content. If it is impossible to create a reasonably clear picture of the contents of the norm, awareness of the expected realization of the norm in practice can become a source of stress and thereby harm the individual's psyche. This is amplified by the fact that there are few possibilities to escape the self-realization demands, and very little opportunity to investigate the nature of their content. Even more thought-provoking, however, is the fact that the criteria for fulfilling the norms are themselves undefined. They possess no finality, and are surrounded by an air of boundlessness.

The game of self-realization roulette never ceases, as new demands will always give the wheel another twist. This further underlines the precarious relationship between performance and authentic self-realization. It simply underpins the argument that the stress of the self-realization demands can exhaust the psyche of the individual and create the conditions for the internalization of depression. Or as Honneth, with direct reference to Ehrenberg, writes:

> The permanent compulsion to draw the material for an authentic self-realisation from their own inner lives requires of individuals an ongoing form of introspection which must sooner or later leave them feeling empty; and the point at which inner experience no longer marks out the path for one's own

> life, even given a strong resolution that it do so, signals in Ehrenberg's view the moment when a depression begins.
>
> (Honneth, 2004: 475)

The relationship between authentic self-realization as a chronic stress factor and depression has thereby been illuminated. Depression begins at the moment when the self is exhausted by the chronic stress factors and thus loses a sense of any adequate future perspectives. However, we have not yet clarified the implications of the fact that depression directly contradicts the contemporary normative conditions of self-realization.

Depression as a social pathology of action and inadequacy

In order to concretize the contradiction between depression and contemporary authentic self-realization, it is necessary to examine the relationship between the currently favoured views of depression and the individual, respectively.

If we begin with the view of depression, the concept seems to have been subjected to an increasing degree of elasticity in its symptom catalogue and consequently, in its practical application (Ehrenberg, 2000: 10). This development has also been detected by Horwitz and Wakefield (2007), who, as mentioned earlier, argue that the expandable view of what counts as depression is the leading cause of the increased rate in depression. Taking this into account, it would appear to be difficult to regard depression as an unambiguous phenomenon with a clear and separate aetiological diagnosis. The elasticity of the depression concept seems to rank it as a 'catch-all phenomenon', under which amorphous symptoms of psychological disorders are grouped in a broad category. As is examined in more detail later, the dynamics in this confusion are determined by two specific factors. First, the introduction of antidepressant medications, especially SSRIs, created a convenient interplay with the terminology of depression (Ehrenberg, 2000: 95). Second, and perhaps most importantly the term 'depression' encompasses a broad continuum of symptoms, ranging from concentration difficulties to dysthymia and suicidal thoughts. As focus has been directed at the symptoms of depression, which has been divided into mild, moderate and severe types, the door has been opened to a whole range of symptoms which were not previously regarded as signs of depression.[1] Under the *ICD-10* classification, tiredness, lack of concentration, insomnia, indecisiveness and, in particular, inhibition (psychomotor retardation) are categorized as symptoms of depression, and thereby define depression itself.[2]

To understand why the concept of inhibition is so important, we can appropriately turn to Daniel Widlöcher. For Widlöcher, the concept encompasses the most important components in the contemporary view of depression. According to Widlöcher, there are two kinds of inhibition: (1) inhibition which affects the thinking of the individual, the symptomatology of which comes to expression in the form of negative thoughts, incommunicativeness, depressive mood, pessimistic feelings etc., and (2) inhibition which involves a reduction in the individual's overall level of activity. This is known as psychomotor retardation: a marked decrease in the subjective ability of depressed persons to express themselves. In Widlöcher's view, the relationship between these two forms of inhibition defines the particular nature of depression (Widlöcher, 2001: 211–212). As the reader may gather, the concept is not very clearly defined. However, strangely enough, its polymorphic character conveys an advantage, in that it makes it relatively easy to apply in practice (Ehrenberg, 2000: 218). This means that inhibition as a general category provides health professionals (doctors, psychologists and psychiatrists) with a kind of multipurpose tool in their initial attempts to pin down depression. In this respect, a lack of activity and energy, the absence of a fresh and rested start to the day, a lack of things which interest the individual in the daily routine, and the absence of joy and good humour are singled out as evidence of a poor quality of life and crystal-clear signs of depression. The concept of inhibition thus becomes utilized as a kind of preliminary means of outlining depression.

A good example of this is found in the Major Depression Inventory (MDI). The MDI is a much propagated, new, brief, self-report measure for depression based on the *ICD*-system, which also allows clinicians to assess the presence of a depressive disorder according to the *DSM-IV* and to assess the severity of the depressive symptoms. Before bringing this system into play, however, it is advised that clinicians present an index of well-being to the patients. This index has been created to initially outline depression on the basis of five different symptoms, which are all evidently connected with the conceptual content of inhibition (Olsen et al., 2003: 353). However, such initiatives do not make the concept any clearer – on the contrary, it would rather appear too diffuse to encompass the entire continuum of depression. At the same time, the concept connotes an absence of action and ability to realize oneself – and thereby passivity. From this perspective, inhibition can be seen as a kind of catch-all concept for the precise opposite of a malleable inner life. Inhibition thus describes a disorder which handicaps the individual through activity-suppressing effects. The central significance of the concept of inhibition can consequently be read in the manner in which depression has been moved away from the terminological framework that corresponds to a conflict perspective. The definition of depression offered by *ICD-10* is practically purged of conflict terminology. Instead, a deficit of activity comprises the principal content of the vocabulary of depression, emphasizing the key role of inhibition in this view of the disorder. It is in this light that it can be postulated that "the individual is confronted with a pathology of inadequacy rather than a disorder based on errors, a dysfunctional universe rather than a universe of law. The depressed individual is broken (en panne)" (Ehrenberg, 2000: 16).[3] Against this background, it would appear that depression appears to describe a condition in which the self has not merely run aground, but is in the process of sinking. To remain in the world of maritime terminology, it may be said that depression "should be regarded as the foundering of the individual as a subject" (Honneth, 2003: 133).

But in order to clarify the concept of depression as the foundering of the individual, it should in my opinion be made clear that depression manifests itself as a defect in the individual's capacity to perform the kind of activity that is specifically linked to its authentic self-realization. From the point of view of the theoretical perspective for which I am arguing, an activity deficit should thus be seen in relation to the contemporary dictum of self-realization. The principal affliction of the depressed person is thereby the inability or inadequate ability to undertake the authentic self-realization demanded by our times. This analytical perspective cannot be allowed to remain unclarified, as I believe one is able to sociologically embed this perspective by turning to the analysis presented by Luc Boltanski and Eve Chiapello (2005 [1999]).

The 'Great Man' and depression

In their sociological magnum opus, *The New Spirit of Capitalism*, Boltanski and Chiapello examine the emergence and social proliferation of a new, third, spirit of capitalism. This new spirit, or the ideology which justifies people's commitment to capitalism and which makes this commitment attractive, rests on a very different normative foundation than did the two earlier spirits. That is, the normative structures of this commitment, the premises of the ideology, have been altered significantly within the last three to four decades, thereby altering the societally anchored conditions of people's engagement with the capitalist system of today. In order to understand how this development has led to a society that stresses authentic self-realization, one must comprehend how this new spirit emerged and in what way it differs from the second spirit of capitalism.[4] In particular, one must understand that critique of capitalism plays a vital part in the transformation from the second to the third spirit of capitalism.

According to Boltanski and Chiapello, capitalism has always been criticized – indeed capitalism needs its enemies (Boltanski and Chiapello, 2005: 27). Without critique, they argue, capitalism would disintegrate. Boltanski and Chiapello claim that critique of capitalism has always been nurtured by two main sources – what they call a social and an artistic critique. Whereas the social critique has the struggle against poverty, social injustice/exploitation and excessive individualism at its core, the artistic critique focuses on how capitalism is disenchanting, technocratic and dehumanizing. That is, the artistic critique elucidates how capitalism oppresses individual creativity, autonomy, spontaneity and authenticity by trying to fit every individual into the same mould (Boltanski and Chiapello, 2005: 37). In the era of the second spirit of capitalism, the artistic critique resonated particularly well. What defined the core of the second spirit of capitalism was namely the *idea* of the business empire, where the great 'leader' reigned (paradigmatically represented by IBM) and where all the employees had a *promise* of long-term employment that, according to the principle of meritocracy, allowed them to gradually realize their personal abilities and skills. Now, in the late 1960s, this organization principle came under immense pressure. There was simply a growing societal discontent with the way in which institutions, organizations, companies and society as such were extremely hierarchic, bureaucratic and disciplining. Hence, this structural arrangement precisely prevented individuals from realizing their personal abilities and skills, so the argument went. Moreover, the leading organizing principle in the second spirit of capitalism oppressed the realization of one's personal understanding of the good life – of one's authenticity. So, by stressing the necessity of emancipating individuals by allowing them to realize their authentic self (in work, at universities, at home, etc.), the artistic critique of capitalism was able to gain ground. Or, as Boltanski and Chiapello argue, capitalism slowly but surely absorbed the artistic critique into its own logic thereby utilizing the normative codes of the artistic critique as its own (Boltanski and Chiapello, 2005: 202). In that way, the artistic critique was especially efficient in paving the way for the transformation from the second spirit of capitalism to the third.

According to Boltanski and Chiapello, the range of this change can be explicated by illustrating which normative expectations of capitalist participation contemporary individuals are confronted with as opposed to those of the second spirit of capitalism. To do so, they utilize the concept of the 'Great Man' (Boltanski and Chiapello, 2005: 112). This ideal concept describes an individual who is successfully capable of internalizing and realizing normative expectations towards sociality. In the second spirit of capitalism, the expected values of the 'Great Man' were those of being effective and enduring in work, having the ability to plan a long-term career and being able to stick to one's guns. Today, the values have changed completely. In contemporary society, the dictum of the 'Great Man' is that of activity – indeed, it overshadows all other individual capacities. It crosses the boundaries between work, private life and leisure time, which means that the individual must maintain a constant level of activity in order to be continuously available for the projects on which he or she is working. However, in addition to availability, the concept of activity also encompasses a number of other normative standards with which the 'Great Man' must comply. These include the requirements to be flexible, mobile, enterprising, creative, polyvalent, adaptable, tolerant, daring, social, innovative and malleable (Boltanski and Chiapello, 2005: 112). The internalization and realization of these normative demands are regarded as necessary, in order for the individual to serve the ideological figure described in the following:

> Life is conceived as a series of projects; the more they differ from one another, the more valuable they are. What is relevant is to be always pursuing some sort of activity, never to be without a project, without ideas, to be always looking forward to, and preparing for, something along with other persons, who are brought together by the same drive for activity.
>
> (Chiapello and Fairclough, 2002: 192)

Projects are always short-term, but the 'Great Man' knows this only too well – indeed, he thrives upon it. The enthusiasm and zeal exuded by a project is built into a short-term template, in which the prospect of the project's imminent termination secures the necessary focus on its successful conclusion. In fact, the 'Great Man' renounces all long-term projects, as these by definition tend to impede the possibility of maintaining a continuous workflow. Long-term thinking hinders, in other words, the possibility of mobility, flexibility etc. In this connection, Boltanski and Chiapello make use of Deleuze and Guattari's 'nomad' concept to describe the most important characteristic of the 'Great Man' (Boltanski and Chiapello, 2005: 162).

The nomad has no fixed base, no ties and no territory, and is therefore perfectly suited to the project culture of network logic. The nomad moves around between the various project units without becoming too comfortable or 'settling down' in a particular project team. The nomad is eternally mobile and rootless, and is constantly moving on. As a result, the nomad is always open to change and capable of adapting to shifting conditions. The nomad loves indeterminacy, without which the psyche cannot be sufficiently adapted and manipulated to ensure that capitalization will proceed optimally. Determinacy, and thereby the possibility of acquiring a particular vantage point, hinders the flowering of personal responsibility and initiative, and thereby impedes the pursuit of the goal of infinite employability. In indeterminate conditions, it is therefore of crucial importance to possess the psychological ability to integrate today's normative standards. An inability to successfully exploit the continuous possibilities of activity is a direct route to the status of 'a little man'. From this perspective, depression becomes a social pathology of action and inadequacy, in which the individual suffers from an inability to initiate authentic self-realization. An individual caught in the talons of depression simply lacks the requisite fuel to rev up the motor of self-realization. As a result, depressed persons are also unable to present themselves as persons worth striving for.

The depressed individual is thus presented as someone who cannot adequately take responsibility for him- or herself, and thereby neglects the self's inherent possibilities of expression. The depressed person is associated with immobility, stagnation and inaction rather than with activity, movement, a forward-looking nature and an overbooked project calendar. Depression thereby represents the negation of a successful (life) project, a repression of the modern freedom to pursue self-realization, and consequently, the incarnation of the negativity of our time (Sørensen, 2002: 169). Moreover, if the demand for continuous self-realization activity cannot be met, the individual will also fail to fulfil the demand to be worthy of socialization and recognition. A condition of depression may consequently be viewed as a block to social integration, in which the unproductive condition of the individual places a radical brake on normal socialization. This psychological morass can be aggravated if the individuals in such a situation have only themselves to consult for guidance on how to escape from the condition, and are thereby thrown into a personal struggle to re-establish their inner (authentic) potential for action.[5]

The social communication of this view of depression presupposes the key role played by the inner self in today's self-realization. As mentioned in the previous section, the nature of the inner self determines the possibility of social success. It therefore rings true when Randall Collins postulates that today's western individuals are encouraged to treat their own selves as a religious cult (Collins, 1992: 55). Ehrenberg analyses the worship of the self in an interpretive scheme in which the innermost self is the sacred totem pole around which the individual must continuously dance. The totem pole thereby symbolizes (and confirms) the view of today's individual as the unrestricted source of its own freedom. But at the same time, the totem pole can be seen as the abyss into which the individual will fall if the constant dancing leads to the exhaustion of the self, and thereby to depression (Ehrenberg, 2001: 51). The dance is thereby neither neutral nor secondary, as it is precisely in the dance that the individual's normative socialization skills are continuously being assessed. If the individual is found wanting in failing to live up to the self-realization demands, the consequences are prompt: the individual is regarded as inadequate, and, in particular, as empty of energy and action – in other words, depressed. This explains Ehrenberg's conclusion:

> Depression is an absence of mental capacity of movement ... which colours all of the individual's feelings with the same grey colour and thereby radically curtails freedom of movement. Consequently, the depressed person's fundamental disorder is the absence of initiative.
>
> (Ehrenberg, 2000: 213)

Here, however, I feel that Ehrenberg is insufficiently precise in his formulation. If the absence of initiative, freedom of movement and capacity to act are to characterize depression in late modern society, this should be seen in the light of the demand for authentic self-realization. The two aspects simply cannot be separated. The point is that the person who lacks initiative may very well be aware of which norms to follow but is unable to fill them with the appropriate content: the depressed person does not perform the dance of authentic self-realization, but stops and perhaps even takes a step back. As a consequence, the movement and progress demanded by our current society ceases. In this respect, one could say that the self-realization possibilities have imploded, and thereby fail to be fulfilled in relation to the general authenticity demands. Here we can clearly see that depression is regarded as a phenomenon of absence: the foundered self lacks the requisite capacity for self-realization, and therefore represents self-realization's underside. This also clarifies what it is that our present era regards as a mentally healthy self-realization: a mentally healthy individual today is one who dances and acts in the service of self-realization, and who is enterprising, active, flexible, mobile, social etc.

Against this background, it is hardly surprising that a depressed individual internalizes a number of techniques of action which serve to re-establish his or her authentic self-realization. These techniques can take on innumerable forms, and are applied in a wide range of contexts: we know of self-help manuals of depression, depression literacy websites and depression focus groups etc. Hence, the market for supplying these techniques is vast and the demand just seems to grow bigger and bigger. However, it appears as if one particular technique stands out from the crowd, namely antidepressants.

Authentic self-realization, antidepressants and depression

In *Comment la dépression est devenue une épidémie* (Pignarre, 2001), the French psychiatrist Phillipe Pignarre explains his view of the 'epidemic' of depression in a quite straightforward manner. According to Pignarre, depression is that which is counteracted by SSRI-antidepressants (selective serotonin reuptake inhibitors). Or in other words, the reason for the rise in the number of cases of depression is simply that antidepressants are efficient remedies for the symptoms which define the condition (Pignarre, 2001: 71). Unsurprisingly, Pignarre's theoretical perspective is shared by his disciple Mikkel Borch-Jacobsen, who writes: "Antidepressants therefore 'recruit' the depressed, and they do so because they work" (Borch-Jacobsen, 2002: 343).[6] The explanation is simple, straightforward and in many respects convenient: depression is a pharmacologically constructed disorder, the increasing frequency of which is exclusively due to the increasing number of individuals who take antidepressant medicine.

Now, it can hardly be questioned that the growth in the use of antidepressants, particularly SSRIs, has had a practically revolutionary effect on the treatment and understanding of depression.[7] Similarly, SSRIs have fundamentally shaken the established conceptual views of healing, addiction and medicine. The unique aspect of these drugs is not just that they have far fewer side-effects than other antidepressants,[8] but that they are effective against all the various kinds of psychological disturbance associated with the disorder (Ehrenberg, 2000: 227).[9] The consequence of the widespread use of these medications has been the establishment of a common dynamic between the continuous expansion of the concept of depression and the areas of application of the drugs (Ehrenberg and Lovell, 2001: 18). As the symptoms of depression assume an ever more polymorphous character, the areas of application of the pills simply fill the vacuum created by this lack of clarity (Ehrenberg, 2000: 251). As a result, the ongoing expansion of the symptom catalogue of depression is accompanied by a continuous search for new and better antidepressants, and thereby, new clients (Dencker, 2000: 7). The new areas of application for antidepressants are harmonized with the multifarious symptom gallery of depression, but the pills also play a normative role in relation to today's demands for self-realization. Because the self-realization demands are made with no clear directions regarding their fulfilment. There is a need for a sort of psychological GPS system which can guide the individual towards the right self-realization destination. In this sense, antidepressants may be regarded as exponents of a technique of action which can lead an erring individual back onto the correct path of action (Sørensen, 2002: 177). Since inhibition, by definition, brings about the opposite of activity, namely personal foundering and inadequacy, antidepressants may be regarded as 'uninhibitors' (*désinhibiteurs*) or simply as initiative pills which eradicate the individual's passivity (Ehrenberg, 2000: 215, 239).[10]

From this perspective, it is thus not the pills in themselves that create the burgeoning rates of depression; in my opinion, it can rather with some justification be claimed that the areas of effectiveness of the pills are grounded in the contemporary normative demands for self-realization. Consequently, they function as indicators of which normative action potentials the individual is expected to be able to realize. Or, to put this another way: SSRI-antidepressants do *not* recruit the depressed, but rather react to the self-realization demands that enable the recruitment of the depressed. When the nature of the demands subjects an increasing number of selves to stress to the point of exhaustion, antidepressants are recruited as the 'stimulating' uninhibitors which will release the individual from the self-realization deficit which is characteristic of depression. In continuation of this, efforts are made to expand our understanding of the nature of medication. If antidepressants play a normative role by causing the individual to become 'de-inhibited' and dynamic, the boundaries between what is regarded as medicine, narcotics and performance-enhancing drugs (doping) become blurred, and the relationship between the normal and the pathological is shifted.

There would in other words appear to be a dilution of the relationship between the normal and the pathological, inasmuch as the areas of application of the pills and the expanded definition of depression infiltrate each other: the dividing line between the normal and the pathological is simply erased (Ehrenberg, 2000: 12). Here the concept of addiction plays an important role. Addiction to SSRIs is not regarded as pathological in the same way as addiction to, for example, narcotics or performance-enhancing drugs, but rather as a form of dependence equivalent to that of the need of diabetics for insulin (Ehrenberg, 2000: 248). If the depressed person can thus be categorized as a kind of psychological diabetic, it helps to pave the way for the use of SSRIs. But what if these pills do not merely re-establish a kind of normal state, or prevent people from dying, as insulin does for diabetics, but actually amplify or improve the state of normality? It is a fact that antidepressant users sometimes feel better afterwards than they did before; that some of the products advertise 'a new self' (Hewitt et al., 2000: 166); that some psychiatrists advocate using the pills as a means to achieve increased psychological well-being in otherwise 'healthy' individuals (Kramer, 1997); and that trials have shown that the pills also affect the psyches of 'healthy' individuals (Sørensen, 2002: 180). Have antidepressants thereby not crossed the boundary we normally place between medicine and doping, in the sense that they do not merely re-establish the normal state, but also disturb it?

The final point I address is the influence antidepressants have had on the concept of healing. The prerequisite for being able to speak of a healed condition must be that the treatment, whether psychotherapeutic or medical, ceases and is no longer necessary. However, the problem is that both the condition of depression and the use of antidepressants show a tendency to become chronic (Ehrenberg, 1995: 148). This means that one cannot claim the depression has been healed, which is why terms such as alleviation and quality of life have become the preferred concepts in the depression debate. Both concepts have the requisite positive connotations, and like the concept of community, exude a pleasant aura (Bauman, 2001b: 1), particularly the concept of quality of life. A good quality of life is after all something to which we would all aspire! Emphasizing the practically universal worthiness of quality of life becomes a way of retaining focus on the individual's authentic self-realization, despite the chronic nature of both the condition of depression and the consumption of anti- depressants. In this way, the medication becomes, not an obstacle in the search for authentic self-realization, but rather a means of preventing a poor quality of life. This is where antidepressants come into their own; they can remove the suffering and contribute towards enhancing the individual's personal quality of life. The question in this context is merely whether there is not a danger of becoming caught in a kind of medical maintenance programme (Ehrenberg, 2000: 261).

Conclusion

As has been intimated in this chapter, today's demands for authentic self-realization can be described as chronic stress factors which have a direct influence on the psychological makeup of the individual, and which can rebound in the form of depression. This contemporary view of depression relies upon the view of the individual currently favoured in the West. If we examine the consequences of this perspective a little more closely, the following would appear to apply. The structure of contemporary western society presents a number of self-realization demands for normative socialization which can be said to constitute a chronic stress factor. The background for societal approval of these demands is the current western concept of the normal individual, characterized in a manner which is the direct opposite of the depressed person. To sum up, we may therefore conclude that the rapid growth in cases of depression is made possible by the combination of these developmental tendencies. Finally, it would appear to be evident that today's response to the increasing frequency of depression is clothed in an antidepressant form, as antidepressants can remove the social pathology of action and inadequacy of the depressed person. From this point of view, the pills function primarily as a means of re-establishment for those whose subjects have foundered. But the idea that antidepressants can reverse the upward trend of the rates of depression would appear to be an example of modern myth-making (Ehrenberg, 2001: 50). As we know from Claude Lévi-Strauss (1995), myths are cultural, order-creating codes, the effects of which are associated with their social foundation. Surely the problem with this order is precisely that it tends to provide a technical solution to a problem which is not exclusively technical in nature. Michel Houellebecq, who introduced this article, will also conclude it; for perhaps all of this, he sarcastically writes, reflects the fact that we live in a time in which all of us in our hearts profoundly wish that "the solution to all our problems – including those of a psychological, sociological or generally human nature – could only be of a technical character" (Houellebecq, 2001 [1998]: 299).

Notes

1 Allan V. Horwitz also points out this phenomenon (Horwitz, 2002: 56). But Horwitz is less interested in what it is that determines the symptoms, and why it is precisely these symptoms that characterize the disorder.
2 *ICD-10* is the World Health Organization's diagnostic manual, in which the characteristics of illnesses function as a vital tool in the identification of psychological disorders. The manual provides a stamp of recognition to psychological disorders, including depression, as genuine diseases.
3 All translations from French are the writer's own.
4 It is not within the limits of this chapter to go into detail on all the aspects of this transformation.
5 As Bauman puts it: "Individually, we stand; Individually, I fall" (Bauman, 2001a: 45).

6 The author is aware of the fact that whether SSRIs are actually effective or not is a much-debated topic. Some experts, for example, truly doubt they are more effective than placebos (see, for example, Kirsch et al., 2002).
7 The American historian of psychiatry, Edward Shorter, makes a similar point in the concluding chapter of his book *A History of Psychiatry*, which he titled 'From Freud to Prozac' (Shorter, 1997: 288). In the conclusion to his book, he writes that over the past two centuries, psychiatrists have "progressed from being the healers of the therapeutic asylum to serving as gatekeepers for Prozac" (Shorter, 1997: 325).
8 This claim has naturally come in for a great deal of criticism (see Breggin and Breggin, 1995), but it is nonetheless obvious that the promotion and consumption of SSRIs relies upon this view.
9 This is clearly in line with Stephen M. Stahl's (2009) general argument that there is a movement towards multifunctional pharmacological drug categorization and that most SSRIs are created to be multifunctional: they should encompass almost all symptoms associated with depression.
10 When directly asked what antidepressants can do for a depressed individual, Ehrenberg replied: "Well, they have a stimulating effect. Everyone knows that" (Ehrenberg, 2005: 27).

References

Bauman, Z (2001a) *The Individualised Society*. Cambridge: Polity.
Bauman, Z (2001b) *Community: Seeking Safety in an Insecure World*. Cambridge: Polity.
Blazer, DG (2005) *The Age of Melancholy: 'Major Depression' and Its Social Origins*. London: Routledge.
Boltanski, L and Chiapello, E. (2005 [1999]) *The New Spirit of Capitalism*. London: Verso Books.
Borch-Jacobsen, M (2002) *Folies à plusieurs: De l'hystérie à la dépression*. Paris: Les Empêcheurs de Penser en Rond.
Breggin, PR and Breggin, GR (1995) *Talking Back to Prozac: What Doctors Won't Tell You about Today's Most Controversial Drug*. New York: St Martin's.
Chiapello, E and Fairclough, N (2002) Understanding the New Management Ideology: A Transdisciplinary Contribution from Critical Discourse Analysis and New Sociology of Capitalism. *Discourse and Society* 13(2): 185–208.
Collins, R (1992) *Sociological Insight: An Introduction to Non-Obvious Sociology*. Oxford: Oxford University Press.
Dencker, SJ (2000) The Need for New and Better Antidepressants: Reboxetine – A New Option. *Acta Psychiatrica Scandinavica* 101(402): 6–11.
Ehrenberg, A (1986) Des stades sans dieux. *Le Debat* 40: 48–61.
Ehrenberg, A (1995) *L'Individu incertain*. Paris: Hachette-Pluriel.
Ehrenberg, A (2000 [1998]) *La Fatigue d'être soi. Dépression et société*. Paris: Odile Jacob.
Ehrenberg, A (2001) Nous sommes dans une culture du malheur intime. *Libération* 17(2): 50–51.
Ehrenberg, A (2005) Det mærkelige molekyle. *Information* February: 24–27.
Ehrenberg, A and Lovell, AM (2001) Pourquoi avons-nous besoin d'une réflexion sur la psychiatrie? In: Ehrenberg, A and Lovell, AM (eds) *La Maladie mentale en mutation. Psychiatrie et société*, 9-39. Paris: Odile Jacob.
Ferrara, A (1998) *Reflective Authenticity: Rethinking the Project of Modernity*. London: Routledge.
Giddens, A (1991) *Modernity and Self-Identity: Self and Society in the Late Modern Age*. Cambridge: Polity.

Hewitt, JP, Fraser, MR and Berger, L (2000) Is it me or is it Prozac? Antidepressants and the construction of self. In: Fee, D (ed.) *Pathology and the Postmodern: Mental Illness as Discourse and Experience*, 163–185. London: Sage.
Honneth, A (2003) *Behovet for anerkendelse*. Copenhagen: Hans Reitzels Forlag.
Honneth, A (2004) Organised Self-Realization: Some Paradoxes of Individualisation. *European Journal of Social Theory* 7(4): 463–478.
Horwitz, AV (2002) *Creating Mental Illness*. Chicago: Chicago University Press.
Horwitz, AV and Wakefield, J (2007) *The Loss of Sadness: How Psychiatry Transformed Normal Sorrow into Depressive Disorder*. Oxford: Oxford University Press.
Houellebecq, M. (1998 [1994]) *Whatever*. London: Serpent's Tail.
Houellebecq, M (2001 [1998]) Elementarpartikler. Copenhagen: Borgen.
Houellebecq, M (2002 [1994]) Udvidelse af kampzonen. Copenhagen: Borgen.
Kirsch, I, Scorboria, A and Moore, TJ (2002) Antidepressants and Placebos: Secrets, Revelations, and Unanswered Questions. *Prevention and Treatment* 5, Article 33.
Kramer, PD (1997) *Listening to Prozac*. London: Fourth Estate.
Lévi-Strauss, C (1995) *Myth and Meaning: Cracking the Code of Culture*. New York: Schocken Books.
Olsen, LR, Jensen, DV, Noerholm, V, Martiny, K and Bech, P (2003) The External and Internal Validity of the Major Depression Inventory. *Measuring Severity of Depressive States, Psychological Medicine* 33: 351–356.
Pignarre, P (2001) *Comment la dépression est devenue une épidémie*. Paris: Hachette.
Shorter, E (1997) *A History of Psychiatry: From the Era of the Asylum to the Age of Prozac*. New York: John Wiley.
Sørensen, AD (2002) Den biologiske psykiatris renæssance og det antidepressive menneske. *Slagmark* 35: 159–183.
Stahl, SM (2009) Multifunctional Drugs: A Novel Concept for Psychopharmacology. *CNS Spectr* 14(2): 71–73.
Taylor, C (1991) *The Ethics of Authenticity*. Cambridge, MA: Harvard University Press.
Taylor, C (1994) The politics of recognition. In: Guttman, A (ed.) *Multiculturalism*, 25–74. Princeton, NJ: Princeton University Press.
Wheaton, B (1999) The nature of stressors. In: Horwitz, AV and Scheid, TL (eds) *A Handbook for the Study of Mental Health: Social Contexts, Theories, and Systems*, 176–197. Cambridge: Cambridge University Press.
Widlöcher, D (2001) Psychogenese de la dépression et mode d'action des medicaments antidepresseurs. In: Ehrenberg, A and Lovell, AM (eds) *La Maladie mentale en mutation. Psychiatrie et société*, 209–218. Paris: Odile Jacob.

4 Return of the age of anxiety

The embedding of a late modern social pathology

Anders Petersen

Introduction

According to Ulrich Beck and Wolfgang Bonss (2001: 63), one of the fundamental tasks of sociology is diagnosis of the times.[1] Actually, one can make the claim that sociology – on an overall level – has always had the ambition to try to diagnose the essential character of society (Lichtblau, 1995). That claim is not hard to support. One just has to direct attention towards the analysis of the founding fathers of the discipline, more specifically their analysis of the transition from traditional to modern society. Marx, Simmel, Durkheim and Weber – they all focused on the consequences of this rupture and the malaises it brought about: anomie, alienation, rational iron cage and tragedy of culture. In relation to the diagnosis of contemporary society, the concepts and analyses of the founding fathers are no longer adequate. We have, as so many authors have reported, moved on to a new historical epoch. A wide range of names has been given to this epoch – post-modernity (Lyotard, 1979); hypermodernity (Lipovetsky, 2005); liquid modernity (Bauman, 2000) and late modernity (Giddens, 1991) – just to mention a few. Whatever conceptualization one prefers, the concepts used to capture the essential character of this epoch have changed and so have the malaises that encapsulate our particular age.[2]

Which malaise, then, is indicative of our historical epoch? A bit more than a decade ago, American sociologist Allan V. Horwitz and American Philosopher Jerome Wakefield tried to capture this in their article 'The age of depression' (Horwitz and Wakefield, 2005).The starting point of their article is actually that we have witnessed a transformation from the age of anxiety to the age of depression. But why?[3] Their main claim is simply that depression is to be perceived as the pivotal mental disorder that informs us in the best possible way about the conditions of living in contemporary society because of two factors: first of all, western countries have witnessed a swelling prevalence in the amount of people who have been diagnosed with depression; second, a steep increase in the amount of people on antidepressant medication has been detected. The argumentation in the article is solid and the claims are well-substantiated.[4] However, a shift seems to be occurring. And although depression is still a significant (and troubling) mental disorder in contemporary society, it appears to have been overtaken by another mental disorder, namely anxiety. Perhaps one can even talk about a comeback for anxiety?

DOI: 10.4324/9781032714356-5

In 1947 (first in New York – then in 1948 in London), W.H. Auden famously proclaimed that time to be 'the age of anxiety' (Auden, 1948). In his lengthy poem Auden, in the form of a dramatic allegory, identifies – and manifests –the basic human problem as man's anxiety in time. Written in the aftermath of World War II, one understands why Auden's poem is permeated with pessimism – especially concerning the psychic condition of his contemporaries. As Edward Callan writes:

> The plot of *The Age of Anxiety* reveals, not character development in the conventional sense, but development within the psychic personality. More specifically, the six parts of *The Age of Anxiety* are six stages in a regenerative journey; and, furthermore, each of the four central acts of the drama presents a search for 'Wholeness'.
>
> (Callan, 1965: 157)

The Age of Anxiety, in Callan's interpretation, thus voices a growing psychic fragmentation. There is a lack of wholeness at stake that is creating immense individual difficulties. People are torn apart and in desperate need of completeness. But alas – their search seems to be in vain. Now, the question arises whether Auden's description of the age of anxiety is adequate when it comes to the age of anxiety that we are witnessing now. I think not. By answering in the negative, I am not questioning whether we in fact live in an age of anxiety. Because I – alongside many others (for example, Wilkinson, 2001; Parish, 2001; Salecl, 2004; Horwitz, 2013) – think that we do. I simply believe that we need another vocabulary to capture the specificities of this age rather than the one provided by Auden. In other words: I want to avoid the risk of portraying anxiety as a historical constant, however comforting that might be. Hence, in this chapter, I will present the outline of an analysis that tries to answer one main question: why is anxiety indicative of our time?

In order to answer this question in an acceptable manner, I will proceed in four stages. First, I will substantiate the main claim of the article and explicate how one can legitimately call our age the age of anxiety. Second, I will elucidate specific kind(s) of anxiety that are sweeping through contemporary western societies and discuss why these kinds are particularly actualized. Third, I will explain why these kinds of anxiety (the kinds that seem to be very prevalent among youth and adolescence) are to be understood as signs of social pathology and not just individualized disorders. Fourth, I will conclude by discussing the main points of this chapter and by elaborating on future research possibilities that this chapter enables.

Why the age of anxiety?

So far I have – in an unhesitant way – addressed anxiety as a particular mental disorder. To most contemporaries, I would claim, this is rather unproblematic. But that has not always been the case. When Søren Kierkegaard embarked on his famous philosophical/psychological (in fact, Kierkegaard called himself a psychologist when writing *On the Concept of Anxiety*, not a philosopher) journey into the concept of anxiety, no mention of anxiety as a mental disorder came to mind. Instead, anxiety to Kierkegaard was to be perceived as an existential and religious (strongly connected with hereditary sin) embedded condition, which individuals had to choose to address when making free choices. Thus, according to Kierkegaard, anxiety was intrinsically linked with freedom. As he writes:

> Anxiety may be compared with dizziness. He whose eye happens to look down into the yawning abyss becomes dizzy. But what is the reason for this? It is just as much in his own eye as in the abyss, for suppose he had not looked down. Hence anxiety is the dizziness of freedom, which emerges when the spirit wants to posit the synthesis and freedom looks down into its own possibility, laying hold of finiteness to support itself.
>
> (Kierkegaard, 1980: 61)

There is quite a long way from this Kierkegaardian perspective on anxiety to mental disorder. The same is true if we move towards cultural understandings of anxiety that reigned in the past. As Allan V. Horwitz writes: "Through much of the twentieth century, anxiety was not only a central condition in medical and psychiatric practice but also a major aspect of Western culture" (Horwitz, 2013: 118). In fact, for most of this century, anxiety was not even formulated as a disease. The cultural aspect of anxiety took precedence over the medical, one could say. According to Horwitz, three major influences can explain this.

First of all, Sigmund Freud's pathbreaking theoretical perspective on anxiety was immensely popular among intellectuals and in the media. In Freud's earlier writings, more specifically in 1894, he coined the term 'anxiety neurosis' (Freud, 1959/1926). According to Freud, this form of neurosis was a distinct syndrome, which were quite different from those of neurasthenia. At that time, neurasthenia was a very popular and successful diagnosis, a nosology instituted by American neurologist George Miller Beard in 1869. The overall reason why neurasthenia – or nervous exhaustion (Beard, 1869) – enjoyed such immense popularity[5] was due to the fact that it described an illness of modern life – increased nervous exhaustion brought about by the emergence of modern industries and big cities. Hence, the aetiology of neurasthenia was to be found in the social permeability of the mind rather than in biomedical alterations of the brain. The problem with the term 'neurasthenia', however, was its scope. It encompassed everything. As Beard wrote:

> If a patient complains of general malaise, debility of all the functions, poor appetite, abiding weakness in the back and spine, fugitive neuralgic pains, hysteria, insomnia, hypochondriasis, disinclination for consecutive mental labour, severe and weakening attack of sick headache, and other analogous symptoms, and at the same time gives no evidence of anaemia or any organic disease, we have reason to suspect… that we are dealing with a typical case of neurasthenia.
>
> (Beard, in Ehrenberg, 2010b: 32)

Freud was dissatisfied with this, and extracted the anxiety neurosis as a particular syndrome from neurasthenia. Or, he grouped a whole range of symptoms and identified them as having different manifestations – heart and breathing problems, panic, psychic obsessions etc. – of the same underlying process. In Freud's interpretation, anxiety neurosis was (and so was neurasthenia) the result of sexual dissatisfaction, and it ultimately "stemmed from the accumulation of more sexual excitation than people could psychically assimilate. Anxiety neurosis were thus especially common among sexually frustrated practitioners of *coitus interruptus*, sexual abstinence, and the like" (Horwitz, 2013: 79). In that respect, anxiety neuroses was more a synonym for culturally imbued distress than for a particular mental disease.

Second, anxiety played (and still plays) a major role in existential philosophy, which – generally speaking – addressed anxiety as a core human predicament. Just think of the writings of existential philosophers Jean-Paul Sartre, Martin Heidegger and Martin Buber, whose thoughts and ideas were highly popular and manifested themselves in the cultural landscape of the 20th century. Of course, the proliferation of their ideas about anxiety did not strike a chord with the vast majority of the western population. But the idea, nevertheless, that anxiety was an inherent part of human life – and that socio-cultural transformations could alter the particular manifestations of anxiety – became axiomatic. Understood as such, anxiety was not to be seen as a medical condition. Third, it was commonplace in especially the middle of the 20th century to perceive anxiety as a natural response to socially and politically generated circumstances. In the post-war period – precipitated by the horrific experiences of Holocaust and Hiroshima – anxiety arose in the face of catastrophic tensions of the cold war, the proliferation of nuclear weapons and uncertainties of the geopolitical situation per se. The greatest hostilities between the USA and the former Communist states are emblematic of this reception of anxiety. One of the central characteristics of the political climate of the time is how anxiety was directly related to something that came from the outside and potentially invaded – and thus disrupted and manipulated – the entire social body. Images of parasites and bacteria were used to delineate how the 'others' could colonize every pore of society. The feeling of anxiety was, undoubtedly, heightened by these circumstances. But there was something that further stimulated this, namely specific societal developments. As Slovenian philosopher Renata Salecl writes: "And then, too, economic crisis became coupled with the crisis of man trying to figure out the idea of the future" (Salecl, 2004: 2). Still, however, anxiety in this guise is not to be mistaken for a specific medical condition or disease: it was a socio-cultural signifier.

All of this has changed. Nowadays, anxiety is mostly perceived as a mental disorder with crippling individual consequences. In order to understand why this has become the case, one cannot avoid dealing with the transformation of the discipline of psychiatry. As historian Edward Shorter has argued, the discipline of psychiatry has – almost since its birth – been biologically/medically oriented. That is, with one major exception, namely what he refers to as the psychoanalytic hiatus (Shorter, 1997: 145). In relation to this chapter, this hiatus is of great importance since it directly refers to the period of time when anxiety was not necessarily perceived to be a medical disorder in need of treatment. As already mentioned, Freud, as well as his contemporary followers, reserved another place for anxiety than the strictly medical. But the Freudian perspective did not last long, which Shorter's final chapter in his history of psychiatry also indicates: the chapter is entitled From Freud to Prozac (Shorter, 1997: 288). Thus, at some point, the medical perspective on anxiety gained prominence, something that actually can be dated to the publication of the *DSM-III* in 1980. The launch of this version of the *DSM* announced what Allan V. Horwitz has called a transformation from dynamic to diagnostic psychiatry (Horwitz, 2002). In the *DSM-III*, all psychoanalytic analysis, language and jargon was removed, thereby altering the focus of psychiatric enquiry. As Horwitz writes:

> In contrast to the dynamic model, diagnostic psychiatry defines diseases through the presence of overt symptoms, regardless of the causes of these symptoms. It regards diseases as natural entities that exist in the body and that generate the particular symptoms a person displays. These diseases became the object of scientific claims that can be made in isolation from the personalities and social contexts in which they arise, an abstraction that would have been unthinkable in the dynamic model.
>
> (Horwitz, 2002: 56–57)

Within the realm of diagnostic psychiatry, the primary causes of mental disorders are not sought in childhood disturbances – or in difficult socio-economic living conditions for that matter – but in disturbed brains and neurochemical activities, all of which manifests itself in various symptoms that can be observed and communicated. In that respect, the main focus is on symptoms that can be classified and collected into a given diagnosis. What is particularly interesting in this transition is, of course, the ways in which anxiety was imbedded in this new philosophy. Horwitz again:

"The *DSM-III* revolutionized conceptions of anxiety" (Horwitz, 2013: 134). First of all, the *DSM-III* separated anxiety from depression and hence chose to distinguish sharply between those two malaises – something which Edward Shorter has problematized (Shorter, 2013). Second, and this is what Horwitz primarily refers to, the *DSM-III* initiated a complete societal implementation of anxiety as a medical, and hence diagnosable, disease that can be treated with pharmaceuticals – first and foremost antidepressants. Due to this development, other languages of anxiety than the diagnostic have, gradually, been replaced. In that respect, the dominant medical language of anxiety is an intrinsic part of what I have elsewhere referred to as the diagnostic culture (Brinkmann and Petersen, 2015). The main characteristic of the diagnostic culture is the fact that psychological problems, human deviance and malaises are predominantly understood as something that can be diagnosed on the grounds of its various symptoms. Hence, anxiety is no longer – by laymen as well as medical professionals – addressed as a moral, ethical, existential or even psychological problem but as a set of symptoms indicative of a medical disorder that needs to be treated and hence removed. In the diagnostic culture, nothing is to be learnt from a period of anxiety – the symptoms of anxiety are merely to be eliminated.

But the revolution Horwitz points at also hints at another pivotal development that the *DSM-III* instigated – namely the beginning of the proliferation of anxiety. Since the 1980s, there is strong evidence that the number of people diagnosed with anxiety and public reports of anxiety have gone up. Epidemiological studies indicate that vast numbers of people in western societies are suffering from anxiety (Horwitz, 2013: 143). This tendency is backed by the birth cohort analysis made by Jean M. Twenge, which shows that the levels of anxiety and anxiety diagnosis reported in the USA between 1952 and 1992 have gone up significantly (Twenge, 2000). More recently, a large Danish survey has shown that anxiety – especially among teenagers and adolescents – is the fastest-growing and most widely proliferated disorder in contemporary Danish society (Flachs et al., 2015). Hence, it seems quite pertinent to call our epoch the age of anxiety. It is my claim, however, that we cannot understand this development only by examining the internal transition of psychiatric thinking. The growing numbers of people diagnosed with anxiety are not just caused by alterations within psychiatric thinking. It is not just because the *DSM* changed its philosophy and shifted focus from aetiology to symptomatology that we are witnessing a bourgeoning rate of people with anxiety. In that respect, I disagree with the argument of Allan Horwitz, who has stated:

> It does not seem plausible that the upsurge in measured rates of anxiety represents a genuine epidemic of anxiety disorders. Instead, the putative growth of anxiety disorders since the implementation of the *DSM-III* seems to stem primarily from the use of diagnostic criteria that fail to actually distinguish natural from disordered anxiety.
>
> (Horwitz, 2013: 144)

There is no doubt about the fact that the successful implementation of new diagnostic criteria of anxiety has paved some of the way for its proliferation. My point is, however, that this cannot account for the whole story. What we also need is an analysis of the socio-structural transformations that have supported the diagnostic understanding of anxiety and hence for its proliferation. Only by engaging ourselves in this are we able to understand why anxiety, in the contemporary age of anxiety, is perceived as an individualized disorder of societal significance. More specifically, we need an analysis of what it is in contemporary anxiety that informs us about current perceptions of order and pathology.

Anxieties in the age of anxiety

So far we have not defined what anxiety is – and that is no easy task. Anxiety is, indeed, a very complex phenomenon and it is beyond the scope of this chapter to go into depth with the many layers of anxiety. What is possible, however, is to give a broad definition of what anxiety entails and then move on to addressing the forms of anxiety that haunt contemporary society.

The condition of anxiety, most researchers would agree, is "comprised of a complex emotional process which involves not only our thoughts, but also our physiology and behaviour" (Wilkinson, 2001: 15). That is, anxiety consists of affective experiences, behavioural responses and bodily reactions. But, as already mentioned, the main arbiters of anxiety definitions in contemporary society are the diagnostic manuals – the *DSM-V* or the *International Classification of Diseases (ICD)-10*. It is in the realm of their medical logic to define anxiety as a syndrome that occurs independently of "any unique qualities of the patients who carry its symptoms or of the period of human history when it appeared" (Horwitz, 2013: 2). Pathological anxiety, then, consists first and foremost of the number and the severity of symptoms that people have in a given period of time. That logic is transferred unto a wide variety of different anxiety categories such as panic disorder (with or without agoraphobia), social phobias, obsessive-compulsive disorder, post-traumatic stress disorder, acute stress disorder, generalized anxiety disorders and many others. These disorders are categorized as being distinct from one another and also from other mental disorders such as depression[6] and somatoform disorders. What is more, the definitions in these manuals make sharp distinctions between those people who have these disorders and those who don't. Again, the pool of symptoms and their severity connected with each of these disorders are decisive of those who are included into the category and those who are not. If we take a closer look at some of the mentioned categories of anxiety, we are able to approach the overall argument of this chapter, namely that these disorders inform us about specific human traits that are socially constituted as pathological in contemporary society. More specifically, three of the most actualized types of anxiety are singled out: social phobia, panic disorder (without agoraphobia) and generalized anxiety disorder. These disorders are defined in the following manner in the *ICD-10*:

Generalized anxiety disorder: Anxiety that is generalized and persistent but not restricted to, or even strongly predominating in, any particular environmental circumstances (i.e. it is 'free-floating'). The dominant symptoms are variable but include complaints of persistent nervousness, trembling, muscular tensions, sweating, light-headedness, palpitations, dizziness and epigastric discomfort. Fears that the patient or a relative will shortly become ill or have an accident are often expressed.

Social phobias: Fear of scrutiny by other people leading to avoidance of social situations. More pervasive social phobias are usually associated with low self-esteem and fear of criticism. They may present as a complaint of blushing, hand tremor, nausea, or urgency of micturition, the patient sometimes being convinced that one of these secondary manifestations of their anxiety is the primary problem. Symptoms may progress to panic attacks.

Panic disorder: The essential feature is recurrent attacks of severe anxiety (panic), which are not restricted to any particular situation or set of circumstances and are therefore unpredictable. As with other anxiety disorders, the dominant symptoms include sudden onset of palpitations, chest pain, choking sensations, dizziness and feelings of unreality (depersonalization or derealization). There is often also a secondary fear of dying, losing control, or going mad.

In order to legitimize why these disorders are singled out, it seems adequate to refer to the fact that these are among the most proliferated anxiety disorders in contemporary western societies (Scott, 2006; Fricchione, 2004). Thus, it is more than likely that a vast number of people – including the readers of this book –can relate themselves to one of these disorders and their symptoms. If we take a closer look at the above-mentioned definitions, this is not particularly odd. By a first glance, these definitions are quite broad, entailing a considerable number of human behaviours and emotions that are being scrutinized as problematic and signs of mental illness. In this sense, it is not difficult to understand why scholars such as Horwitz refer to processes of pathologization when explaining the proliferation of these disorders (Horwitz, 2013: 158). By pathologization, it is understood that diagnostic manuals such as the *ICD* and the *DSM* are failing to distinguish between natural and disordered anxiety, thereby promoting specific symptoms as pathological and hence instigating a breakdown of our conventional distinctions between problems in living and psychiatric disorders (see also Lau, 2012). This perspective posits that the ongoing cultural process of pathologization implies that many traits and behaviours that used to be considered normal human problems (sorrow, guilt, shyness, disruptive behaviour etc.) are now conceptualized as mental disorders that can be diagnosed and treated medically and therapeutically.[7] Perhaps the transformation of shyness into social phobia is the best indication of this process of pathologization, at least when it comes to issues of anxiety. As Christopher Lane (Lane, 2007) and Susie Scott (Scott, 2006) have shown, shyness has become an unhealthy state of mind in contemporary society and thereby transformed into a diagnosable mental illness in the form of social phobia. What was hitherto considered 'just shyness' has hence found its way into the specific diagnosis of social phobia, something that is largely enabled by the prevailing psychiatric mind-set of the diagnostic manuals, both Lane and Scott argue. The consequence is, according to the authors, that instead of providing clear-cut boundaries between natural and abnormal anxiety, the medical model of the diagnostic manuals in fact gives much leeway in pathologizing what was previously considered to be normal behaviour. What is more, this has paved the way for an increasing medicalization of shyness, as particularly Scott argues, and is thereby to be viewed as a central aspect of an overall development of medicalization of – and hence managing – social deviance per se that we are witnessing in late modern society (Scott, 2006: 148).

The pathologization of these kinds of anxiety is, no doubt about it, partly responsible for their widespread proliferation. But again, this explanation cannot account for the entire development. The process of pathologization per se, does not explain why these particular mental disorders are socially constituted as pathological. Or, to be more precise, it does not explain why these particular symptoms are understood as signifiers of mental illness in contemporary society. In this respect it is pivotal to be aware of the fact that mental disorders, when inscribed in the diagnostic manuals, are constituted by symptoms. Unlike somatic illnesses, in which symptoms are signs of a particular disease – blood in the stools is indicative of colon cancer (but is not necessarily cancer per se) – the symptoms of mental illnesses *are* the disease. The variety, length and severity of the symptoms account for the disease that can be diagnosed. So in this respect, it seems quite important to base the analyses of our particular age of anxiety on the symptoms that constitute the aforementioned kinds of anxiety. When invoking such a gaze on the definitions of general anxiety disorder, social phobia and panic disorder one rather obvious element of the symptoms arises. They evolve around individual loss of control of one's life, particularly concerning the individual mind (sense of self) and the body. This loss manifests itself in different ways in the different forms of anxiety, ranging from feelings of depersonalization, low self-esteem and nervousness to light-headedness, blushing and dizziness. This loss of control is not restricted to any particular situations, albeit social phobias and panic disorder are more likely to occur in social situations in which the individual is to take part.

Of course, a loss of control is also a pertinent part of other mental disorders – for example, depression. In depression, the gradual experience of losing control over one's life is often followed by feelings of helplessness and a sense of hopelessness, true hallmarks of depression (Ratcliffe, 2015). American psychiatrist Dan G. Blazer even goes as far as to state, "The swelling prevalence of depression in Western society perhaps reflects and increasingly dominant hopelessness within society" (Blazer, 2005: 154). In Blazer's account, the connection between the ascent of depression and the loss of hope can be analysed in detail by extracting eight themes associated with the loss of hope. These are: loss of story, loss of language, loss of self, loss of unity, loss of trust, loss of orientation, loss of meaning and, finally, nihilism (Blazer, 2005: 154–158). Without going into detail with these eight themes, I would like to raise two questions concerning Blazer's thesis. First: Is contemporary western society really experiencing a general loss of hope? I would answer in the negative. I would rather argue – as I will do in the next paragraph – that we are witnessing a significant change in the social norms and rules that is altering the societal conditions for the emergence of social pathologies such as depression and anxiety disorders. Second: Can we rank the loss of hope put forward by Blazer alongside the loss of control that I argue is the common feature of the anxieties in question? Again, I would argue no. The difference is that Blazer claims the bourgeoning rates of depression are caused by the overall loss of hope while I claim that the above-mentioned anxieties – and hence the loss of control connected with them – are constituted by and are a reaction to new societal conditions of what it means to be a human being in contemporary society. The main point is that these forms of anxiety are reflecting types of individual loss of control – feelings and behaviours – that are socially unwelcome in the cultural climate of contemporary late modern society. But, at the same time, the cultural climate in contemporary society, I will argue, is fostering the societal conditions that support the emergence of these types of anxiety. The question is, in which way?

Anxieties as signs of social pathology in contemporary society

The concept of social pathology has, ever since it was proliferated and popularized by Emilie Durkheim, been controversial. The mere idea that society can be sick, and that society can cause harm to individual organisms and psyches, is not straightforward and critique has been raised. In his relatively critical article about the notion of social pathology, French sociologist Alain Ehrenberg writes the following:

> The idea underlying the adjunction of the adjective 'social' to the substantive 'pathology' is that mental pathologies are the product of our social relationships, that they reveal something about our mores and lifestyles, and that there is a moral, social and political lesson to be drawn from this type of pathology.
>
> (Ehrenberg, 2013: 11)

Although Ehrenberg does not discard this idea entirely, he does not embrace it either. In fact, he is critical about the idea of society producing the conditions through which mental pathologies are created. As he has written in some of his previous work: "we are witnessing a change of the social status of psychic suffering – and not a *psychological aggravation* of the condition of individuals in 'depressive society'" (Ehrenberg, 2010a: 9). In fact, Ehrenberg is arguing that the altered social status of psychic suffering – here understood as increased awareness and public attention – has paved the way for the bourgeoning rates of mental illnesses that we are confronted with in contemporary society.

In a similar vein, German social philosopher Axel Honneth is also challenging the scope of the concept of social pathology (Honneth, 2014). He does so by investigating the concept via the thoughts of German social-psychologist Alexander Mitscherlich and Sigmund Freud. In Honneth's perspective, both of these theorists are too narrow in their analytical scope. He writes:

> At first, Mitscherlich ties the existence of a social disease to the existence of a conspicuous number of the members of society suffering from symptoms of a psychic abnormality to such a degree that they consult in droves physicians or therapists. Without this first indicator of a suffering from psychic functional impairment, experienced en masse, there seems to be no reason, in Mitscherlich's picture, to look for deeper disturbances in the process of social integration. Similarly, for Freud, whose cultural diagnoses clearly set the example for Mitscherlich's inquiry, the neurologists first need to register a rapid increase in a specific class of only psychologically explainable illnesses before the sociologically invested analyst can go on to search for their causes in the societal apparatus.
>
> (Honneth, 2014: 686)

At a certain level, there is nothing wrong with these observations, Honneth argues. The problem arises, however, if one establishes a too intimate bond between conspicuous societal tendencies and the increase in symptoms that are manifested in widespread illness among individuals. And Honneth thinks both Freud and Mitscherlich fall prey to this mistake. If the analysis of social pathologies rests almost entirely on this premise, the argumentation is going to be too vague – even flawed, Honneth claims. In order to speak of social pathologies, or of diseases of social life, Honneth believes a transition to the "independent organizational unit of society, which is irreducible to the sum of its individual members' behavior" (Honneth, 2014: 689), is required. Thus, we need to broaden our analytical scope substantially and utilize the concept of social pathologies accordingly. However, as mentioned, Honneth is not claiming that the rise in mental pathologies or psychic suffering is indifferent in the analysis of social pathologies. As he writes: "There would be no reason to give thought to potential 'diseases' of society if the failures of individual socialization did not generally reflect themselves in behavioral abnormalities of the members of society" (Honneth, 2014: 690). Thus, it is all about the scope of things and hence about the usage of the concept of social pathologies.

In my perspective, both Ehrenberg and Honneth are directing attention to important issues. But I also disagree with them. In relation to Ehrenberg, I simply think he is off the mark in only considering the changed social status of psychic suffering when accounting for increased rates of mental illnesses. I mean, there is hardly any doubt about the fact that psychic suffering has a totally different social status now compared to 40 years ago. Hence, there is an increasing societal awareness about psychic suffering as well as an extended perception of what psychic suffering really is. I have already mentioned the process of pathologization as one pivotal aspect of this development. But, there is also a societal development that one has to take into consideration when accounting for the bourgeoning rates of, for example, different kinds of anxiety, I will argue. In relation to Honneth, I almost entirely concur with his reasoning. One cannot reduce the analysis of social pathologies to increasing levels of mental illnesses. Social pathologies might very well manifest themselves in other – and more collective – ways than in individual psychic malaises. This does not entail, as Honneth is well aware, that we should neglect the analysis of increased levels of individual psychic suffering as signs of social pathologies. In fact, I would argue, the need to make these analyses is a matter of utmost importance, especially in the light of contemporary society trying to reduce particular psychic malaises to individual problems. That is, there is a widespread tendency in contemporary society to individualize problems that could, in fact, be seen as structurally stimulated.

It is in line with this reasoning that I argue the following. In our historical epoch, not only the above-mentioned types of anxiety are manifesting themselves as the seamy side of a societally recognized normality but also the bourgeoning rates of these anxieties are present because of increasing societal pressure to perform ceaselessly. What is normality, then, in our late modern society? American sociologists Luigi Esposito and Fernando Perez have answered this question by putting late modern society and contemporary neoliberal society on the same footing. They write:

> subjects in a neoliberal society are considered normal and functional only when they show a willingness to compete with others for the things they need or desire and when they assume 'personal responsibility' for their own problems. In contrast, any person who fails to display these qualities is assumed

> to fail not only as an economic actor but also as a responsible being. In fact, failing to display these sorts of behavioural and/or attitudinal qualities is very commonly attributed to some type of personal dysfunction or pathology.
>
> (Esposito and Perez, 2014: 421)

The claim is quite straightforward. Being normal – and hence functional – is only possible if one internalizes the inclination to compete with others and by assuming personal responsibility for all aspects of one's own life. The functional aspect of being normal is quite narrowly understood. Functional equals being able to perform adequately on the ever-changing labour market, hence being able to address the required competences and normative demands. Only the functional are able to compete with others, which is why the internalization of the necessary competences and normative demands are crucial. So, which are the required competences and normative demands? We know that a clear-cut definition of the required competences is impossible. It is hard to predict the future. Therefore, vague categorizations are used. These are, more often than not, connected with – and understood as the same thing as – the normative demands put forward in our historical epoch. In order to understand these, we can turn to French sociologists Luc Boltanski and Eve Chiapello.

In their seminal study on the emergence of the new spirit of capitalism, Boltanski and Chiapello have coined a comprehensive list of normative demands individuals in contemporary society are confronted with in order to be attractive for the labour market. These, all collected under the heading of endless activity, are: flexibility, polyvalence, adaptability, mobility, connect-ability, versatility and the ability to be open, friendly, funny, self-aware and easy-going. All of these qualities – in fact put forward as demands – are markers of a persons' employability – what Boltanski and Chiapello refer to as 'markers of great men' (Boltanski and Chiapello, 2005: 114). Thus, great – employable – men [and women] are able to internalize these qualities and employ them in competition with others in regard to who is the most attractive person for a particular position. Small men [and women] – or what they refer to as 'little persons' – on the contrary, are incapable of being flexible, versatile etc., which ultimately grounds them as unemployable and hence without the necessary means of entering competitive relationships (Boltanski and Chiapello, 2005: 119). Thus, if we follow the claim of Esposito and Perez, the little persons in Boltanski and Chiapello's terminology are attributed to being dysfunctional or even pathological. If we look at the definitions of the above-mentioned types of anxiety, the analysis is – I believe – quite easily legitimized. The markers of great men are totally absent in the definitions of the types of anxiety. Instead of flexibility and adaptability, fear and nervousness are the hallmarks of anxiety. Instead of being an easy-going and self-aware, low self-esteem and depersonalization characterize these anxieties and so on. No one who is struggling with these symptoms is capable of internalizing the normative demands required to be a great person. In that respect, the absence of taking responsibility for one's life – and thus not being able to compete with others on the grounds of these normative demands – is considered to be the exact opposite of normality and therefore pathological.

I would also argue, however, that the demand in itself to live in accordance with these normative demands – and hence the ongoing attempt to internalize them – can lead to the above-mentioned anxieties. What is crucial in this understanding is the fact that the normative demands have been institutionalized. In this respect one could talk about the role of the media – the Facebook generation etc. where the demands to constantly compete and show that one leads a good, healthy and interesting life is affecting people 24/7. This is combined with the fact that, in contemporary institutional settings – such as kindergartens, schools and universities – the pupils and students are constantly confronted with curricula that support the overall idea of internalizing these normative demands (Pedersen, 2011). That is, they are confronted with the idealizations of these demands and hence with the overall positive outcome of their display. In that respect, they are also confronted with the negative outcome of a lack of their successful internalization. The constant awareness of this – and the mere confrontation with these powerful demands – is, in fact, putting immense pressure on individuals to perform accordingly. This pressure is actually augmented by the fact that these demands – however difficult they might be to internalize – are wrapped in positive connotations. Because who would not like to act responsibly in respect to one's own life? Who would not like to be considered a great person? Who would not like to be flexible, adaptable, funny etc.? We all would – but the fact of the matter is that more and more people are showing signs of the exact opposite. And, especially concerning the types of anxiety in question here, more and more young people and adolescents are struck down with this 'disorder'. One of the reasons why that is, I would claim, is exactly because of the fact that they are institutionally confronted with the demands. Young people today are increasingly reacting negatively to what I refer to as the chronic stressor of adhering to these normative demands (Wheaton, 1999). According to Canadian sociologist Blair Wheaton, chronic stressors are defined as ongoing pressure on a person's mental well-being caused by difficulties of coping adequately with this pressure. In this respect, I would argue that one central explanation of why more young people are showing signs of and given the diagnosis of anxiety is due to the fact that the pressure – the chronic stressor – to internalize these normative demands is causing the opposite. They lose control instead of gaining control over these normative demands. So, instead of leading to flexible, adaptable young people who are able to compete with each other and ultimately become employable, an increasing amount of young people are facing anxieties.

Instead of dealing with the social aspects of these pathologies, the common reaction against this development is individualized treatment. That is, various forms of psychopharmacology and cognitive behavioural therapy are the most prescribed forms of treatment for these anxieties. The overall logic of these types of treatment is the individual removal of the symptoms connected with the pathological behaviour. The symptoms are distressing and should hence be eliminated. That is, the focus of the treatment is elimination of symptoms in order for the individual to return to a life free of symptoms. In that respect the treatments are adhering to the ideal of individual responsibility for one's problems in life without taking any particular social aspects of the symptoms into consideration. The anxieties in question are simply malaises that no individual should endure – therefore they should be eradicated.

The future of anxiety

In her psychoanalytically informed analysis of anxiety in contemporary society, Renata Salecl not only delivers a cultural critique of what, in her mind, paves the way for increasing anxiety but also warns us about the dangers of perceiving anxiety as something we should do our utmost to eliminate. Anxiety – understood in the right way – is not only, she contends, a negative emotion but also a fruitful phenomenon we should learn from. She ends her book by writing: "Society without anxiety would similarly be a dangerous place to live in" (Salecl, 2004: 148). In what way dangerous, we might ask? I would argue that are two ways of answering this question. The first answer is quite straightforward. Anxiety is, or at least could be, a compelling yardstick for measuring socio-political developments. That is, if we do not have anxiety as a kind of a backstop for political and social incentives and policies, we are lacking a very powerful stop-sign. In that respect, one could actually argue that we need even more anxiety today, considering the current political and socio-cultural developmental tendencies. The second, I believe, is more interesting in relation to this chapter. This answer concerns the ways in which the presence of anxiety is orienting and informing us about the quasi-anthropological human need for boundaries. In fact, the above-mentioned analysis of what it entails to be a human being – or a subject – in contemporary society, is very much a story about blurring boundaries. It is not a question of missing boundaries, but instead of social rules and norms that are dependent on extremely elastic boundaries. My contention is that the social rules and norms that I have been discussing are so powerful and compelling because they scrutinize – and in a certain sense constantly erase – limitations. In contemporary society there should be no limits as to what you can do – as long as you follow the prerequisites of the social norms and rules, that is. Hence, there is a socio-cultural inclination not to let yourself get bothered or constrained by limitations –indeed, an institutional demand not to be caught in the straitjacket of socially or culturally imposed confines. Especially for young people, when it comes to questions of education and future job-realizations, the demand to constantly explore the ever-changing potentialities is present. It is only by doing so that they are able to flourish and realize themselves in a satisfying manner. Ultimately, then, I will argue, the mere idea of blurry boundaries is so powerful because it is heralded as individual freedom. Richard Sennett has, when talking about the cultural norm of adaptability, addressed this aspect. He writes: "we imagine being open to change, being adaptable, –as qualities of character needed for free action – the human being free because capable of change" (Sennett, 1998: 48).

In such a socio-cultural constellation, there is, of course, no room for anxiety. Anxiety is, for lack of better words, a party-pooper to the contemporary understanding of free – and hence normal – individual adaptation to the presiding social norms and rules. Therein lies the danger, I would claim. The danger of upholding the idea that anxiety is only to be perceived as a restriction to individual freedom and not as a marker of the necessary limitation to this freedom. So, is there such a thing as a future for anxiety? I would argue that there are severe dangers involved in neglecting anxiety and only envisaging it as something we should eradicate. Perhaps we should pause and learn from the massive proliferation of anxieties in contemporary society instead of just trying to reject its pedagogical values by addressing them as individual malaises and hence not social pathologies. Perhaps!

Notes

1 The other two main tasks are: theoretical construction of concepts and empirical testing of theoretical assumptions.
2 I do not wish to pretend that all sociologists agree that the discipline should engage itself in diagnoses of the times. English sociologist Mike Savage has written an article entitled "Against epochalism" that argues for the serious pitfalls of this endeavour (Savage, 2009).
3 In a later article, "How an age of anxiety became an age of depression", Allan V. Horwitz has elaborated on this argument (Horwitz, 2010).
4 In the next chapter, this line of argumentation will be analysed and debated.
5 In his study *Suicide*, Emile Durkheim mentions neurasthenia several times and comments on its societal proliferation (Durkheim, 2006).
6 We are well aware of the fact that depression is the most common coexisting disorder in patients with most types of anxiety disorder. This is not, however, the same as saying that these disorders are similar. In the diagnostic manuals they are sharply separated.
7 One pivotal aspect of the diagnostic culture is precisely the emergence of multiple diagnoses that encapsulates an increasing selection of human behaviour as signs of mental pathology. Among the more curious diagnoses that have entered the *DSM-5* is hoarding disorder, nicotine dependency disorder and premenstrual dysphoric disorder (PMDD). Now, these conditions might be problematic but are they really mental disorders? Or have they become pathologized due to a lack of thorough distinction between the normal and the pathological?

References

Auden, WH (1948) *The Age of Anxiety*. London: Faber & Faber.
Bauman, Z (2000) *Liquid Modernity*. Cambridge: Polity Press.
Beard, G (1869) Neurasthenia, or nervous exhaustion. *The Boston Medical and Surgical Journal*, 80: 217–221.
Beck, U and Bonss, W (eds) (2001) *Die Modernisierung der Moderne*. Frankfurt am Main: Suhrkamp.
Blazer, DG (2005) *The Age of Melancholy: 'Major Depression' and its Discontents*. London: Routledge.
Boltanski, L and Chiapello, E (2005) *The New Spirit of Capitalism*. London: Verso.
Brinkmann, S and Petersen, A (eds) (2015) *Diagnoser – perspektiver, kritik og diskussion*. Aarhus: Klim.
Callan, E (1965) Allegory in Auden's The Age of Anxiety. *Twentieth Century Literature*, 10: 155–165.
Durkheim, E (2006) *On Suicide*. London: Penguin.
Ehrenberg, A (2010a) Society of discontent or discontent in society? https://www.booksandideas.net/Society-of-Discontent-or.html (accessed 25 June 2016).

Ehrenberg, A (2010b) *The Weariness of the Self: Diagnosing the History of Depression in the Contemporary Age*. Montreal and Kingston: McGill-Queen's University Press.
Ehrenberg, A (2013) The notion of social pathology: A case study of Narcissus in American society. In: Keohane, K and Petersen, A (eds), *The Social Pathologies of Contemporary Civilization*, 11–23. Farnham: Ashgate.
Esposito, L and Perez, FM (2014) Neoliberalism and the commodification of mental health. *Humanity and Society*, 38(4): 414–442.
Flachs, EM, Eriksen, L, Koch, MB, Ryd, JT, Dibba, E, Skov-Ettrup, L and Juel, K (2015) *Sygdomsbyrden i Danmark – Sygdomme*. København: Sundhedsstyrelsen.
Freud, S (1959/1926) *Inhibitions, Symptoms and Anxiety*. New York: W.W. Norton.
Fricchione, G (2004) Generalized anxiety disorder. *The New England Journal of Medicine*, 351: 675–682.
Giddens, A (1991) *Modernity and Self-Identity: Self and Society in the Late Modern Age*. Cambridge: Polity Press.
Honneth, A (2014) The diseases of society: Approaching a nearly impossible concept. *Social Research: An International Quarterly*, 81(3): 683–703.
Horwitz, AV (2002) *Creating Mental Illness*. Chicago, IL: Chicago University Press.
Horwitz, AV (2010) How an age of anxiety became an age of depression. *Milbank Quarterly* 88: 112–138.
Horwitz, AV (2013) *Anxiety. A Short History*. Baltimore, MD: Johns Hopkins University Press.
Horwitz, AV and Wakefield, JC (2005) The age of depression. *The Public Interest*, 158: 39–58.
Kierkegaard, S (1980) *On the Concept of Anxiety*. Princeton, NJ: Princeton University Press.
Lane, C (2007) *Shyness: How Normal Behavior Became a Sickness*. New Haven, CT: Yale University Press.
Lau, RWK (2012) Understanding contemporary modernity through the trends of therapy and life-skills' training. *Current Sociology*, 60(1): 81–100.
Lichtblau, K (1995) Sociology and the diagnosis of the times, or the reflexivity of modernity. *Theory, Culture and Society*, 12: 25–52.
Lipovetsky, G (2005) *Hypermodern Times*. Cambridge: Polity Press.
Lyotard, J-F (1979) *La condition postmoderne: Rapport sur le savoir*. Paris: Éditions de Minuit.
Parish, J. (2001) The age of anxiety. *The Editorial Board of the Sociological Review*, 48(2_suppl): 1–16.
Pedersen, OK (2011) *Konkurrencestaten*. København: Hans Reitzels Forlag.
Ratcliffe, M (2015) *Experiences of Depression: A Study in Phenomenology*. Oxford: Oxford University Press.
Salecl, R (2004) *On Anxiety*. London: Routledge.
Savage M (2009) Against epochalism: An analysis of conceptions of change in British sociology. *Cultural Sociology*, 3(2): 217–238.
Scott, S (2006) The medicalisation of shyness: From social misfits to social fitness. *Sociology of Health and Illness*, 28: 133–153.
Sennett, R (1998) *The Corrosion of Character: The Personal Consequences of Work in the New Capitalism*. New York: Norton.
Shorter, E (1997) *A History of Psychiatry: From the Era of the Asylum to the Age of Prozac*. New York: John Wiley and Sons.
Shorter, E (2013) *How Everyone Became Depressed*. Oxford: Oxford University Press.

Twenge, JM (2000) The age of anxiety? Birth cohort change in anxiety and neuroticism, 1952–1993. *Journal of Personality and Social Psychology*, 79(6): 1007–1021.
Wheaton, B (1999) The nature of stressors. In: Horwitz, AV and Scheid, TL (eds) *A Handbook for the Study of Mental Health: Social Contexts, Theories, and Systems*, 176–197. Cambridge: Cambridge University Press.
World Health Organization (2015) ICD-10. https://icd.who.int/browse10/2015/en (accessed 3 October 2024) (accessed 25 June 2016).
Wilkinson, I (2001) *Anxiety in a Risk Society*. London: Routledge.

5 'Clap along if you feel like a room without a roof'

Understanding the pursuit of happiness as ideology

Anders Petersen

Introduction

Why is it that the prevailing ideal of happiness – not only to many academic scholars but also to a wider public – presents itself as a significant problem in contemporary society? Although the main point of the discourse is encouraging and positive – be happy! – it is frequently criticized for being inflammatory, provocative, and even oppressive, leading to the exact opposite of its intentions, namely increasing unhappiness (cf. Bruckner, 2000). Evidence of the skewed nature of the happiness ideal is sometimes presented by pointing to the societal discontent that bourgeoning rates of mental disorders such as depression, anxiety, and stress are manifestations of and to how "The lure of happiness will find a comfortable place in the buying and selling of medication to alter mood" (McMahon, 2007: 479). Yet the demand to be happy is a problem not only for those who are unhappy, suffer from mental malaise or try to medicate themselves into happiness. In fact, one can argue the opposite. As Sam Binkley claims in his *Happiness as Enterprise: An Essay on Neoliberal Life*,

> Happiness is a problem for those who do not have a problem: it operates not as an abnormality one discovers within oneself through techniques of introspection and self-assessment in the closed spaces of clinics and asylums, but as a potential to be exercised in the open spaces and otherwise healthy moments of everyday life.
>
> (Binkley, 2014: 18)

Sociologically speaking, Binkley points at something pivotal. It is not happiness per se that is interesting. The most widespread notions of happiness – that it refers to an *individual* experience, feeling, emotion, instance, and so on – does not qualify as something of sociological interest.[1] It is rather, as the late Zygmunt Bauman has persuasively argued, the opposite of a social fact in the Durkheimian sense. What makes happiness a phenomenon worthy of sociological interest, then, is what Binkley refers to as the 'potential to be exercised' and

DOI: 10.4324/9781032714356-6

which Bauman describes – in an interview with Michal Hviid Jacobsen – in the following manner:

> It is the pursuit of happiness, and particularly the selection of objects on which that pursuit is targeted and whose appropriation/consumption is expected to be and consequently experienced/described as the moment of happiness, that deserves to be categorized as social facts calling for and receiving sociologists' attention.
>
> (Bauman, in Jacobsen, 2014: 87–88)

In this chapter, I will show how analytically fruitful it is to understand happiness – the potential that people need to pursue and are expected to work hard to materialize and objectify – as an ideology. I will argue that a significant part of the problem with the current ideology of happiness is that its internalization is presented as an individual endeavour whose successful implementation relies on personal capabilities of controlling socio-structurally supported norms and social rules that are in fact uncontainable. Thus, the ideology of happiness informs us about important aspects of what it entails to be a human being in the late modern society of performance.[2]

The main title of this chapter is taken from Pharrell Williams's popular and contagious song from 2014, *Happy*. The song struck a chord with a huge audience, and a lot of people clapped along and joined Williams's message. Williams's call to understand oneself as 'a room without a roof' refers to the contemporary ideal of addressing oneself and one's options in life as unlimited. The sky is the limit, so to speak. The second line of the chorus reveals the profound nature of this ideal: "Clap along if you feel like happiness is the truth". The truth of the happiness ideology, I will argue, resides in the concept of freedom it reflects: one is only free when embracing the absence of individual limitations, thereby tolerating, controlling, and living without constraints.

The position I defend in this chapter is that the development of the happiness ideology is supported and driven by particular social norms and rules that have emerged with the onset of late modern performance society. In justifying this thesis, I should like to proceed in five sections. I shall, in the first section, give an account of what I mean by happiness *ideology*. Ideology is, of course, a heavily loaded concept imbued with theoretical and empirical connotations, hence necessitating a definition that I can apply in this context. In the second section, I shall explain the societal context in which the happiness ideology can spread, which is followed by the third section in which I dissect the social norms and rules one can perceive as supporting the overall happiness ideology. Then, in the fourth section, I will elucidate some of the problematic aspects of the happiness ideology, focusing on the strains and tensions it places on people in contemporary late modern performance society. In the fifth section, I will make some concluding remarks and propose new research questions that I believe should be addressed.

The potential/pursuit of happiness as ideology

Presenting a single and coherent definition of *ideology* is impossible. Rather, the concept lends itself to multiple definitions, consequently creating some confusion about what it actually entails. It is, however, possible to differentiate between two distinct meanings of *ideology*, covering two traditions: one inspired by Marx/Marxism, another by culturalist conceptions. In the Marxist tradition, ideology

> is defined as the sphere of representations, ideas, and conceptions versus the sphere of actual production, as the imaginary versus the real, as the way individuals 'may appear in their own or other people's representation' versus the way 'they really are, i.e., operate, produce materially', and hence work under definite material limits, presuppositions, and 'conditions independent of their will'.
>
> (Ricoeur, 1976: 18)

The quotations in this excerpt are from Marx's *The German Ideology*. Of course, this is no random pick that Paul Ricoeur makes. By choosing so, he wishes to emphasize the elements of false consciousness, distorted representation, and oppression in this notion of ideology. When seen in this light, ideology is to be conceived as a form of *superstructure* that encompasses and surmounts everything else.

Contrary to the Marxist conceptualization, culturalist conceptions perceive ideology in a more positive vein as *infrastructure*. That is, forms of social representations that are shared by a large number of people in a certain group (society) but are not individually oppressing per se (cf. Dumont, 1977). Rather, ideology presents itself as a guideline – an infrastructure – that people, collectively, can tap into and use to steer their life. In short, the culturalist conception "stresses its group integration and identity preservation function" (Chiapello, 2003: 159). In 1999, Eve Chiapello, whom I just quoted, wrote a much-debated book with Luc Boltanski called *The New Spirit of Capitalism* (Boltanski and Chiapello, 1999). In the book, they argue for the reconciliation – or synthesis – of the aforementioned conceptualizations of ideology in order to understand the specifics of the new spirit of capitalism. Drawing on the work of Paul Ricoeur (1976), Boltanski and Chiapello are able to present a more-nuanced concept of ideology that takes its productive and enabling force and its distortive functions into consideration. Hence, ideology presents itself as something that presents people with a variety of (collectively embedding) action possibilities and disables them through the blurring of viable alternatives.

Where Boltanski and Chiapello (1999) use this analytical construction of ideology to develop their ground-breaking theory of the new spirit of capitalism, it is my intention to use this concept of ideology with reference to the contemporary pursuit of happiness, where everyone has to exercise their happiness potential and materialize it. Of course, my analysis cannot be as sophisticated as Boltanski and Chiapello's, but I intend to illuminate how fruitful this analytical endeavour is. Let me explain. In contemporary late modern performance society, the pursuit of happiness and the exercise of one's happiness potential are certainly producing integration – and hence accounting for a specific social order or logic that people tap into and (happily) identify with. The obvious downsides to happiness are hard to find. At the same time, however, the pursuit of happiness is distortive because the potential to exercise happiness has become a societal demand that everybody has to strive for if they wish to achieve professional and private success. In the next section, I shall lay out what supports this ideology.

From a society of discipline to the performance society

In order to gain a more in-depth understanding of the happiness ideology, we need a deeper insight into the societal context in which it prevails. To achieve this, I will take my point of departure in explicating how our particular period in time differs from earlier epochs. In this chapter, I will thus focus on how the transformation from a society of discipline (the early 19th century until the late 1960s)[3] to the society of performance, which we live in today (see Petersen, 2016), has brought about new social norms and rules that people have to take into account.

Perhaps Michel Foucault, in his *Discipline and* Punish (Foucault, 1991), has made the most famous description of the society of discipline. The structuring aspects of the society portrayed by Foucault – panopticism, the organization and manufacturing of docile bodies, rigid institutional discipline, and so on – are in many ways fundamental to our understanding of what societal discipline entails. No doubt, Foucault's characterization is convincing. But it is also open to criticism of being one-sided. One might say that Foucault's focus is on the distortive aspects of society while neglecting its integrative functions. Perhaps one should ask the question whether the society of discipline – how odd that may sound – also has an emancipatory side to it that people collectively relate to. Without using the concept of ideology, German sociologist Peter Wagner has argued that no societal epoch – or form of modernity, as he refers to – is truly accounted for by solely referring to its production of disciplinary mechanisms. History is, to put it popularly, more nuanced than that. Therefore, Wagner suggests, the analysis of societal epochs – and of the transformations between them – has to stand on an analytical platform that allows a more-nuanced picture to be taken into account. According to Wagner, then, the overall point of departure for such an endeavour must be that each historical epoch always has to be understood in terms of ongoing ambivalence between realized autonomy and discipline (Wagner, 1994: 15). Here it is important to understand a central analytical prerequisite, namely that what constitutes discipline and autonomy varies according to the historical epoch in which they occur. More precisely, the social logics that are institutionally materializing themselves in every epoch differ. So rather than focusing on aspects of discipline only, the more potent question to ask is how the society of discipline also involves opportunities of realizing individual autonomy.

In my opinion, we can gain insightful knowledge about this by approaching the literature of the epoch in question that deals explicitly – and implicitly – with how the overall organization of work is socially institutionalized. Here it makes good sense to turn to William H. Whyte's classic *The Organization Man* from 1956. A central tenant of Whyte's analysis is the emergence of a particular social ethic that can be said to be the moral foundation on which the society of discipline lays. Whyte explains:

> By social ethic I mean that contemporary body of thought which makes morally legitimate the pressures of society against the individual. Its major prepositions are three: a belief in the group as the source of creativity; a belief in 'belongingness' as the ultimate need of the individual; and a belief in the application of science to achieve the belongingness.
>
> (Whyte, 2002: 7)

The social ethic that Whyte detects is comparable to the 'other-directed' character that David Reisman coined 50 years later, in *The Lonely Crowd* (Riesman, 2001). Reisman and Whyte are talking about not only the emergence of a new social norm that relates itself to work but also the social proliferation of a broader social ethic: an ethic that is morally legitimated and supported by the overarching structures of society and one that people ought to live by. Note, however, that neither Reisman nor Whyte is particularly happy with the materialization of this social ethic. In fact, Whyte's book can be seen as an enthusiastic attempt to scrutinize every little detail of this by pointing out its detrimental consequences. In Whyte's terms, this overly bureaucratized manner that the organization of social life – and work in particular – has gained societal currency completely undermines the favoured 'rugged' individualism and thus hinders individuals from realizing their own kind of autonomy and individuality. In other words, it is distortive and an expression of excessive discipline. The genuine realization of people's autonomy, Whyte believes, is possible only if they are freed from the straitjacket of this social ethic. Only then would the inner forces and freedom of each and every individual be liberated, something that would also be beneficial to firms and businesses and hence to the successful development of these (Whyte, 2002: 16).

In a book titled *The New Individualists: The Generation after the Organisation Man*, American sociologists Paul Leinberger and Bruce Tucker empirically trace this development by interviewing exponents of the new individualists. Their informants have no desire to follow an 'outer-directed' social ethic; instead, they are preoccupied with being what the authors refer to as 'man-made selves' (Leinberger and Tucker, 1991: 225). Human-made selves are driven by a firm belief in the dismantling of every structure or institution that – in any form or sense – prevents them from realizing their own self and hence their own version of the good life. More specifically, Leinberger and Tucker detect a desire in their informants to compose their life on the basis of its 'artistic' parts. This does not imply, however, that the informants refer to their 'desires' to be artists, musicians, or performers. But it means that all the informants have artistic dreams about "realizing their creative potential" (Leinberger and Tucker, 1991: 226). The realization of this creative potential is not restricted to specific life situations. Rather, it transgresses the boundaries of work, family, and leisure time. Furthermore, the social ethic of the human-made self addresses important issues of identifying oneself in relation with others – or, rather, seeing oneself as being different from other people: not to be a copycat. Now, this desire to be different from others is not a question of vanity. In fact, Leinberger and Tucker write this ethic is "founded on a genuine moral imperative – the *demand* to express the authentic self" (Leinberger and Tucker, 1991: 12).

In relation to understanding which social rules and norms the society of performance is founded on, Leinberger and Tucker's (1991) research is essential. By stressing the aforementioned moral imperative, they do point us in the right direction. However, they do not go into much detail with defining what an authentic self really is and hence do not give us a thorough grasp of this moral imperative. Canadian philosopher Charles Taylor can help us here. He has, more than anyone else, described what the contemporary ethic of authenticity consists of. According to Taylor, being authentic entails following certain specific rules:

> There is a certain way of being human that is my way. I am called upon to live my life in this way, and not in imitation of anyone else's. But this gives a new importance to being true to myself. If I am not, I miss the point of my life, I miss what being human is for me.
>
> (Taylor, 1989: 28–29)

Originality and being true to oneself are hence the hallmarks of authenticity, the realization of which one is called upon to achieve. Missing out on what being human is for me is a shame. Indeed, one could say that it is shameful. But why? Because the socio-structural conditions in the contemporary performance society are geared towards accompanying people to realize their autonomy in the guise of authenticity. Or so the story goes. To accept this story would, of course, be a blatant example of embroidering the truth. For example, it is hard to imagine that the pivotal concern of Pierre Bourdieu's informants from his monumental study *La Misère du Monde* would be that of authenticity (Bourdieu, 1993), at least in the manner I am discussing it here. The same goes for members of the new precariat class that Guy Standing has written so forcefully about (Standing, 2012).

But even with the aforementioned taken into consideration, it still seems as if the ideal of authenticity has acquired a distinctive pitch and force in contemporary society. Thus, Taylor seems to be on the right page when he says we are called to live our lives authentically. That, however, does not relieve us of asking pivotal questions: Who does the calling that convinces people to search for their authenticity? Is there a religious undertone supporting this prerogative? Or is it a secularized notion? *Both* might be the answer. But I am content with reflecting on the latter, because the calling to realize one's authenticity not only is hovering over people's heads like a cloud but also has been transformed into an institutional demand. As Axel Honneth writes,

> At first hesitantly and subsequently on a massive scale, individuals were confronted with the expectation that they present themselves as being 'flexible'

> (to cite the contemporary jargon) and willing to develop themselves if they wished to achieve success in their profession or in society.
> (Honneth, 2004: 472)

The shift from the possibility of realizing one's authenticity to an institutionalized demand is fundamental. It addresses the analytical point I would like to make, namely that realizing – or performing – one's authenticity has become distortive and functions as a form of discipline in itself. When individuals in the performance society are expected to activate their authentic selves to satisfy institutional demands, they are acting in accordance with societal norms and rules. They must perform authentically. This implies that the notion of the authentic self is stretched out: it is not only an individual matter but also a public raw material that can be worked up and moulded into fulfilling certain criteria of success. But as Honneth highlights, the content of these demands is not random but instead quite specific. Only by being flexible, one is able to achieve social and professional success. However, as I have argued in my latest book (Petersen, 2016), we cannot thoroughly grasp the institutionalized demands on this basis alone. Rather, we have to expand our understanding significantly. This implies a more detailed description of the performance society, one in which these demands are linked with the prevailing ideology of happiness.

The social norms and rules espousing the happiness ideology

As shown, there is a strong link between authenticity and performance. But what is meant by performance? Performance is, of course, something one does. It is a form of action. One performs at work, in school, as a footballer, and so on. The important aspect of performance in the performance society is that one is equivalent with one's performances. That is, one identifies oneself with one's performances and is identified with them. The performances are the markers of identity that one is being judged for and with. We could use the work of Judith Butler (2005) to say that it is via our performances that we give an account of ourselves. Through the performances we make, we take stock of who we are. And through our performances, we show others who we are. Performances are thus to be perceived as the perpetual making of our curriculum vitae (CV) – an unending enterprise that we must undertake. What is more, these CVs are constantly examined – by ourselves and by others. And these exams never cease. We cannot allow ourself to get stuck. Getting stuck has consequences: to stay put is to be left out and furthermore to be marginalized (see also Brinkmann, 2017). Hence, to keep our authentic self in motion and develop, we have to perform constantly and nurture the accounts of who we are.

This endeavour is backed by the 'numbers' and the content of the social norms and rules that one has to internalize to live authentically and hence pave the way for a successful life. Nowadays, not only is authenticity sugar-coated with demands to be flexible but also one has to be adaptable, mobile, polyvalent, active, proactive, effective, positive, social, outgoing, and robust. Although the meaning of these norms, as I will return to later, might be blurry, their existence is tangible. Ordinary people, in their everyday life, are confronted with these and the demand to internalize them. Now, one does not necessarily have to embrace all of these demands, but the total neglect of some of these is the same as sentencing oneself to complete failure. The incentives to keep on incorporating these demands are thus quite powerful, and the enticements to perform accordingly are just as blatant. And this is important, because the internalization of these demands is projected outwardly via the performances that one makes. Perpetual performances, then, show that one is authentically adhering to the societal demands. It shows that one is able to decipher the overarching logic of the demands, namely that one should be in constant movement. It shows the desired and demanded development and progress. It makes sure that standing still is not an option. Resting on one's laurels or taking a time-out is not possible in the performance society, because standing still in the performance society is, as I have illustrated, a mortal sin. It is a sin that endangers the social logic related to the ideal of performance, namely that one should not be constrained by any limitations. Rather, one should perceive oneself as 'a room without a roof'. This perception, I argue, is fortified by the fact that these social rules and norms are institutionalized.

Hence, the demand to exercise them is evident in job ads, in the job or dating markets, talked about in social gatherings, or communicated on (social) media, and they have found their way into our kindergartens, schools, and universities. From toddler to teenager to high school student to university student, one is learning to strive for (almost to covet) and hence to internalize these demands via different programmes, teaching modules, and educational schemes that have been promoted politically. In that way, they have materialized themselves as social rules and norms that have political leverage as well as sociocultural and economic leverage. They have become ethical duties we collectively tap into. These norms and social rules are, in other words, those we mutually recognize as the ones we need to internalize in order to become successful individuals – to become winners instead of losers. And who does not want to be successful and win? Who does not wish to be happy? The same logic applies to these two elements, which is why it is possible to analytically intertwine them. They are bound by the same manifestation, namely that they present themselves as truths. As Pharrell Williams sings, happiness *is* the truth. It's a truism. And it's a truth that is anchored – and hence presents itself as morally profound – in the prevailing concept of freedom in the performance society. Pursuing happiness and exercising the potential to be happy are the right things to do. Moreover, it is not simply a manifestation of one's ability to follow the path towards a successful and authentic life. Rather, it is a way of achieving freedom. Richard Sennett has persuasively written about an understanding of freedom that triumphs in the realm that he refers to as flexible capitalism. He states:

> We imagine being open to change, being adaptable, as qualities of character needed for free action – the human being free because capable of change.
> (Sennett, 1998: 47)

By slightly rewriting this quotation, it becomes possible to extract the understanding of freedom that dominates in the performance society. Here we imagine that the human being is free because they are exercising their potential to pursue happiness. The integrative function of the happiness ideology, its social representation, is that everybody is able to understand the positive inclinations of this concept of freedom. Intuitively as well as logically, the impact of the message is crystal clear. It resonates well. Therefore, it is no wonder that people morally back and support it. The main constituents of the ideology of happiness are namely presenting themselves in a fairly straightforward manner. Happiness – understood as the unlimited and hence free pursuit of performance possibilities – is possible and pleasurable if one only adheres to the ideals of the performance society. According to this ideology, then, happiness can be 'measured' by one's ability to constantly perform successfully and hence inscribe oneself in the group of winners. That takes a lot of effort. Within the realm of this ideology, happiness is embedded in the will to take responsibility for being a competent person constantly capable of following the routes to success. But the distortive and oppressive function of the ideology of happiness remains. We can address this via Pascal Bruckner's claim: "Unhappiness is not just unhappiness: It is, worse still, the defeat of happiness" (Bruckner, 2000: 17). True, but the absence of pursuing happiness – and hence refraining from achieving one's potential to do so – is also the same as being unfree. And that seems even worse than being unhappy. Because if caught in the manacles of unfreedom, the accompanying consequences are not only those of a lack of happiness but also those of sensations of individual incompleteness. As Bauman has stated,

> The spectre hovering over a society of would-be performers-by-decree is the horror of finding oneself deficient – inept and inefficacious; as well as its immediate effects – loss of self-esteem and its prospective sequels: outcasting and exclusion.
>
> (Bauman, 2016: 420)

The grim reality of things seems to be that more and more people are finding themselves on the dark side of the performance society – not because of ill faith but because they cannot adequately manoeuvre in and tackle the demands presented to them. In fact, one could say that they are being trampled by the constant demands to perform and to be happy. But as I have already mentioned, the problems associated with the happiness ideology lie not only in its distortive function but also in its integrative function. How is that?

Happiness as controlling the uncontainable

If the analysis so far is correct, the internalization of the social norms and rules of the performance society is central to pursuing and exercising one's potential for happiness. The ability to adequately control these norms and rules is therefore pivotal to achieving happiness. But a serious problem arises when taking a closer look at these norms and rules.

At first glance, they might present themselves as straightforward and even appetizing. Being flexible, adaptable, mobile, polyvalent, social, positive, and so on has a nice ring to it – the crème de la crème of desirable qualities. It is almost as if obvious points of resistance are suspended. Instead, a glossy picture is being painted in which people trying to adhere to the norms and social rules are depicted as malleable and easy-going. Or, the road to success is paved with a gradual dosage of flexibility. And that might be the case. However, the contents of these norms and social rules are also blatantly inconclusive. That is, one never reaches the endpoint of being flexible, adaptable or mobile. Instead, their completion becomes a never-ending journey that individuals are demanded to embark on. Being flexible, for example – as Richard Sennett has shown – is a question of eternal bending without sight of any fixed platform or safe haven to return to (Sennett, 1998). The same goes for adaptability and mobility – and the rest of the social rules and norms, for that matter. In relation to the pursuit of happiness and the potential to exercise this, individuals in the performance society are therefore confronted with the demand to control something that in fact cannot be controlled. The norms are constantly on the move – they continually expand – and the attempt to keep up with them therefore requires the total abandonment of unmitigated control. Or perhaps one could say that being in control resides in the acceptance of not being in control. Within the realm of the performance society, this is, of course, perceived as a good thing. It is in the interest of this type of society to keep people on their toes and not expect happiness to come to them easily. Therefore, the logic of the performance society forces it to expand the zone of its pursuit of happiness to infinity and hence to invest in the complete disappearance of fixed entities of happiness. People have to strive for it – in that same manner that they have to strive for and dream about the next commodity in line that serves as a particular object or marker of their happiness.

The endless performances have to somehow materialize into something, yet these objects or markers are, more often than not, flighty. Affirmed by popular culture and consumer ideals, happiness every so often boils down to the incessant hunt for various happiness opportunities. As Bauman stated,

> We have been brought up to think about happiness, by marketing, by advertising, by ever new temptations, seductions and so on, ever new fashions, to think about happiness as an uninterrupted row of better and better pleasures.
>
> (Bauman on Al Jazeera talks)

Within the realm of the performance society, I believe it is safe to claim, the yardstick of measuring the success of one's potential to exercise the pursuit of happiness is the freedom to capture new ground devoid of unpleasantness. Pleasures are, almost by definition, only pleasurable. And they are confined by time. A consequence of this is that happiness always is to be explored in the future and never to be located in the past. Faith in progress – and thereby in the idea of endless happiness possibilities – is associated with looking towards the future. In a forward-looking performance society, who wants to situate their happiness in the past? It is as if the words of John Wayne, which adorn his headstone, summarize the social condition well:

> Tomorrow is the most important thing in life. Comes to us at midnight very clean. It's perfect when it arrives and it puts itself in our hands. It hopes we've learned something from yesterday.
>
> (Wayne, 1971: 82)

Of course, today is already pregnant with tomorrow, and we ought to learn from days gone by. It is, however, the *is-not-yet* that holds currency and really matters. The past is not to be dwelled on, but the future has to be conquered. Tomorrow is 'clean and perfect' – not yet infested with the germs and bacteria of human intervention – and therefore the only logical place to position our pursuit and exercise our potential of happiness – in an authentic manner, naturally. But to take a firm grip on the future and establish the grounds for our pursuit of happiness, certain conditions seem to be needed. One is that *confidence* in the possibility to make this journey towards the future has to be secured. The future has, somehow, to be seen as a place we can rely on. Another is *hope* in the ability of the future to establish the platform for a 'happier' place than that of the past. The big question is whether this is the case. Zygmunt Bauman once wrote that the

> colonization of the future is bound to remain forever disconcertingly provisional and non-definite; the future is, after all, the site of the self-same uncertainty which has prompted the colonizing thrust in the first place.
>
> (Bauman, 1992: 54)

So the future has always been a blurry and uncertain place. It seems, however, that the future has become more intangible and complicated than before. At the same time, mastering it is pivotal. Nowadays, it is not the past but the future that is breathing down our necks. If this is the case, the integrative function of the ideology of happiness is problematic. The basic idea on which it rests is precisely that it really is possible to become happier by the minute – as long as we actively master the future. As long as we invest ourselves in the pursuit of happiness and indulge in better pleasures. Seen in this light, the societal demand of the performance society to do so – and hence the request of constantly exercising the possibility of happiness – is not only highly demanding but also deeply problematic.

Conclusion

In this chapter, I have tried to show the fruitful endeavour of perceiving the happiness imperative in the performance society as an ideology. By doing so, I hope to have accounted for some ways that this ideology is both integrative and distortive and for the fact that the problem with the ideology does not reside only in the latter category. Of course, the problematic aspect of the ideology becomes all too obvious when confronted with its production of unhappy people and even mental suffering. But the ideology, in itself, is also problematic due to the vagueness of the demands its completion is founded on. That is, the ideology of happiness rests on premises that forces each and every one of us – on a daily basis – to stretch and bend ourselves enormously in order to master something that is extremely difficult to concretize. But alas, we do it anyway. Why? Because the ideology of happiness has teamed up with the concept of freedom that imbues the performance society. Only by pursuing and exercising one's potential for happiness is one free. And who wishes not to be free? A rhetorical question, indeed. But perhaps a question that forces us to contemplate even more on what happiness is and how new ideas about happiness might question the structural demands of the performance society.

Notes

1 I am aware of the fact that this claim cannot be said to cover the sociological interest in happiness writ large. As David Bartram has shown (Bartram 2012), the sociological contribution to happiness studies has, during the last couple of decades, evolved immensely, thus broadening the range of perspectives that sociologists are interested in while dealing with issues of happiness.
2 I shall explain this term in the third section of the chapter.
3 In making this distinction, I am using Peter Wagner's historical separation of epochs of modernity (Wagner, 1994: 16–18).

References

Bartram, D (2012) Elements of a Sociological Contribution to Happiness Studies. *Sociology Compass*, 6(8): 644–656.
Bauman, Z (1992) *Mortality, Immortality & Other Life Strategies*. Cambridge: Polity Press.
Bauman, Z (2016) From 'Official' to 'Do it Yourself' Fear. *Revue Internationale De Philosophie*, 3: 413–420.
Binkley, S (2014) *Happiness as Enterprise: An Essay on Neoliberal Life*. New York, NY: State University of New York Press.
Boltanski, L and Chiapello, E (1999) *Le Nouvel Esprit du Capitalisme*. Paris: Gallimard.
Bourdieu, P (ed) (1993) *La Misère du Monde*. Paris: Seuil.
Brinkmann, S (2017) *Stand Firm*. Cambridge: Polity Press.
Bruckner, P (2000) *L'Euphorie Perpétuelle: Essai sur le devoir de bonheur*. Paris: Grasset.
Butler, J (2005) *Giving an Account of Oneself*. New York, NY: Fordham University Press.
Chiapello, E (2003) Reconciling the Two Principal Meanings of the Notion of Ideology. The Example of the Concept of the 'Spirit of Capitalism'. *European Journal of Social Theory*, 6(2): 155–171.
Dumont, L (1977) *Homo Aequalis: Genèse et épanouisssement de l'ideologie économique*. Paris: Gallimard.
Foucault, M (1991) *Discipline and Punish. The Birth of the Prison*. London: Penguin Books.
Honneth, A (2004) Organized Self-Realization: Some Paradoxes of Individualization. *European Journal of Social Theory*, 7(4): 463–478.
Jacobsen, MH (2014) Sociology and Happiness: An Interview With Zygmunt Bauman. *The Journal of Happiness and Well-Being*, 2(1): 85–94.
Leinberger, P and Tucker, B (1991) *The New Individualists: The Generation After the Organisation Man*. New York, NY: HarperCollins Publishers.

McMahon, D (2007) *The Pursuit of Happiness: The History from the Greeks to the Present.* London: Penguin Books.
Petersen, A (2016) *Præstationssamfundet* (The Achievement Society). København: Hans Reitzels Forlag.
Ricoeur, P (1976) Ideology and Utopia as Cultural Imagination. *Philosophical Exchange*, 7(1): 17–28.
Riesman, D (2001 [1961]) *The Lonely Crowd.* New Haven, CT: Yale University Press.
Sennett, R (1998) *The Corrosion of Character: The Personal Consequences of Work in the New Capitalism.* New York, NY: W. W. Norton & Co.
Standing, G (2012) *The Precariat: The New Dangerous Class.* London: Bloomsbury Academic Publishing.
Taylor, C (1989) *The Ethics of Authenticity.* Cambridge, MA: Harvard University Press.
Wagner, P (1994) *A Sociology of Modernity: Liberty and Discipline.* London: Routledge.
Wayne, J (1971) Playboy Interview: John Wayne. *Playboy Magazine*, May 1971: 80–82.
Whyte, WH (2002 [1956]) *The Organisation Man.* Philadelphia, PA: University of Pennsylvania Press.

6 Depression

Emotion and (or) dis-connection in late modern society

Anders Petersen and Bert van den Bergh

Introduction

It is by no means uncommon that academic scholars, journalists and even poets use the epithet 'age of' to signal how a certain feature is particularly characteristic of the times in which we live. In this chapter, we argue that it makes sense to address our current epoch as an 'age of emotions'. Broadly speaking this entails that emotions, in many shapes and forms, have been widely recognised as decisive factors in social, cultural, economic and political realms in ways that were not the case before. For example, emotions are proven to play a key role in otherwise rational aspects of life such as political orientation and elections, as Arlie R. Hochschild so forcefully has demonstrated in her account of how people's deep emotions are decisive when constructing their political identity and casting their vote (Hochschild, 2016). In a more specific sense, emotions have historically been singled out as particularly informative about the psychic constitution of the times in which we live. W. H. Auden in 1947 famously declared that this epoch was an 'age of anxiety' (Auden, 1948). Written in the aftermath of World War II, this pessimistic statement is not surprising: Anxiety was a normal human response to extraordinary circumstances.[1] Recently, journalist of *The Guardian*, Oliver Burkeman, has pondered whether we currently live in an 'age of rage', in which people are – simply put – angrier than before, and in which social media is supporting and encouraging the ventilation of people's rage and fury in a hitherto unseen manner. In relation to this chapter, the statement made by Allan V. Horwitz and Jerome C. Wakefield, based on an increasing prevalence of the phenomenon in question, that contemporary society should be understood as an 'age of depression' is noteworthy (Horwitz and Wakefield, 2005). This characteristic begs the questions of how depression has become such an influential and prevalent disorder in our times and how – even if – we should understand the phenomenon as an indicatory emotion of our epoch?

Both as a sign of our times and as an emotion, depression is a particularly interesting phenomenon to study. This is not least due to its long and prolific history. As literary scholar Clark Lawlor has stated, it seems as if depression has been around forever and that depression has been 'fashionable throughout its history' (Lawlor, 2012: 2). For centuries, Lawlor explains, depression has been a socio-cultural weighty condition that a significant amount of people has been emotionally affected

DOI: 10.4324/9781032714356-7

by. Similarly, however, he also implies that the understanding of depression – as a fashionable type of suffering – has changed proportionate to various socio-historical transformations. That is, depression is by no means a static description of a specific type of human suffering. Depression changes and 'relates' to the societal circumstances it is situated in. If we focus on contemporary late-modern society, two things hold true. First of all, there seems to be no doubt about the fact that the dominating understanding of depression, by and large, is equivalent with the medically informed definition of *Major Depression Disorder* found in the *DSM* (Diagnostic and Statistical Manual of Mental Disorders). In here, depression is perceived as a biomedical disease that people suffer from. Second, we are witnessing a societal proliferation of the diagnosis of depression unseen in history. WHO has expressed that a veritable depression alarm is ringing loudly worldwide, and that more than 264 million people of all ages now suffer from depression (WHO, 2021).

The combination of these facts is interesting. It informs us about a situation in which a biomedical understanding of depression has inserted itself in the societal discourse about what depression is, and that this understanding has internalised itself in the lives of many people. How are we to fathom this? In this chapter, we shall address this by following four main steps. First, we shall explore how depression has come to be understood as a *biomedical disorder* that is treated as a specific diagnosable disease, and then show how this understanding has been criticised. Second, we elucidate how – and against the backdrop of what – contemporary depression can be understood as an *emotion*. Third, we will attempt to nuance the understanding of depression as emotion by arguing that when one zooms in on the phenomenon – that is on the *experience* of depression – one comes to understand depression as elementary *disconnection*. Fourth, and based on this deepened understanding, we shall show how the alleged 'depression epidemic' can be sensibly linked to a certain *subject-position* in contemporary culture. Lastly, we will discuss some important implications of this nuanced understanding of depression.

A voice to depression

However, before we take the first step, we aim – in a preliminary way – to 'give voice' to the emotion of depression by tapping into David A. Karp's *Speaking of Sadness: Depression, Dis-connection, and the Meanings of* Illness (1996). This very influential study, written by someone who is a sociologist as well as an 'experience expert', was based on interviews with 50 depression patients, to whose voices Karp added his own. The second edition was published in 2016, containing a new introduction in which Karp emphasises the need to provide a 'counternarrative' to what happened in the two decades since the publication of the first edition of his book: a continuation of the structural 'muting' of the voices of depression experiences. Even more strongly in this second edition, Karp underlines the urgency to tell the story of depression as an 'illness of isolation' (Karp, 2016: 38, 4, 7):

> It was impossible to listen to depressed people without being struck by the frequency with which themes of 'isolation', 'withdrawal', and 'disconnection'

came up. As with all feelings and emotions, isolation is experienced in different degrees and hues. Some individuals feel obliged to withdraw from virtually all arenas of social life. Most people though, unless they become hospitalized, struggle through their daily obligations, sometimes heroically maintaining a facade of 'normalcy'. Others may continue to associate with friends and family while nevertheless feeling disengaged, uncomfortable, marginal, and profoundly alone.

(Karp, 2016: 101)

There is a strong need to withdraw and at the same time a huge distress because of the state of isolation. Karp calls this the 'central paradox' of the depression experience (Karp, 2016: 101). Common metaphors people use to describe their depressed state are: being trapped, being caged, suffocating, being in a lightless tunnel, descending into a bottomless pit, drowning, sinking to death, dying. The following words are also often used in the description: darkness, black hole, cold, fog and vacuum (Karp, 2016: 83ff). Depression is a process of impoverishment. It can deepen itself to an utterly debilitating state. "There was near consensus', Karp writes, 'that depression, during its bleakest moments, utterly robs them of concentration, motivation, and energy. Even the simplest acts can become impossible" (Karp, 2016: 95).

Two important questions may be posed here. First: What connection could there be between this widespread 'illness of isolation' and the contemporary cultural context of hyperindividualist, strongly competitive late capitalism? And second: What is the influence here of the more direct context of 'depressive disorder': the world of professional mental health care? We will address the latter question first.

Depression – a quick historical introduction

As described above, it is possible to capture significant characteristics of the emotion of depression. However, the phenomenon of depression has – historically speaking – been fashioned by other elements than what constitutes its emotional ingredients. Or perhaps one could even say that the understanding of depression has been colonised by a particular way of thinking about it. In this respect, there is no doubt about the fact that one single discipline, namely psychiatry, has forcefully shaped the understanding of depression for decades, expounding the definition that most people are familiar with in contemporary society. The specific categorisation of mental disorders placed in concrete manuals that health professionals such as GP's should use in their practices is also a psychiatric endeavour. In 1952, *The American Psychiatric Association* published their first classificatory manual, in which a number of specific mental disorders were listed. Since then, this manual has become pivotal in particularly Western understanding of what a mental disorder is and is often referred to as 'the diagnostic bible of psychiatry'.

It is also in the *DSM*, at a very specific period in time, that a landslide in the history of mental disorders is marked, namely with the introduction in 1980 of the *DSM-III*. Robert Spitzer, the main architect of the *DSM-III*, led a campaign to ensure that the understanding of mental disorders would involve classifying them in discrete categories with precise descriptive diagnostic criteria. In his book on the societal and human consequences of psychiatry, Nikolas Rose explains that the *DSM-III* consisted of

> 265 categorical diagnoses, each defined as a set of apparently observable behaviours, seeming not requiring interpretation and hence, so it was hoped, equally evident to psychiatrists from different schools of thought. It construed each of these diagnostic categories as a distinct disorder, believing that each would, eventually, be underpinned with a unique aetiology, and amenable to a specific treatment.
>
> (Rose, 2019: 81)

It is rather uncertain whether the hopes Rose writes about here have been fulfilled. One thing is certain though, and that is that the focus of the *DSM-III* represents a veritable paradigm shift, altering the epistemological and ontological focus of the *DSM*-II. Perhaps sociologist Allan V. Horwitz has explained this in the best possible way when he states that the introduction of *DSM-III* represents a shift from dynamic to diagnostic psychiatry (Horwitz, 2002). By dynamic psychiatry, Horwitz refers to the Freudian inspired terminology and understanding that *DSM*-II was imbued with, and which did not put much focus – if any at all – on diagnostic criteria for each mental disorder. This furthermore entails a hitherto unseen focus on symptoms. Within the realm of dynamic psychiatry, mental pathologies were not considered discrete symptom-based diseases (Horwitz, 2002: 38). He writes:

> What is important is that in the dynamic view symptoms were never *direct indicators* of underlying disorders; instead they were *symbolic expressions* of conflicts that involved the entire personality. Symptoms in themselves were not important because similar symptoms can represent many different underlying disturbances.
>
> (Horwitz, 2002: 44–45)

In the *DSM-III* – and onwards – it is all about symptoms and diagnostic psychiatry has won the battle of what mental disorders are. Aetiology plays second fiddle when this entirely medical understanding of mental disorders – including depression – is embedded. The intellectual role model of this paradigm shift was not Freud but German psychiatrist Emil Kraepelin, who initiated the modern classificatory system of psychiatric disorders. In his perspective, mental disorders were to be perceived as brain disorders, and that perception paved the way for understanding depression as such (see Grob and Horwitz, 2010: 144).

It is a justified claim to make that this perception of depression is embedded in the *DSM*. Here, depression is listed as a mood disorder. Mood, in this respect, is characterised as a *persistent* emotion – an emotion that has mentally as well as bodily consequences, but which is believed to be located in the brain. This persistent emotion called depression can be diagnosed by ways of various symptoms. In the current version of the *DSM* – the *DSM*-5 – the following criteria make a diagnosis of depression. Five or more of these symptoms must be experienced during the same two-week period and at least one of the symptoms should be either depressed mood or loss of interest or pleasure:

1 Depressed mood most of the day, nearly every day.
2 Markedly diminished interest or pleasure in all, or almost all, activities most of the day, nearly every day.
3 Significant weight loss when not dieting or weight gain, or decrease or increase in appetite nearly every day.
4 Insomnia or hypersomnia nearly every day.
5 Psychomotor agitation or retardation nearly every day.
6 Fatigue or loss of energy nearly every day.
7 Feelings of worthlessness or excessive or inappropriate guilt nearly every day.
8 Diminished ability to think or concentrate, or indecisiveness, nearly every day.
9 Recurrent thoughts of death, recurrent suicidal ideation without a specific plan, or a suicide attempt or a specific plan for committing suicide (APA, 2013).

In many ways, this cluster of symptoms has become the authoritative arbiter of how depression should be considered in contemporary society, thus generating a remarkable consensus about what depression is and a common language for discussions about depression worldwide. Depression, as such, is an individual disease in the brain.

Of course, this interpretation of what constitutes depression, the one-sided focus on clusters of symptoms indicative of depression, has been widely criticised. From within the discipline of psychiatry, especially Edward Shorter's critique of this development is worth mentioning. In his book *How Everyone Became Depressed* (2013), he calls this development "an appalling story of scientific error that has resulted in a public that believes itself to be, more or less, depressed" (Shorter, 2013: 2). It is appalling, Shorter argues, because since 1980, the biomedical model of depression has been disconnected from the ancient concept of melancholy, thereby totally embracing the false idea that low mood and an inability to experience pleasure are the main components of depression. This leads, he states, to the wrong conclusion that depression is a 'mood disorder situated solely in the brain and mind that antidepressants can correct. But this is not science; it is pharmaceutical advertising' (Shorter, 2013: 5). In other words: depression is that which can be amended with antidepressants, and antidepressants work by affecting neuro-transmitter substances in the brain.

Alan Horwitz and Jerome Wakefield have voiced another vital form of critique of this development, a critique from outside of psychiatry, in their book *The Loss of Sadness* (2007). Here they argue that 'the age of depression results from a faulty definition of depressive disorder' (Horwitz and Wakefield, 2007: 6), entailing that the *DSM* definition of depression

> fails to take into account the context of the symptoms and thus fails to exclude from the disorder category intense sadness, other than in reaction

> to the death of a loved one, that arises from the way human beings naturally respond to major losses.
>
> (Horwitz and Wakefield, 2007: 14)

The emotion of sadness has, they argue, been transformed by psychiatry into depressive disorder, hereby creating a situation in which every form of (intense) sadness is equivalent with depression.

Overall speaking, it seems fair to state that the emotional component of depression in contemporary society – as defined by psychiatry – is narrowly affiliated with the understanding that (intense) sadness, however its context, is to be perceived as a sign of mental disorder. It is a disease. This biomedically centred perception of depression has been driven by the proliferation of diagnostic psychiatry, hereby also supporting the understanding that antidepressants are the primary levers of depression. In that respect, it is utterly understandable that the emotions connected with depression are perceived as something one should get rid of – by alleviating them via antidepressants – as soon as possible. But the crux of the matter is that the nature of these emotions – the fact that they are unwanted – cannot be understood unless we elucidate the societal context in which they thrive. The proliferation of depression in current times is thus not only a matter of diagnostic psychiatry operating with a flawed definition of what depression is – one that conflates emotions such as sadness with depression – but also to be found in central structures of our late-modern society.

Depression as a 'forbidden' emotion in contemporary society

To give a thorough account of why the emotion of (intense) sadness is pathologised as depression, we thus need to perceive how the dominant discourse on depressive disorder is intrinsically linked to the prevailing late-modern conception of the subject as *Homo oeconomicus*: the *Me Ltd*, the enterprising subject or the subject as enterprise (Foucault, 2008; Kirchgässner, 2008; Keohane, Petersen and Van den Bergh, 2017). This conception is often referred to as 'neoliberal', but we prefer the adjective 'ultraliberal', thereby implicitly referring to the long history of this type of subjectivity, which goes back way further than the mid-20th century. We understand late modernity as *accentuated* modernity, which means, among other things, an individualism intensified in a very specific way. The successful entrepreneur-subject is the authentic person. 'Authenticity' then is taken as dynamic self-realisation of an autonomous, empowered, motivated, future-oriented and above all *resilient* individual (Bröckling, 2007; Petersen, 2011; Van den Bergh, 2013a, 2013b, 2017; Evans and Reed, 2014; Slaby, 2016; Graefe, 2019). Depression now, in these late-modern or ultraliberal times, appeared more and more strongly as the flipside of this *Homo oeconomicus*. The depressed person is commonly understood as the in-authentic individual, suffering from a failing self-realisation or from *la fatigue d'être soi* – in English: 'the weariness of the self' (Ehrenberg, 1998).

The perspective of French sociologist Alain Ehrenberg is illuminating. According to him, the depression epidemic or pandemic is not a sign of decline but of transition. It does not entail a pathology of economic or social malaise, but rather one of abundance. Ehrenberg uses the term *pathologie du changement*, a pathology of change (Ehrenberg, 1998: 121). The global spread of depression, in other words, marks the shift from modernity to late modernity, and thereby one from a modern to a late-modern form of subjectivity. At the first page of Introduction of *La fatigue d'être soi*, he presents the two key questions of his depression study: "Why and how has depression imposed itself as our major personal misery? How does this reveal the mutations of individuality at the end of the 20th century?" (Ehrenberg, 1998: 9).

Depression, he states, is the pathology of a society with a new normativity. Since the 1950s, economic competition, sporty contest and passionate consumption are the templates, which determine the individual, his/her lifestyle and mode of self-manifestation. Traditional bonds and fixed values no longer make up the groundwork for the development of the individual. One has to rely above all to oneself and needs to expand, be successful, be outstanding and assert oneself as a self-confident consumer. In this way, we have come to live in post-neurotic times: the late modern subject no longer is led by prohibition, conflict and guilt, but rather by incitement, failure and shame (Ehrenberg, 1998: 16ff, 2010: 19f). It is the ethos of self-realisation and responsibility, which moves him/her. The thing to do no longer is the restraint and sublimation but the mobilisation and expression of the personal passions. The individual needs to display initiative, motivation, resolution, purposiveness, versatility, resilience and communicativeness. And within this context depression comes to the fore as exactly the opposite, so as failing in what is being called for. It means being an inadequate individual. Depression, in Ehrenberg's words, is 'the fatigue of becoming oneself', or 'the disease of responsibility' (Ehrenberg, 1998: 10).

Interestingly, the developments in 20th-century psychiatry, Ehrenberg argues, corresponded to this transformation of normativity. Gradually the reference to conflict – which since the end of the 19th century underpinned the concept of the subject – subsided and made way for a model of weakness or failure. Concerning depression, the symptoms of (intense) sadness and mental anguish pulled back in favour of fatigue. This is a shift, which is not discussed by Horwitz and Wakefield who stick to the strong link between depression and intense sadness. Ehrenberg questions this link and widens the interpretation by relating depression to the overall societal development. Ehrenberg's perspective amounts to a reversed version of how to contemplate weakness: one no longer is weak because one suffers, rather one suffers because one is weak. Lack of initiative became the principal defect of the depressed person. And the new antidepressants that were launched in the 1970s and 1980s, and became highly successful in the 1990s, the so-called SSRI's, aim at reverting this, at restoring the enterprising spirit of the disheartened. Prozac, writes Ehrenberg, 'is not the pill of happiness, but that of initiative' (Ehrenberg, 1998: 203; see also Ehrenberg, 2010: 215). The idea, taken root in the 1980s, that mental and behavioural disorders could be treated solely with biological remedies, became the norm. "Sick nerves are today a neurochemical imbalance", Ehrenberg writes (Ehrenberg, 1998: 189). Seen in this light, the amelioration of a state of depression must be biomedical. Furthermore, the lack of trying to ameliorate this state is the same as embracing ones weakness, inability and lack of responsibility. In contemporary society, this is the quintessence of what is forbidden.

Depression as disconnection

However intriguing the perspective introduced by Ehrenberg is, one has to ask whether it captures the personal accounts of experiences of depression. Going back to Karp's typification of depression as 'illness of isolation' one could say that the feeling of being robbed of concentration, motivation, and energy is rooted in the deeply felt impossibility of connecting to the world and to others. Karp speaks of "the downward spiral of hopelessness, withdrawal, the erosion of the self, the still more powerful feelings of hopelessness, the even greater impulse to withdraw, and so on" (Karp, 2016: 91). Also in other personal accounts of depressive episodes, we encounter a feeling of *existential isolation* at the heart of the disorder. Famous example of this is American author William Styron typifying the depressive state in his acclaimed *Darkness Visible: A Memoir of Madness* (1992: 46) as an 'immense and aching solitude'. Or British author and journalist Sally Brampton indicating her position as depressed person in *Shoot the Damn Dog: A Memoir of Depression* (2008: 1) with the words 'the most isolated place on earth'. Also American psychologist and author Andrew Solomon refers to such a state in his compendium *The Noonday Demon: An Anatomy of Depression* (2002: 436f), a rich mixture of autobiography and theory: "So many people have asked me what to do for depressed friends and relatives", he writes there, and "my answer is actually simple: blunt their isolation". These three works belong to a genre, which strongly came to the fore in the 1980s: autobiographies which only cover one or more depressive episodes the writer had. This genre could be called 'automelangraphy' (Van den Bergh, 2013b).

On the cover of the Dutch automelangraphy *Kikker gaat fietsen: Of over het leed dat leven heet* (*Froggy Goes for a Ride: Or on the Suffering that is Life*), by professor of modern French literature Maarten van Buuren, a frog in a crystal ball is displayed. The frog refers to a children's book series, which is well-known in the Netherlands, the crystal ball represents the nature of the depressive condition: still being there, but no longer being part of things. Van Buuren writes: "Apparently depression especially erodes my communicative and social powers, or rather: the depression perverts these from something protective into something menacing" (van Buuren, 2008: 58). Depressed mood or 'dis(at)tunement' – we will explain the latter term later in this chapter – often goes along with a loss of basic trust. In this state, British phenomenological philosopher Matthew Ratcliffe reports in *Experiences of Depression*, people often mention 'feelings of being vulnerable, exposed, threatened, or unsafe' (Ratcliffe, 2015: 220; see Karp, 2016: 102). One is there, but no longer participates. One is, as it were, in outer space. Or rather: the strange space in which one is placed makes the normal world into an outlandish, frightening thing. One is isolated. Important to note is, that sadness or inhibition is not so much the cause but rather the outcome of this.

There are three key traits returning over and over again in personal reports of depression experiences: disturbed relationality (existential isolation), disturbed temporality (closed future, empty present, insisting past) and disturbed corporeality (heaviness, slackness, rigidity). These three are closely connected. And these three are hardly present in the *DSM*-definition of *Major Depressive Disorder*. As such, the definition displayed in the *DSM* is nothing more than a fairly loose collection of symptoms, which lacks phenomenological coherence. Ratcliffe calls the *DSM*-description 'remarkably cursory' and marks the fact that in the *DSM* feelings of isolation are not classified as major symptoms but as possible accompaniments as a capital mistake: "Impaired interpersonal relations are not an 'effect' of depression experiences but absolutely central to them" (Ratcliffe, 2015: 218). One is out of tune and out of the world. The open future has been closed. The bodily bridge to the world has been blocked. One slackens, freezes, stagnates. Seen in this light, it becomes obvious that the *DSM*-definition does not grasp this cohering interplay of symptoms. It does not really tap into the experience of depression. One may wonder why this is the case. In the next section, we will return to this captivating question.

Let us take a closer look at the experience of depression. We will do this by discussing Ratcliffe's work a bit further and by turning subsequently to the writings of Thomas Fuchs, a German psychiatrist and philosopher. In his *Experiences of Depression*, Ratcliffe uses the central phenomenological distinction between 'emotional feelings' and 'existential feelings' (Ratcliffe, 2008). Both are bodily feelings, but emotional feelings occur in an intentional domain, whereas existential feelings happen in a pre-intentional sphere. The former have a specific object, the latter are background orientations that structure experience, they establish "a background sense of belonging to the world and a sense of reality", they are "ways of finding oneself in the world" (Ratcliffe, 2008: 38ff, 7, 2015: 55ff).[2] These latter feelings are most susceptible to phenomenological reflection, Ratcliffe states in *Feelings of Being*, when they change (Ratcliffe, 2008: 40). And this, according to Ratcliffe, is exactly what happens in a dramatic way in depression. Depressive disorder involves an 'existential change', a fundamental transformation of the 'sense of belonging' and the 'sense of reality'. One is isolated, positioned in a strange, uncanny domain which can hardly be described and which is cut off from the shared world of the others. The experience of isolation goes along with that of confinement (Ratcliffe, 2015: 31ff). One is captured in a bell jar, so to speak. Ratcliffe writes: "The world is not 'gone'. Instead, one is irrevocably cut-off from a realm that others continue to inhabit'. All this entails a deep feeling of 'estrangement" (Ratcliffe, 2015: 69, 202).

Also working within the phenomenological tradition, Thomas Fuchs argues that the dominating discourse on depression as a brain disorder or a cognitive aberration should be put 'on hold' if we are to 'retrieve the hidden layers of our own experience'. There is no other way, Fuchs claims, we need to 'change our concepts' (Fuchs, 2013: 226). The WHO has called depression a 'hidden burden' (www.who.int), and in spite of all the talk about this disorder many today still connect that burden with the word 'taboo'. But the 'burden' of depression is 'hidden' and 'taboo', not so much because we turn away from it or keep silent about it, but rather because it is ineffable, since we lack the proper narrative for it. We need to put the ultraliberal conception of subjectivity and connected ideas of 'the good life' on hold and re-tap into the tradition of phenomenology in order to be able to get back to the matter itself, that is the primordial pre-reflective, pre-intentional, pre-subjective level of (inter)affective, (inter)corporeal *attunement*.

Today, not only the prevailing notion of depression but also – and obviously connected to it – the dominant ones of affectivity, corporeality and subjectivity prevent a more suitable understanding of what we call mental disorders, including major depressive disorder. By putting these notions 'between brackets' – the phenomenological *epochè* – one clears the way for the approach of what is presently concealed, namely something that has a fundamentally *relational* character. Corporeality then can become intercorporeality, affectivity interaffectivity and subjectivity can be understood as basically intersubjectivity. *Homo sapiens* is first and foremost a *Homo resonans*. Thinking along these lines, depression becomes a deeply relational problem. The disorder of mood becomes a disorder of attunement, so a problem of 'detunement' or 'distunement'. The 'mood disorder' depression is thus basically a *participation* disorder at a very elementary level, as Fuchs acknowledges: "the patients lose the participation in the shared space of affective attunement" (Fuchs, 2013: 228). Or in the words of Ratcliffe: depression involves a loss or corrosion of "a changeable sense of belonging to the world that is pre-subjective and pre-objective" (Ratcliffe, 2015: 56).

Depression and the *Homo oeconomicus*

If depression, as shown above, should indeed be understood as disconnection and not as individualised, persistent ill mood, we have to understand what depressed people are in fact disconnected from. Only then are we able to understand this disconnection at a deeper level. As we wrote earlier, the *DSM* does not really tap into the experience of depression. Is that perhaps because it has other interests? Do these interests lead to a perspective for which the event of elementary attunement is 'out of order'? Is the basis of the way of thinking that carries the *DSM*-framework perhaps the idea of the *Homo oeconomicus*?

In the work of French philosopher Dany-Robert Dufour (2003) the *Homo oeconomicus* is presented as the 'isolist' subject. We will now connect this isolism of the ultraliberal subject with the existential isolation of the depressed person, thereby hoping to clarify why a liberal perspective that has isolist subjectivity as its basis must have a blind spot for the existential isolation of the depressed. Dufour understands the late-modern subject position as outcome of a longlasting (cultural) historical process, which he calls 'the liberal cultural revolution' (Dufour, 2007). Liberalism then is not conceived primarily as an economic or a political but as a *cultural* phenomenon. The mentioned revolution entails a gradually intensified liberation of the passions, a liberation which within the late capitalist context of the globalising 'free market' paradoxically also increasingly means a mobilisation and colonisation of those passions. Dufour names this market the 'Divine Market' (Dufour, 2007). After all, its word is law, in all sorts of ways, including the subjectification of the individual. 'Revolution' here implies inversion: the Augustinian order of *amor Dei* en *amor sui*, divine love and self-love is reversed bit by bit. This inversion or perversion is accomplished in the 18th century via – among others – Bernard Mandeville, Adam Smith and Marquis de Sade, after having been started in the mid-17th century by Blaise Pascal.

Take the radical stance of Marquis de Sade as a prime (because finalising) example. By the end of the 18th century, he heralded the pursuit of radicalised self-interest in his ultra-libertarian literary work. The term Sade uses a couple of times for this radicalisation is 'isolism'. A striking term. Isolism is the extremist combination of egoism and hedonism. According to Dufour, it is this Sadean isolist spirit, which since the global economic crisis of 1929 increasingly gave colour to our 'free market'-society. We live in a world that is more and more becoming Sadean, Dufour states provocatively (Dufour, 2009: 11). Our late-modern, late capitalist world is strongly marked by isolism, and this isolism, so the thesis goes that we want to present here, can be linked directly to the existential isolation of the depressed person. Depression then becomes isolism that starts to hurt badly. The widespread depressive malaise shows that the isolist subject position is intolerable and unliveable. It is a depressogenic position.

Our late-modern cultural society is a context of liberated and at the same time mobilised passions – an ultradynamic and hyperindividualist society. This society as a whole is *verstimmt*, says the German sociologist and philosopher Hartmut Rosa (2016: 739). The word *verstimmt* has two meanings: it refers to a collective discontent and to a basic dis(at)tunement. The late-modern 'discontent in civilisation' no longer relates to *Triebverzicht*, constraint of desire, like Sigmund Freud explained a century ago, neither to a loss or lack of autonomy, like Ehrenberg stated a decade ago, but to *Resonanzverlust* or a lack of attunement, so Rosa contends in his *Resonanz: Eine Soziologie der Weltbeziehung* (*Resonance: A Sociology of Our Relationship to the World*). "*Die Moderne ist verstimmt*", he writes there, modernity is out of tune or distuned (Rosa, 2016: 739). In his first major work *Beschleunigung* (*Acceleration*), Rosa analysed the dynamics of late-modern society as something, which becomes ever more self-destructive. Depression there comes to the fore as key pathology of our epoch, because it is a pathological form of a collective basic experience, namely that of 'raging standstill' (Rosa, 2005: 40ff, 385ff). Depression is called a 'pathology of time': it is the key disorder of *our times*, late modernity; it is the outcome of the *time pressure* that characterises this era; and it is the deep experience of deadlock or *futurelessness* in the middle of all of this societal dynamism.

Rosa's interpretation of depression between 2005 and 2016 moves from one in terms of ossification and autonomy loss – in that respect Rosa initially is close to Ehrenberg[3] – to one in terms of alienation and resonance loss. In the trajectory from *Beschleunigung* to *Resonanz*, Rosa starts questioning what Ehrenberg refrains from questioning: autonomy as the major thing. The German sociologist finally does not opt for an 'autonomy politics' but for a 'resonance politics', a politics in which autonomy loss or lack is no longer the main problem and the strong orientation on autonomy is even considered to be part of the problem.

Resonance appears in Rosa's work as a basic human need (Rosa, 2016: 293ff). It means a relation in which the related firstly speak with their *own voice*, secondly are *open to the otherness* of the other, and thirdly are prepared to be *transformed* by the relation. In our contemporary 'isolist' society, so the main thesis of Rosa goes, this basic need is structurally thwarted. Therefore, we are massively *verstimmt*: discontented and distuned. This 'alienation' comes to a head in the phenomena of depression and burnout, which Rosa calls 'radical forms of alienation' (Rosa, 2016: 307ff). Not loss of autonomy but elementary disconnection is the main problem in contemporary culture.[4]

Conclusion

In this chapter, we have shown how depression in contemporary society is, by ways of diagnostic psychiatry and under the influence of the *DSM*, understood as a persistent mood disorder that is classified as a mental disease. As such, the emotion of (intense) sadness is pathologised as depression, one can say. This conceptualisation imbues contemporary society, thus stipulating depression as a diagnosable disorder, located in the brain of individuals treatable by ways of pharmaceuticals. However, we have also shown how depression – instead of being identified as this type of individualised emotion – could (perhaps should) be perceived as disconnection. In fact, perhaps we are better off understanding depression as disconnection, utilising terms such as estrangement and distunement in getting a clearer picture of how the depressed person is in relation to the world of today. Understood as such, it is specified that depression is inter-relational – and can even be perceived as a consequence of the times in which we live that structurally support the emergence of depression: contemporary society produces depression as deranged isolism. As such, depression is also a political issue. We can elaborate on this by returning to the aforementioned analysis of Dany-Robert Dufour.

The alleged freedom of a society embracing liberalism is in fact a new form of slavery, Dufour states; it is the servitude of 'anti-authoritarian totalitarianism' (Dufour, 2011: 14). This slavery is our addiction: "We have become our own proper tyrants, we have become the slaves of our passions/pulsations" (Dufour, 2011: 277). By forwarding this analysis, Dufour has been labelled a 'neo-reactionary' in France – a label he obviously rejects. No room for nostalgia, he says. Rather, Dufour makes a distinction – referring to Herbert Marcuse – between necessary and unnecessary repression: the latter concerns the subjection of the other and needs to be contested, the former relates to the disciplining of the passions and is connected to a long tradition that we need to guard and recall (Dufour, 2011: 31, 148). Hence, no neo-reactionary or neo-conservative discourse, but a way of thinking that Dufour terms *neo-resistant* and *conservatoire*, neo-resistant and conserving. For the only regime that is truly revolutionary, as the young Karl Marx already expressed, is the capitalist system. The key thing is to resist this perpetual turnover and take 'conserving measures' (Dufour, 2011: 303ff). In this way, the tradition that was demolished by ultraliberalism can be recovered and regained, in order to enable us to build a world of postliberal, non-isolist, 'sympathetic individualism' (Dufour, 2011: 358). Perhaps one could call this endeavour 'Eros and the Social Pathologies of Contemporary Civilization' as it would elaborate on the thoughts unfolded in this chapter. This requires a re-evaluation of Marcuse's famous work *Eros and Civilization* published in the 1950s, together with his thoughts in *One-Dimensional Man*, published in the 1960s. The same goes for both volumes on 'capitalism and schizophrenia' by Gilles Deleuze and Felix Guatarri, *L'anti-Oedipe* and *Milles plateaux*, published in the 1970s. What can be said today about these thoughts on affectivity, madness and capitalism after the rise of 'neo-liberalism' in the 1980s and after its victory in the 1990s plus the consolidation of its power in the last two decades?

The resonance politics that were mentioned earlier in this chapter aim, above all, for an *affective re-tunement*, or an erotic re-tunement, if one likes, a re-disciplining or re-orchestrating of Eros, to put it again in musical terms. Resonance politics envision a post-repressive, post-oedipal, post-liberal, post-growth society. To be able to come to such a thing – and that is one of the key 'messages' of this chapter – it is crucial that affectivity is interpreted differently from the way one tends to do today. The same goes, obviously, for the 'mood disorder' or 'affective disorder' of depression. We need a turn from affectivity to inter-affectivity, from hyperindividuality to inter-subjectivity, and in terms of interventions a shift of focus from action/activation techniques (like pharmacotherapy and CBT) to passion/attunement techniques.[5] As David A. Karp writes at the end of his depression book: there is an urgent need 'to redefine ourselves in *relational* rather than individualistic terms' (Karp, 1996: 187). Taking affect as being at the deepest level an inter-relational phenomenon means having to understand depression as being at the deepest level a political problem.

Notes

1 Quite recently, it has been argued by one of the authors of this chapter that our current historical epoch, albeit in a different manner than announced by W. H. Auden, should be understood as an age of anxiety (Petersen 2017).

2 Ratcliffe refers here to the Heideggerian concept of *Stimmung*, mood or attunement.

3 In the follow-up study *La société du malaise*, Ehrenberg states that the world has become American, that is liberal, something that we need to accept concretely instead of rejecting it abstractly (and vainly). This liberal world calls for an 'autonomy politics', to address the 'new inequality', that is an inequality which is not so much a collective destiny of groups but rather, and increasingly distinctly, a matter of individuals, involving the unequal distribution of personal capacities (Ehrenberg 2010: 299ff). In his recent *La mécaniques des passions* (2018), Ehrenberg investigates how the world turning 'liberal' is linked to the rise of cognitive neuroscience.

4 Writing in these 'Corona times', it is almost impossible to speak about basic attunement and resonance politics without addressing the problems that are connected to this other pandemic. Obviously, we cannot go into detail here concerning the links of the latter with the 'depression pandemic'. One could state that COVID-19 functions as an amplifier: many issues and problems that were already present in our ultraliberal playing field are intensified or spotlighted. Summarising this, one could say: *Homo oeconomicus* bumped again painfully – and differently – into *Homo resonans*. The isolism of the former can be typified as an existential self-quarantine. It is the prescribed ultraliberal

modus vivendi of having to be weaponised and resilient in a 'dangerous' world. In the situation of real lockdowns and enforced quarantines, the hidden open space of elementary attunement suddenly was not so hidden any more because it was gone, or blocked, or contaminated, and thereby let itself painfully being felt. It is an elementary space, which cannot be missed. In that respect as well, COVID-19 gives us food for thought.

5 On cognitive therapies as opposed to what he calls 'resynchronisation therapy', see Fuchs (2013: 220, 2014: 410ff). And see Ratcliffe (2015: 71ff) on cognitive approaches to depression.

References

American Psychiatric Association (APA) (2013) *Diagnostic and Statistical Manual of Mental Disorders*, Fifth Edition. Washington, DC: APA.

Auden, WH (1948) *The Age of Anxiety*. London: Faber & Faber.

Brampton, S (2008) *Shoot the Damn Dog: A Memoir of Depression*. New York: W. W. Norton & Company.

Bröckling, U (2007) *Das unternehmerische Selbst: Soziologie einer Subjektivierungsform*. Frankfurt am Main: Suhrkamp.

Dufour, DR (2003) *L'art de réduire les têtes: Sur la nouvelle servitude de l'homme libérale à l'ère du capitalisme total*. Paris: Éditions Denoël.

Dufour, DR (2007) *Le divin marché: La révolution culturelle libérale*. Paris: Éditions Denoël.

Dufour, DR (2009) *La cité perverse: Libéralisme et pornographie*. Paris: Éditions Denoël.

Dufour, DR (2011) *L'individu qui vient ... après le libéralisme*. Paris: Éditions Denoël.

Ehrenberg, A (1998) *La fatigue d'être soi: Dépression et société*. Paris: Éditions Odile Jacob.

Ehrenberg, A (2010) *La société du malaise*. Paris: Éditions Odile Jacob.

Ehrenberg, A (2018) *La mécaniques des passions: Cerveau, comportement, société*. Paris: Odile Jacob.

Evans, B and Reid, J (2014) *Resilient Life: The Art of Living Dangerously*. Cambridge: Polity Press.

Foucault, M (2008) *The Birth of Biopolitics: Lectures at College de France, 1978–1979*. New York: Palgrave/Macmillan.

Fuchs, T (2013) Depression, Intercorporeality and Interaffectivity. *Journal of Consciousness Studies*, 20 (7/8): 219–238.

Fuchs, T (2014) Psychopathology of Depression and Mania: Symptoms, Phenomena and Syndromes. *Journal of Psychopathology*, 20: 404–413.

Graefe, S (2019) *Resilienz im Krisenkapitalismus*: *Wider das Lob der Anpassungsfähigkeit*. Bielefeld: Transcript Verlag.

Grob, GN and Horwitz, AV (2010) *Diagnosis, Therapy and Evidence: Conundrums in Modern American Medicine*. New Brunswick, NJ: Rutgers University Press.

Hochschild, AR (2016) *Strangers in Their Own Land*. New York: The New Press.

Horwitz, AV (2002) *Creating Mental Illness*. Chicago, IL: Chicago University Press.

Horwitz, AV and Wakefield, JC (2005) The Age of Depression. *The Public Interest*, 158: 39–58.

Horwitz, AV and Wakefield, JC (2007) *The Loss of Sadness: How Psychiatry Transformed Normal Sorrow into Depressive Disorder*. Oxford: Oxford University Press.

Karp, DA (1996) *Speaking of Sadness. Depression, Disconnection and the Meanings of Illness*. Oxford: Oxford University Press.

Karp, DA (2016) *Speaking of Sadness. Depression, Disconnection and the Meanings of Illness* (2nd Edition). Oxford: Oxford University Press.

Keohane, K, Petersen, A and Van den Bergh, B (eds.) (2017) *Late Modern Subjectivity and its Discontents: Anxiety, Depression and Alzheimer's Disease*. London: Routledge.

Kirchgässner, G (2008) *Homo Oeconomicus: The Economic Model of Behaviour and Its Applications in Economics and Other Social Sciences*. New York: Springer.

Lawlor, C (2012) *From Melancholia to Prozac: A History of Depression*. Oxford: Oxford University Press.

Petersen, A (2011) Authentic Self-Realization and Depression. *International Sociology*, 26 (1): 5–24.

Petersen, A (2017) Return of an Age of Anxiety: The Embedding of a Late Modern Social Pathology. In: Keohane, K, Petersen, A and Van den Bergh, B (eds) *Late Modern Subjectivity and its Discontents: Anxiety, Depression and Alzheimer's Disease*, 24–40. London: Routledge.

Ratcliffe, M (2008) *Feelings of Being: Phenomenology, Psychiatry and the Sense of Reality*. Oxford: Oxford University Press.

Ratcliffe, M (2015) *Experiences of Depression: A Study in Phenomenology*. Oxford: Oxford University Press.

Rosa, H (2005) *Beschleunigung: Die Veränderung der Zeitstrukturen in der Moderne*. Frankfurt am Main: Suhrkamp.

Rosa, H (2016) *Resonanz: Eine Soziologie der Weltbeziehung*. Berlin: Suhrkamp.

Rose, N (2019) *Our Psychiatric Future: The Politics of Mental Health*. Cambridge: Polity Press.

Shorter, E (2013) *How Everyone Became Depressed: The Rise and Fall of the Nervous Breakdown*. Oxford: Oxford University Press.

Slaby, J (2016) Kritik der Resilienz. In: Wüschner, P and Kurbacher, FA (eds) *Was ist Haltung?* 273–298. Würzburg: Königshausen & Neumann.

Solomon, A (2002) *The Noonday Demon: An Anatomy of Depression*. London: Vintage.

Styron, W (1992) *Darkness Visible: A Memoir of Madness*. London: Vintage.

Van Buuren, M (2008) *Kikker gaat fietsen! Of over het leed dat leven heet*. Rotterdam: Lemniscaat.

Van den Bergh, B (2013a) Depression: Resisting Ultra-Liberalism? In: Keohane, K and Petersen, A (eds) *The Social Pathologies of Contemporary* Civilization, 81–102. Farnham: Ashgate Publishing.

Van den Bergh, B (2013b) Self-Fulfilment or Self-Erosion? Depression as Key Pathology of Late Modernity – Extended Version. In: Araoz, G, Alves, F and Jaworski, K (eds) *Rethinking Madness: Interdisciplinary and Multicultural Reflections*, 87–110. Oxford: Inter Disciplinary Press.

Van den Bergh, B (2017) Sadean Depression and the Work of Culture. In: Keohane, K, Petersen, A and Van den Bergh, B (eds) *Late Modern Subjectivity and its Discontents: Anxiety, Depression and Alzheimer's* Disease, 41–68. London: Routledge.

World Health Organization (WHO) (2021) Depression. Available online at: www.who.int/news-room/fact-sheets/detail/depression.

Part 2

Liberalism and disenfranchisement

7 Introduction to Part 2

Søren Christian Krogh

Part 2 contains two central texts from Anders Petersen's work on the connection between (neo)liberalism and disenfranchisement. In both texts, Petersen demonstrates how a specific form of disenfranchisement has emerged among employees in liberal capitalist societies, i.e., disenfranchisement as a process that deprives contemporary employees of the ability to express criticism of their working conditions without fear of reprisal. Petersen thus aims to re-vitalize and re-actualize the long-standing tradition in sociology of critically analysing the complex and intersecting social forces that shape individuals' opportunities and experiences in modern capitalist societies, a tradition that can be traced all the way back to classical sociology. For example, in the work of Max Weber (2009), we learn how the rise of capitalism and bureaucracy can lead to the loss of individual autonomy and the dominance of instrumental rationality over moral values. Likewise, the critical analyses of capitalist societies led to Èmile Durkheim (2005) theorizing, among others, anomic suicide. Later on, we see the evolution of this sociological tradition in modern sociology in the work of scholars like Michel Foucault (1995). Here, it is argued that modern societies have developed sophisticated mechanisms of discipline and surveillance that control and regulate individual behaviour, often through subtle forms of power and coercion that limit individual freedom and expression. In contemporary sociology, highly acclaimed sociological analyses, such as that of Luc Boltanski and Ève Chiapello (2005), the flexibility and adaptability of capitalism as the dominant social order. Undoubtedly, critical scrutiny of liberal capitalist societies has been, and still remains, crucial to the field of sociology.

What makes Petersen's contribution to this research area stand out is his unique analysis of disenfranchisement processes in modern capitalist societies. First, Petersen's analysis of disenfranchisement differs from the majority of studies into forms of disenfranchisement, such as studies into felon disenfranchisement (see e.g., Manza & Uggen, 2008), as Petersen explores disenfranchisement as a deprivation of the ability to express criticism of working conditions without fear of reprisal (Petersen and Willig, 2011, 2013). Second, Petersen provides extensive and nuanced analyses of how and why this exact form of disenfranchisement has emerged among employees in liberal capitalist societies and places his analyses firmly within wider sociological debates of flexibility, autonomy and performance within contemporary society. Finally, another key finding in Petersen's work on

DOI: 10.4324/9781032714356-9

the connection between liberalism and disenfranchisement is how the issue of disenfranchisement is not solely a characteristic of large enterprises and companies but appears, in fact, widespread within the public sector as well. In this part of the book, Petersen's work on disenfranchisement is presented in two texts. In the first text, Petersen and Willig (2011) argue how demands for flexibility – here understood as the ability to constantly bend and shape one's work performances and identity to ever-shifting requirements – can be analysed as a process of disenfranchisement. More specifically, demands for flexibility weaken the sense of stability and security at work, cause insecurity about skills and ability to perform, and render employees incapable of raising criticism without fear of reprisals. In the second text, Petersen and Willig (2013) show the extent to which a pervasive culture of evaluation – particularly within the public sector – leads to disenfranchisement, self-criticism and a culture of fear and last but not least, negatively impacts the service provided (in this case child-care). Petersen and Willig thus put forth a new and much-needed contribution to the conventional and established literature on evaluations in which evaluations are mainly understood as positive tools that enhance learning, innovation and skills.

Both texts of the present chapter have been co-written with Petersen's close colleague and childhood friend Rasmus Willig. The influence of the pair's studies of disenfranchisement in contemporary society is instantly recognizable in much of Willig's writings. Throughout his work, Willig has been occupied with understanding the role of criticism and how possibilities for criticism are regulated within what he describes as the 'infrastructure of critique' (Willig, 2012). Like Petersen, Willig is also occupied with understanding why criticism in contemporary society has an intrinsic inclination to turn inwards and become directed at ourselves and our own shortcomings, flaws and imperfections rather than at social structures, policies, cultures, working conditions etc. (Willig, 2009, 2014), an inclination that Willig (2013) has described as the U-Turn of Criticism. Moreover, Willig has also demonstrated the extent to which the issues of flexibility, adaptability, (self-)criticism and disenfranchisement provide useful tools for critically scrutinizing changes in the Danish labour market as a whole, particularly in terms of the renowned Danish flexicurity model (derived from combing the words flexibility and security). In short, the flexicurity model seeks to allow for a relatively flexible labour market (particularly in terms of hiring and firing) while simultaneously providing citizens with a comprehensive social security system (unemployment support, free education, health care etc.). However, as Willig and Erjnæs (2018) demonstrate, the entire Danish labour market model is under threat by a combination of weakened social security measures along with the rise of a growing 'flexism regime' that causes self-censuring, fear of reprisal for criticizing working conditions, stress and isolation among employees. Consequently, it is no wonder that the scholarly partnership of Petersen and Willig was consolidated by a desire to further our understanding of how experiences of disenfranchisement appear within liberal countries of contemporary society.

References

Boltanski, L and Chiapello, E (2005) *The New Spirit of Capitalism*. London: Verso.
Durkheim, E (2005) *Suicide. A Study in Sociology* (Simpson, G, ed). London: Routledge.
Foucault, M (1995) *Discipline and Punish: The Birth of the Prison*. London: Vintage Books.
Manza, J and Uggen, C (2008) *Locked Out: Felon Disenfranchisement and American Democracy*. Oxford: Oxford University Press.
Petersen, A and Willig, R (2011) The demand for flexibility as a process of disenfranchisement. *Distinktion: Journal of Social Theory*, 12(3), 343–362.
Petersen, A and Willig, R (2013) Evaluations as a Process of Disenfranchisement. In: Keohane, K and Petersen, A (eds) *The Social Pathologies of Contemporary Civilization*, 175–192. London: Routledge.
Weber, M (2009) *The Protestant Ethic and the Spirit of Capitalism* (Swedberg, R, ed). New York: WW Norton & Company.
Willig, R (2009) Self-realization options: Contemporary marching order in the pursuit of recognition. *Acta Sociologica*, 52(4), 350–364.
Willig, R (2012) *Disenfranchisement. An Essay on the Infrastructure of Critique*. London: Peter Lang.
Willig, R (2013) *Kritikkens U-vending* [The U-Turn of Criticism]. Kopenhagen: Hans Reitzels Forlag.
Willig, R (2014) Emancipation. From Introvert to Extrovert Critique. *Advances in Applied Sociology*, 04(07), 190–196.
Willig, R and Ejrnæs, A (2018) *Flexisme* [Flexism]. Kopenhagen: Hans Reitzels Forlag.

8 The demand for flexibility as a process of disenfranchisement

Anders Petersen and Rasmus Willig

Introduction

To claim that the concept of flexibility is more and more central in modern forms of organizational thinking and political control is hardly controversial. Briefly put, the concept deals with eradicating resistance to change and requiring adaptability in reaction to varying political demands and a rapidly changing market. Framed in this context, flexibility is, in the dominant organizational literature, almost exclusively presented as a positive managerial concept (e.g., Child, 2005; Cook, Macaulay, and Coldicott, 2004).

The demand for employees to show flexibility is not merely a characteristic of large enterprises and modern companies (Krause-Jensen, 2010), but one that is also present in public-sector institutions, and can even be traced in municipal day nurseries and kindergartens. In a series of focus group interviews with Danish kindergarten teachers, managers and staff representatives, it became clear that the idea of flexibility has been incorporated into society's most basic reproductive stages.[1] The idea had, in other words, been internalized by the kindergarten teachers (Willig, 2009). The demand to show flexibility is not, however, unproblematic. It has proved difficult to handle for many kindergarten teachers, and also appears to have had consequences for the children. The demand has been accompanied by the impression of unceasing change at the institutions concerned, which thereby come to be perceived as workplaces that are never stable, but insecure. Efficient working procedures are altered and cease to function appropriately. The situation is experienced as highly confusing, and even the simplest procedures and tasks can come to take a long time, either because they have been radically altered or because the responsibility for them has been shifted elsewhere. Furthermore, the kindergarten teachers report that they no longer have a clear impression of the pedagogical perspectives and tools that are demanded. They appear to have lost a sense of which performances and skills will convey recognition. The consequence of this is that the kindergarten teachers talk about the absence of the necessary stability to secure the children's development, which has been placed under severe pressure. According to the kindergarten teachers, this pressure has brought about a considerable deterioration in conditions for the children. This pressure is, however, equally manifested through the fact that the frequent protests of the kindergarten teachers

DOI: 10.4324/9781032714356-10

concerning their conditions have been completely futile. They feel that their criticism has received no response, and they speak of experiencing a gradual sense of disenfranchisement as their critical voices are ignored or deflected. Several are also afraid to speak out, as they feel this may lead to serious censure or even dismissal.

In this chapter, our main focus is on some of the problematic aspects of flexibility that the kindergarten teachers conveyed. Our core contribution is hence an analysis, based on empirical data, of how imposed flexibility can have severe individual implications. This chapter is structured in seven steps. First, we are defining the central concepts of this chapter; namely, disenfranchisement (Section "Disenfranchisement") and flexibility (Section "Flexibility as autonomy?"). While the concept of flexibility is theoretically informed, the concept of disenfranchisement draws upon a previous study in which it formed as part of the development of a new critical theory that attempted to trace the developmental processes that, on a micro-sociological level, dismantle critique or entirely suppress or render impossible criticism of modern working conditions. However, common to the choice of concepts is that they have been undertaken on the basis of the results of the focus group interviews (Section "Methodological reflections").

We will then discuss the findings of the focus group interviews, in which we will show how the idea of flexibility has not only become established as a requirement but also taken on a coercive character, with the result that several of the affected staff feel that they have lost their sense of enfranchisement. This represents not just a loss of enfranchisement in professional terms, but also a very basic feeling of being unable to speak out critically against the rising demands for ever-greater adaptability, mobility and creativity – all of which arise in the wake of the central idea that everyone must show flexibility (Section "Results of the focus group interviews"). Following this brief empirical account, we will turn our attention to Axel Honneth's perspective on the relationship between recognition and work. Here it becomes clear that the diagnosis, which Honneth outlines, brings about greater insecurity with respect to the performances, skills and abilities that can lay claim to recognition. This transition to a society that accentuates the idea of being flexible and service-oriented helps to explain why several kindergarten teachers speak of the extreme psychological pressure they experience when they are constantly required to demonstrate new forms of performance. The surprising aspect, however, is that this psychological pressure is perceived as a process of disenfranchisement in which the respondents feel that it could be detrimental to their careers, or even place their jobs in jeopardy, if they were to speak out critically about the increasing demands to show greater flexibility (Section "Changeable forms of recognition"). However, Honneth's exposition also needs to be located in a more contemporary organizational context. In this connection, the famous analysis of Luc Boltanski and Eve Chiapello, in which project work is the principal organizational motif, can help to explain why several of the interviewed kindergarten teachers feel that they have lost their sense of enfranchisement. Project work demands flexibility: projects are formulated consecutively, with a new project always overlapping previous ones (Section "Flexibility as the motor of the project motif"). The theoretical reflections of Honneth,

Boltanski and Chiapello provide a more general understanding of the reasons why flexibility can be identified as a powerful process of disenfranchisement – one that deprives the participating respondents of their sense of being able to criticize the many changing political demands for more and more services, or new ways to organize their pedagogical work (Section "The demand for flexibility as a powerful process of disenfranchisement").[2] The conclusion is that many of the interviewed kindergarten teachers feel that each time they are just beginning to gather critical arguments against new processes of change or new forms of cutbacks, the target for their criticism is shifted. We end this chapter by summarizing its central arguments (Section "Conclusion").

Disenfranchisement

This chapter is part of a larger theoretical and empirical work focusing on how the criticism of modern human beings is dismantled, leaving them as disenfranchised citizens (Willig, 2007; 2009). The research project focused on kindergarten teachers, but could just as easily have dealt with primary or secondary school teachers, nurses, police officers or people in other public-sector professions.

Kindergarten teachers, however, constitute a useful illustrative group, as they are located on the front line of society's institutions. This is where the future citizens take their first steps – both literally and figuratively. Briefly put, kindergarten teachers are required to be enfranchised adults who take care of un-enfranchised children and turn them into enfranchised adults. In recent years, however, kindergarten teachers have been subjected to what might be termed a series of processes of disenfranchisement, which has not only robbed them of their capacity to act but also caused them, against their will, to reproduce these same processes towards the un-enfranchised children in their care.[3] The enfranchised person may be defined as one who is able to voice criticism, as it is through criticism that individuals assert their influence and their choices. The enfranchised person is thus not a member of a critical elite; on the contrary, within the framework of this definition, the critic is both democratized and generalized. The enfranchised person is an ordinary human being who can make choices and offer or withhold consent on the basis of critical considerations (Willig, 2009). An enfranchised person may therefore be regarded as an individual who is able to utter criticism without fear of legal or normative sanctions or reprisals. Conversely, processes of disenfranchisement may be described as processes, which cause one or more individuals to fear reprisals in the form of sanctions. A process of disenfranchisement may furthermore be defined as a series of acts or changes that produce alterations in the sense of enfranchisement of a person or group (Willig, 2009).

The process is negative in the sense that it deprives the individuals concerned of the ability to criticize, causing them to lose their sense of identity, and to feel powerless and paralysed. Such loss of enfranchisement may in extreme cases lead to a loss of personality on the moral–psychological level. The individuals concerned lose the ability to construe their biographies (i.e. their life-stories) in a way that seems meaningful (Willig, 2009). The concept of disenfranchisement cannot, however, stand alone. It must be associated with other theoretical and empirical phenomena if it is to possess concrete semantic content. The question is, then, what are the processes that lead to disenfranchisement?

On a more general theoretical level, the increasing demand for flexibility is assumed to have both positive and negative consequences for the extent to which individuals feel able to express themselves critically. In traditional hierarchical companies, critique often has to travel long distances to be heard, and in some cases there may even be no infrastructural pathways for criticism. Modern, flexible companies have in many cases taken on board this criticism of the traditional hierarchical corporate structure, which has difficulty involving its employees, but flexible forms of organization can also mean, firstly, that it can be difficult to know where to direct your criticism, and, secondly, that the requirement to be flexible can make employees feel insecure and thereby unable to express themselves critically.[4]

Flexibility as autonomy?

It is hardly polemic to claim that "autonomy – the extent to which employees exercise discretion in their work – has been an important subject in both public and scholarly debate on organizational flexibility and labour market stratification" (Edlund and Grönlund, 2010: 213). The interest in autonomy at work was developed against the backdrop of scientific management, which epitomized the 20th-century era of mass production. Scientific management – as famously put by Frederick W. Taylor – was based on two basic principles, namely the fact that work could be divided into standardized units, and that the detailed planning of work and the division of labour should be undertaken by management (Taylor, 1972). From Taylor's perspective, efficiency could only be obtained through enforced standardization of methods. That is, workers should adapt themselves to the standardized working conditions determined by management, thereby altering their status from craftsmen to a tool of the management. What becomes clear in this perspective, as famously shown in Braverman's (1974: 137) interpretation of scientific management, is not only that autonomy is related to skill and power, but also that management possessed a monopoly of knowledge that could be used to control workers. Scientific management, in other words, was first and foremost a method of de-skilling.

With the abolition of Tayloristic principles – which came about with the proliferation of the flexible organization – a reinstatement of craft skills, empowerment and worker autonomy is suggested to have taken place (Castells, 1996). It is argued that in a globalized world, organizations must adhere to a lean and flexible mode of organization in order to adapt themselves to volatile markets. As Piore and Sabel stated in their 1984 seminal work on the flexible organization, the need for flexibility would turn the Tayloristic principles upside down, resulting in multi-skilled workers, team work and increasing autonomy amongst workers (Piore and Sabel, 1984: 278). What instigated the end of Fordism and Tayloristic principles was thus, within this perspective, the adherence to flexible modes of organization. This would increase workers' autonomy – give them back their skills, so to speak. In that sense, the proliferation of flexibility was viewed as something purely positive.

A multifaceted discussion of this phenomena came to light in the same year as Piore and Sabels' praise of flexible organizations, namely via John Akinson's famous term the 'flexible firm' (Atkinson, 1984). This term played a very prominent role in shaping the debate about labour market flexibility and employment restructuring in the 1980s. One might say that the central thrust of the argument was that employers were

> increasingly segmenting their workers between a permanent 'core' of full-time employees, and a 'periphery' of part-time, temporary, subcontract and 'outsourced' workers. The 'core' provides 'functional flexibility' through lowered job demarcations and multi-skilling, while the 'periphery' provides 'numerical flexibility'.
>
> (Pollert, 1988: 281)

As Arne L. Kalleberg suggests, however, the debate about this rather simple 'core periphery' model "has focused mainly on whether it is an accurate representation of employers' labor utilization strategies" (Kalleberg, 2001, 480), and not so much on how employers attempt to balance the advantages and disadvantages associated with them. Hence, the historically and structurally conveyed division between functional and numerical flexibility has been subjected to rather one-sided analysis. Functional flexibility has been connected with organizational performance; that is, how this kind of flexibility equips employees with multiple skills, so that they can be redeployed from one task to another (see Appelbaum and Batt, 1994). Research on numerical flexibility, on the other side, has mostly been concerned with employers' attempts to 'reduce costs by using workers who are not their regular, full-time employees' (Kalleberg, 2001: 482).

In the context of this particular study, however, the focus has been on how functional flexibility has been connected with the internalization of various types of individual flexibility. In that sense, our main objective has been to analyse some of the human consequences of functional flexibility. There seems to be no doubt that there are different approaches to, and hence many possible interpretations of, the consequences of the proliferation of this flexible mode of organization. At one end of the scale, we find those who, in line with Piore and Sabel, praise functional flexibility as a desirable characteristic of firms and employees (see Anell and Wilson, 2000). In a fairly unambiguous manner, functional flexibility is viewed by this group as promoting worker autonomy and thereby creating the possibility for workers to make full use of their expertise and creative competencies. Moreover, in this perspective, functional flexibility is identified as one of the single most important factors in creating success for companies (Peters, 1992). At the other end of the scale, however, we find those who are more critical towards this concept and the consequences of its widespread implementation. At this end, we find the work of Richard Sennett. Sennett's perspective on flexibility and flexible organization is strongly linked with the emergence of what he calls flexible capitalism (Sennett, 1998: 2006). According to Sennett, the social, political, economic and cultural adaptation to flexible capitalism not only is on a structural level but also has serious implications for the working human being as such. In his much-debated work *The Corrosion of Character*, Sennett (1998) traces the term 'flexibility' – in the English language – to the 15th century. The meaning of the term originally derived from the observation that a tree bending in the wind always springs back to its original position once the wind stops blowing. Flexible human behaviour ought, in Sennett's perspective, to have the same tensile strength: people should be able to adapt to different circumstances without being broken by them. Nowadays, however, the term has taken quite a different turn. As Sennett writes: "Society today is searching for ways to destroy the evils of routine through creating more flexible institutions. The practices of flexibility, however, focus mostly on the forces bending people" (1998: 46). Drawing on Sennett's work, we are thus able to define functional flexibility in a rather broad sense, which, however, has some very concrete demands attached to it. Hence, functional flexibility, as it is expressed here, refers to the ability to constantly bend and shape your work performance to match "the shifting demands of the day". In that sense, functional flexibility also implies the forced incorporation of many related concepts, such as the ability to be adaptable, creative and mobile. From this perspective, then, flexibility is less concerned with the optimization of worker autonomy per se, but is rather a tool used to equip workers with very specific skills.

Methodological reflections

The empirical examples presented here derive from a series of focus group interviews conducted in the years 2008 and 2009. In the first series of interviews, 20 focus group interviews were held over four days, with a total of 110 participants. In the second series, 28 focus group interviews were held over seven days, with a total of 138 participants.[5] The first series of focus group interviews encompassed kindergarten teachers, kindergarten managers, staff representatives and daycare centre managers, while the second series involved staff representatives and joint staff representatives. The interviewed persons all live in medium-sized towns in Denmark,[6] and the group of joint staff representatives was drawn from the whole country.

The focus group interview was chosen because this method is particularly good at mapping and identifying the common interpretations and understandings that different groups generate towards a given subject. A much-quoted definition of a focus group is that it is "a research technique that collects data through group interaction on a topic determined by the researcher" (Morgan, 1996: 130). This very broad definition implies three things: focus group interviews are used to collect data, as opposed to their use in marketing, where the method is applied as a means to sell ideas, products, political content, and so forth; group interaction is the main source of data; and the researcher/moderator plays a significant role in creating the group discussion that generates the data (Kitzinger, 1995). In view of the fact that group

interaction is the main source of data collection; we need to define which kinds of group interaction we pay attention to. In our study only oral interaction was accounted for, leaving out gesticulations, body language and so forth. Accordingly, we strongly encouraged all the participants in the focus groups to talk to each other, ask questions of each other, comment on each other's experiences, and be critical towards each other in relation to the topic in question. The methodological point being that we were not interested in the sum of individual utterances, but in the accumulated interpretations of the group (see Kitzinger, 1995: 299). This technique has, of course, a strong influence on the forms of knowledge that focus group interviews can produce, and hence on which forms of knowledge they cannot produce.

Firstly, knowledge produced through group interaction is always formed within the particular context of the group interaction itself. That is to say, the participant's interaction is limited to the particular setting – a setting that may be deemed superficial, because it was neither chosen by the participants themselves nor to the liking of all of the participants.

Secondly, the knowledge produced through group interaction is influenced by a certain power structure within the group. Symmetry of power is unlikely to occur within a group setting – a factor that determines which of the participants actually produces the knowledge. These conditions certainly exclude the knowledge, which might have been produced if we had interviewed the participants in a one-to-one situation. The particular in-depth information that it is possible to extract in normal interviews is thus impossible to produce in focus group interviews. In order to compensate for this lack, the role of the moderator in focus group interviews is therefore vital, not only to encourage interaction but also to make sure that as many of the participants as possible participate in the knowledge production. As this theme may be perceived as being relatively delicate and sensitive by the participants, it was considered advisable to take a gentle approach to initiating the focus group interviews regarding the kindergarten staff's perception of which processes of disenfranchisement were most prevalent.

Two ethical strategies were utilized for this purpose. Firstly, it was emphasized that all statements would be anonymized; and secondly, the serious nature of the subject was defused via a series of oral presentations (see also Mariampolski, 1989: 7; Greenbaum, 1990).[7] The ethical considerations involved in focus group interviews are much similar to those of doing interviews. There are, however, some particular ethical aspects that need to be taken into account when conducting focus group interviews, of which one crucial consideration is the possibility of keeping the participants anonymous. The problem does not so much lie in the written presentation of the material – since, as authors, we can always change people's names, and so forth – as in the actual conducting of the focus groups. Once a particular utterance is out in the open it cannot be controlled, leaving the speaker in a potentially delicate situation towards the other participants (Smith, 1995: 483). In such a situation, power asymmetry is obviously a risk that the moderator would be unlikely to be able to keep in check. In the study in question, we openly informed potential participants about this possible "risk" of participating in a focus group interview. On the basis of this information, the participants could decide whether they actually wanted to be a part of the interview or not, given the specific circumstances of such an interview. None declined to participate, which we assume was the result of both precisely provided information on our part and of the huge interest on the part of the participants to be part of the process. Another ethical/ practical aspect of the focus groups conducted was that of introducing the participants to the intended area of study. That is to say, the participants were made familiar with various analyses of more general processes of disenfranchisement, which they could reflect upon and compare with their own situations. These analyses then served as a springboard and source of inspiration for the first group discussion, which dealt with the participants' experience of various processes of disenfranchisement. The participants were encouraged to look upon the focus group interview as a laboratory in which they could analyse their work situations, consider alternatives and reflect critically on their often very stressful daily lives (for this approach, see also Watts and Ebutt, 1987: 31).[8]

It is clear that our focus group research can be subjected to different sorts of criticism – one being that we lack reading for difference in the facilitation of the groups. That is, the focus groups were not designed to subject our particular theoretical perspective to empirical pressure. It was simply not our motif to do so.

Another reservation one could make is the way in which we introduced the participants in the focus groups to the processes of disenfranchisement. Now, one of the more complicated aspects of doing focus group interviews is presenting the participants to the topic in a 'neutral' or 'objective' way – especially if the topic is of a delicate nature (Folch-Lyon and Trost, 1981). Thus, our presentation might have caused the participants to think about their working situation in a narrow manner, hence creating a certain bias in the data. This directly leads to a reservation that could be made; namely, the level of agreement among the participants. The research leaves the impression that there were no differences and too much coherence between the participants on the subject in matter. So were there no ambivalences? When trawling the empirical data for evidence of clear-cut satisfaction with the imposed flexibility or even on how employees might use the demand of flexibility to their own advantage, we come up short. The interaction within the focus groups simply does not communicate this. Now this surely raises the question as to whether the usage of focus groups alone suffices to analyse processes of disenfranchisement. We are fully aware of this methodological weakness in our study, something that probably could have been rectified by the supplementary usage of ethnography and/or individual interviews. By applying these methods we might have got a more nuanced picture. To this, we should even add that despite the fact that relatively many focus group interviews were undertaken, they were all conducted within the same region in Denmark, which implies that the dissatisfaction is locally based. This means that the case cannot be generalized, but can only provide theoretical inspiration.

Results of the focus group interviews

When applying our analytical grid to the many focus group interviews, they revealed numerous processes of disenfranchisement. But one of the most dominant, and repeatedly discussed by the participants, was the idea of flexibility. As a result of this concept, many had the feeling that they had barely finished implementing the last set of organizational initiatives before new ones were on the way. The process of development of the institutions, pedagogical methods and ways of organizing the work was incessant, with the consequence that the kindergarten teachers lost their sense of having a stable workplace, but rather perceived it as being subject to continual change. According to this study, this resulted, amongst other things, in the alteration of otherwise well-functioning working methods, which thus became dysfunctional. It was seen as very difficult to gain one's bearings in the work, and even the most basic procedures and functions could take a very long time, either because they had been radically altered or because the responsibility for the work processes had not been clearly located. Many of the respondents appeared to have lost track of things and had difficulty in obtaining a clear picture of the many administrative initiatives. As this short extract so vividly expresses:[9]

Lone: "The problem with the new structure is that the boundaries are so fluid. This puts me under stress. We are constantly adapting to new policy initiatives, and each time we have to learn new roles, which is difficult for many people. We are constantly breaking down our working procedures. We haven't even managed to implement the last set of requirements before new ones are imposed. This creates internal discord, and people start criticizing each other. But if we criticize the management or the politicians, we are told that we should see 'resources' instead of 'limitations'. And that's how the criticism is swept under the carpet".

Hanne: "Yes, what about just letting us have some bloody peace – just let us keep our routines so we are not ordered to show adaptability all the time".

The group of interviewed kindergarten staff had been and still are exposed to constant pressure to adapt to new developmental goals. The political demand to show flexibility, which was initially regarded as a temporary measure, has become a permanent reality. The demand for flexibility can appear quite liberating in situations where entrenched dogmas, rigid institutions or outdated systems have wholly or partly placed obstacles in the way of all innovative activities, but once flexibility becomes a permanent condition, it reveals, according to the respondents, a character that is almost akin to that of prostitution: be prepared to take up any position.

One kindergarten teacher compares this experience, in stark terms, with feeling like a puppet: "I don't know when I'm in, or when I'm out. I don't know what I have become. Sometimes I am just a puppet, while at other times I have a say in decisions and can exert an influence". Note that she says, "I don't know what I have become". This phrase gives some indication of the extreme psychological pressure to which she is subjected by the role of "puppet", in which she is required only to nod, move as directed by the strings, and not ask questions: merely be a puppet. In the eyes of the kindergarten teachers, the municipal administration does not interpret questions as a sign of sincere interest, but rather of a lack of understanding, or even direct resistance to new initiatives. With a puppet you can do what you like. You can put new clothes on it whenever you want, and it will not protest. When she says, "I don't know when I'm in, or when I'm out", she means that she does not know whether she is inside or outside the right group. Is she included or excluded? Is she recognized or not? Another extract stipulates this point:

Lise: "When discussing our work environment we are not allowed (by management) to say something too critical. It has to be so cosy all the time. 'A wise man once said that it takes two men to create a conflict'. This is, very often, how our meetings begin and then all critique ceases. But when we are so amiable not a damn thing happens".

Tove: "Exactly, and one of the things that bothers me the most is the fact that there is no transparency when it comes to our critique. Everything that is being criticized in different settings seems to vanish. And then it all ends up with being management that evaluates the results instead of the employees because the timeframes are so narrow. It is the emperor's new clothes".

The kindergarten teachers feel that they are constantly being forced to put on new clothes. They must not only be ready to accept new roles – show individual flexibility on the count of functional flexibility – but also must do so without asking critical questions. However, none of them can see the point of the new political initiatives. The metaphor of the emperor's new clothes is actually very useful to analyse their perception of the situation. They feel as if they are forced into adjusting and criticizing something, which is really not there. Furthermore, when the members of this professional group are asked to be flexible, this in many cases means that they must relinquish their professional integrity and identity; that is, the fundamental enfranchisement that enables them to speak out and thereby retain their sense of who they are. The kindergarten teachers' talk, as shown in the extract, about working routines constantly being broken down, and that this brings about an erosion of the protective barrier that such routines create. Routines create a sense of security, because they work. They become automatic, which means that the kindergarten teachers can relax while they are carrying them out – this, they tell us in the interviews, is the benefit of experience. When these routines are broken down, on the other hand, the sense of stability and security is swept away, and with it the security to criticize, since such routines comprise the very heart of the kindergarten teacher's professionalism. An attack on this professionalism, and thereby on the profession itself, is therefore, it seems, also an attack on the foundations of critique. Critique relies for its arguments and references on professional conviction; it is, so to speak, underpinned by the professional arguments, which make it possible to speak of professional authority and anchoring. Professionalism is the foundation, which creates a sense of security despite the external pressure; a strong professional foundation can withstand the worst storm or attack.

The concept of showing flexibility does not, as one might think, cause critique to adapt to the new situation and the new professional foundation, but rather to disappear entirely. Due to the willingness to show flexibility, and the increasing demands to do so, a new professionalism never manages to take root before it is once again time to embrace change. Furthermore, the willingness to show flexibility has no objective, according to the kindergarten teachers; it is no longer a means, but has become an end. Reorganization has become good thing in itself. Once the goal has disappeared, so has the object of critique. We may seek to hit the target, the kindergarten teachers explain, but the target is gone.

Changeable forms of recognition

It is precisely this feeling of constantly having to relinquish previously learned skills that is the source of many problems. For many of the kindergarten teachers, it feels like a veritable loss of identity. By applying Axel Honneth's theory on recognition, we are able to clarify why it is so difficult for the interviewees to constantly adapt to new forms of recognition. For Honneth, the theoretical links between the concepts of work and recognition are to be found in the normative, structuring capitalist performance principle (Petersen and Willig, 2002: 274), according to which any member of society has the right to be recognized for his or her contributions to society's reproduction; that is, contributions that can be regarded as work (Petersen and Willig, 2002: 275).

According to Honneth, the performance principle arises in extension of the concept of honour, under which the individual valuation of work was reserved for a minority of the members of society. As the honour principle erodes, recognition becomes something that may be awarded to any modern individual who can meet the demands of society in relation to what society deems worthy of such recognition. So instead of a particular, bound concept of honour associated with certain fixed forms of status, individual performances are now emphasized in parallel with the growth of the industrial division of labour. This historical transformation produces a meritocracy in which more members of society can obtain social recognition as working citizens, on the basis of their respective performances.

It is clear that this new principle has had an ideological component from the start, since a described task could only count as a contribution to society's reproduction after being evaluated in relation to the hierarchy of values established by the male bourgeoisie. In this respect, the liberation of recognition was from the outset based on the dominance relations of specific groups, as a result of which many forms of work were denied any possibility of recognition. By extension, we can view struggles for recognition within various professional groups as battles, which strive to articulate the demands of the performance principle, namely the right to recognition for the groups' own abilities and skills, and for performances that have not yet achieved the recognition they should rightfully be assigned. Thus, Honneth, like Hegel and Marx, believes that work is not merely economic in nature, but can also be viewed in terms of self-realization, in as much as it is assigned an emancipatory potential. From such a perspective – in which the concept of work is not merely reduced to an instrumental category but also expanded to include an externalization of the individual's essential creativity and talents – it becomes possible to practise a different type of social criticism that can investigate not only the material conditions of individual physical work but also the psychological conditions for individual self-realization. Honneth, however, has only in a fragmentary manner indicated how recognition relations play out in the context of modern capitalist society. Before we can proceed to give the idea of flexibility a more substantive content, we should therefore briefly summarize some of the more contemporary social diagnostic statements that we find in Honneth's work.

In his essay, Honneth (1995) identifies two primary processes, which have contributed to reducing the value of industrial work. The first of these is the growth in the service sector, in which reflexive activities have replaced industrial, mechanical activities. These activities differ from earlier forms of performance, partly because they are extremely heterogeneous and uncertain and partly because the entire service sector lacks clear criteria for economic efficiency, which can be made the yardstick of recognition. Secondly, industrial work has lost not only the economic status, which can form the basis for recognition, but also its collective status. The traditional biography of the individual, in which recognition was accorded on the basis of continuous, lifelong performance, is under pressure from an ever-changing job market. Consequently, industrial work, understood as a cultural and ethical medium in which the worker obtains a sense of identity, achieves recognition and acquires a self-image as a morally acting person and a bearer of rights, is placed under severe pressure. In Honneth's own words:

> Traditional patterns of self-realization lose their cultural support in the life-world's long practiced forms of recognition. [...] Everyday cultural praxis is freed step-by-step from its received value commitments and traditions without them having already been replaced by comprehensive patterns of orientation, within which the individual subjects' attempts at self-realization could find intersubjective recognition.
>
> (Honneth, 1995: 229)

According to Honneth, therefore, the normative performance principle, which has hitherto served as a source of integration, is in the process of dissolution. As we saw, this is due not just to the demise of industrial work but also to the increased opportunities to obtain incomes that are difficult to justify, examples of which include the violent rises and falls of the stock market, the speculative property market, and the increasing number of competitions in which success is due to simple forms of economic luck, and which cannot therefore be justified by the performance principle. Honneth's social diagnostic point is that the performance principle has now in general become too narrow to encompass types of work that cannot be assigned recognition value in connection with the reproduction of society. The conclusion is that we are likely to witness a growing number of symbolic struggles for recognition in relation to the issue of what may be considered work, and that there will be an increase in forms of mental illness related to the new organization of work, as it becomes harder to orient one's behaviour in relation to performance that conveys recognition and thus, at a fundamental level, confirms one's identity (Petersen and Willig, 2002: 274).

How are we able to transfer Honneth's observations on the devaluation of industrial labour to pedagogical work? There is nothing industrial about crèches and kindergartens, but the pedagogy applied there has moved from being predominantly oriented towards the collective to becoming more individually focused. In this transition to multiple and heterogeneous tasks, it is striking that the kindergarten teachers state that their tasks are continually altering, and that it is difficult to assess them from the point of view of whether they represent good or bad pedagogy. In this context one could argue that, due to the profession's qualitative nature, it is almost impossible to fundamentally determine what is good or bad pedagogy, and therefore that the profession will always have difficulty in presenting its educational performance in clear and unambiguous hierarchies of recognition. However, it is also clear that the profession has been subject to more pronounced demands to undertake various kinds of evaluations. These evaluations, so the kindergarten teachers tell us, have had a dramatic impact on the respondents, since the respondents internalize the many evaluative questions and attempt to pursue them. The result is that the many different evaluative standards create confusion concerning what deserves recognition as a good pedagogical work. By extension, it also becomes clearer why several of the kindergarten teachers said that they had difficulty criticizing the evaluative goals, since they simply changed all the time.

In many ways, there is a paradox here. A greater degree of flexibility ought to lead to an increase in the plurality of forms of recognition, but instead it creates confusion concerning what is deserving of recognition. It is a similar story with the evaluations to which the kindergarten teachers are subjected. The intention of these evaluations is to clarify the educational goals to be pursued and thereby provide rewards, but instead they lead to greater confusion, as they are perceived as being continuous and lacking in any conclusion. This empirical observation harmonizes very well with some of the more recent theoretical discussions and empirical findings arrived at by Honneth and his colleagues in recent years (Honneth and Hartman, 2006; Kocyba, 2000; Neckel, 2000; Voswinkel, Holtgrewe, and Wagner, 2000). Honneth's second observation can also help to explain why many kindergarten teachers feel that their profession is under extreme pressure. It is no longer 'enough' merely to be a kindergarten teacher. There are now many different specialties within the profession, and it can therefore be perceived as more difficult to arrive at a collective consensus on what should constitute the struggle for recognition. This places the collective professional struggle under pressure, and several of the respondents also saw this as a significant weakening of their professional identity. This is logical, in the sense that a differentiation of the kindergarten teachers' profession could potentially lead to more disagreements and conflicts of interest within the profession, which might weaken the struggle for the recognition of more equitable working conditions. But while the respondents predominantly focused on this negative aspect, it is also worth noting that the kindergarten teaching profession has grown, and that it is precisely the differentiation of the profession's professional qualities that has also helped to strengthen it. In the focus group interview study, the disagreements between the various specialized branches within the profession and in pedagogy generally were often compared with 'chicks pecking at each other'. These situations occurred, according to the kindergarten teachers, whenever there were cutbacks and internal conflicts about who should cut more or less. In these situations, several of the teachers spoke of how they had forgotten that their criticism ought to be directed externally, against the cutbacks, and not internally, against themselves.

This thus brought about a U-turn of the criticism on two levels. Firstly, the kindergarten teachers informed us that they directed their criticism at the profession, accusing it, for example, of not being progressive enough or of being unable to oppose the many new demands. Secondly, the interviews make it clear that several of the kindergarten teachers personalized the criticism and accused themselves of not being able to live up to the demand for flexibility. In this context, it is worth noting that the criticism served as a means of creating great insecurity concerning the profession and the abilities and skills of individual teachers.[10] This criticism was therefore in some respects an unintended means of devaluing their performance, and as a consequence their sense that their achievements were recognized.

Flexibility as the motor of the project motif

While Honneth's work helps to explain why kindergarten teachers find it difficult to pin down the criteria for what conveys recognition, and the consequences of this, Boltanski and Chiapello (2005) help us to understand the social grouping that celebrates the idea of flexibility. We thereby obtain a theoretical explanation of why functional flexibility is presented as a natural (and positive) characteristic, which kindergarten teachers are also expected to practise.

As an empirical basis for their comprehensive analysis of the rise of the new spirit of capitalism, Boltanski and Chiapello utilize so-called neo-management literature,[11] and find that references to a loose network logic occupy a particularly central place in this literature. Briefly put, this logic, also known as project-oriented logic, is supported by a dictum of functional flexibility, by which is meant that the crucial feature of project-oriented logic is the demand for constant activity and constant adaptation (Budgen, 2000: 150). These demands are in fact so trenchant that they overshadow all other individual abilities, skills and talents, and in this way seem to permeate every aspect of life, dissolving the boundaries between work, private life and leisure. As a result, individuals must continually maintain a high level of activity, so that they are always available for projects and accessible by network contacts. But in addition to the demand for continuous availability, Boltanski and Chiapello also feel that the concepts cover a number of other normative demands that individuals must meet in order to achieve recognition, including demands to be flexible, mobile, enterprising, creative, polyvalent, adaptable, tolerant, bold, social, innovative and malleable (Boltanski and Chiapello, 2005: 112). The internalization and realization of these normative demands is regarded as necessary in order for the individual to serve an ideological motif in which the following basic conditions apply. According to Chiapello and Fairclough:

> Life is conceived as a series of projects, the more they differ from one another, the more valuable they are. What is relevant is to be always pursuing some

> sort of activity, never to be without a project, without ideas, to be always looking forward to, and preparing for, something along with other persons, who are brought together by the drive for activity.
>
> (2002: 192)

Projects, in this context, are always short-term. The enthusiasm and zeal exuded by a project is built into a short-term template, in which the prospect of the project's imminent termination further underlines the focus on its successful conclusion. In fact, the individual renounces all long-term projects, as these by definition tend to impede the possibility of maintaining a continuous workflow. Long-term projects hinder, in other words, the possibility of showing mobility, flexibility and so forth. In this context, Boltanski and Chiapello make use of Deleuze and Guattari's (1988) "nomad" concept to describe the most important characteristics of this new individual (Boltanski and Chiapello, 2005: 145). The nomad has no fixed base, no ties and no territory, and is therefore perfectly suited to the project culture of network logic. The nomad moves around between the various project units without becoming too comfortable or 'settling down' in any particular project team. The nomad is eternally mobile and rootless and is constantly moving on. As a result, the nomad is always open towards change and capable of adapting to shifting conditions. The contrast with the capitalist demands of previous eras is striking. In the past, working life was deeply rooted in institutionalized frameworks, and focused on stability and long careers. This organization of work was anchored in a series of collective agreements that were strongly reinforced by the powerful social position of the trade unions. Now, this situation appears to be history: "With careers much less organized, people are compelled to keep returning to the market, where their value is assessed at different stages of their working life" (Boltanski and Chiapello, 2005: 314).

Since the market has become the primary source of organization for the assessment of the individual in working life, no form of long-term organization is invited. What the market demands are individuals who can think in a short-term and project-driven manner. This new working climate is not necessarily seen as obstructive, but rather as conducive to the provision of continual possibilities for self-realization, and thus a guarantee of lasting employability. In fact, it is this employability by which the network logic stands or falls. Since individuals are forced to return to the market to have their value assessed, they must also have something to bring with them to the market, or else they cannot remain employable, much less active, and thus cannot meet the normative requirements for the new project individual (Boltanski, 2002: 19). It is naturally difficult to transfer this logic directly to the working situation of the kindergarten teachers. Their work is not immediately project oriented, and it is therefore impossible to conceive of kindergarten teachers as project nomads moving from project to project. Nonetheless, kindergarten teachers would appear to be subject to a number of the normative demands of project logic, as, through the constant emergence of new political and organizational initiatives, they are continually being confronted with the consequences of the project-oriented life. The breaking down of old working practices and the building up of new ones is accompanied by the expectation that kindergarten teachers can easily manoeuvre in shifting organizational contexts. They are in other words expected to be able to adapt. More strikingly, however, they are also expected to view the changes as potential resources, not limitations. They are thus expected to regard the destruction of well-functioning working methods as a positive development, and thereby view adaptation as a virtue, since it will enable their 'self-realization' in the work. In this way, the demand for flexibility is elevated to an ultimate, positive characteristic. However, this is not how the interviewed persons themselves regard the development; for them, the many changes mean that they are losing their grip on their primary tasks, due amongst other things to the fact that their criticism of the changes is ignored. The consequence is that the kindergarten teachers lose their sense of enfranchisement.

The demand for flexibility as a powerful process of disenfranchisement

One of the seemingly overlooked problems is not the idea of functional flexibility in itself, but what happens when this becomes compulsory. When routines are constantly being broken down, degradation also takes place in the psychological bulwark, which these routines comprise. Routines create a sense of security, because they, according to the interviewed kindergarten teachers, function as easily recognizable repetitive actions, which do not require reflection. They have been thoroughly rehearsed, as a result of which many of the respondents say they can relax while performing them. When these routines are broken down, on the other hand, this sense of stability and security is removed, including the security to criticize, since such routines comprise the very core of the kindergarten teacher's professionalism.

An attack on this professionalism, and thereby on the profession itself, is also an attack on the foundations of critique. Critique relies to a large extent for its arguments and references on firmly-anchored professional conviction; it is, so to speak, underpinned by the professional arguments. Professionalism is the foundation, which creates a sense of security despite external pressure. The idea of showing flexibility, according to the focus group interviews, does not, therefore, as one might think, result in critique merely adapting to the new situation and the new professional foundation, but instead apparently causes it to disappear entirely. Due to the demand for flexibility, a new professionalism never manages to take root among the kindergarten teachers before it is once again time to embrace change. The demand to show flexibility does not appear to have a goal; it is no longer a means, but has become an end. Reorganization is presented as being a virtue in itself. But once the goal has disappeared, so has the object of critique. The interviewed may seek to hit the target, but the target is gone.

In one of her most recent studies, the American sociologist Arlie Russell Hochschild concludes that the modern employee is deemed worthy of recognition in relation to the extent to which he or she shows initiative and industry, "seeks a response to his personal behaviour', 'is sensitive to alterations in mood and level of attentiveness' and 'adapts his personality to the situations and people with which he is involved" (Hochschild, 1997: 189). The qualities deemed worthy of recognition are therefore based precisely on an emotional register that prioritizes responsive skills such as flexibility and adaptability. This matches well with what the kindergarten teachers say, namely that they are required to "see 'resources' instead of 'obstacles'" (Willig and Korsbæk Sørensen, 2010). They must be responsive rather than passive or aggressive; that is, they should not advance criticism that might hinder an ongoing reorganization process. The kindergarten teacher must prove his or her worth by showing commitment to projects, while being aware that such projects both temporary and volatile. They must be able to present themselves as flexible, mobile and creative, and in a position to establish new and valuable contacts, which will secure the next project. It is a question of being light, adaptable, flexible and in tune with the contingent demands of our times. According to Boltanski and Chiapello, these are the new values with which individuals must accord in order to achieve recognition (Boltanski, 2002: 14).

Only a certain type of individual, according to Richard Sennett, can thrive under such unstable conditions, in which the idea of flexibility is one of the most prevalent ideals. Such individuals must be able to meet three requirements. Firstly, they must be able to move from task to task. They must be able to improvise their biographies, or even survive without any long-lasting image of their own personalities. Secondly, they must not emphasize their own skills but should highlight potential abilities rather than achieved results. Thirdly, they must be able to let go of their work. Even those modern individuals who perform well at the workplace cannot be certain of retaining a job (Sennett, 2006: 11–12). Sennett puts this very precisely: "This is task oriented rather than fixed-function labour. Linear development is replaced by a mind-set willing to jump around" (Sennett, 2006: 44). Although Sennett derives this conclusion from interviews with employees of software companies, the many focus group interviews appear to display exactly the same pattern; the kindergarten teachers have difficulty finding stability in their work with the children. The three characteristics, which are present only in the particular type of person who thrives under such organizational conditions, are in direct contradiction with what is required to create a secure and stable environment for children's development. The kindergarten teachers have apparently been trapped in the idea that flexibility as permanent change is an inevitable condition and a prerequisite for being part of the project society. They have the clear impression that others should preferably see them as participants in a permanent process of change. It is not the result of this process of change that is the source of recognition, but rather the permanent process itself. The means has, in other words, become the end, with the result that many people feel they have lost their bearings. The study has led us to the hypothesis that flexibility can be characterized as a powerful process of disenfranchisement as soon as it goes from being a possibility to a compulsory condition. Once the idea of flexibility assumes a coercive nature, the anticipated sanctions and reprisals also become evident. Those who might consider criticizing the idea fear being excluded and categorized as unworthy of recognition and being seen as dynamically and functionally pathological (for a similar point, see also Dejours, 1980: 47). They feel under pressure not only in relation to their profession but also in relation to their own identities, in so far as some of them feel manipulated or, as we have seen, have come to regard themselves as mere puppets.

Emmanuel Renault describes this process as a "fragilization of the identity" (Renault, 2000: 84), which he defines in a concise and precise manner: "The fragilization of identity consists of the feeling that individuals have when they cannot manage their jobs in accordance with the conception they have of their identity in the work" (2000: 87). The cause of this fragilization, according to Renault, lies in the overall logic promoted by modern management strategies; namely that of one-sided competition, focusing solely on increased efficiency and productivity. In Renault's perspective, this means that the social function of work disappears, which may cause the individual to completely lose his or her identification with the work. The result is intensified psychological pressure on the individual. Renault's hypothesis is that the increasing fragilization of identity paves the way for what he calls "a transmutation of the identity" (Renault, 2000: 92), by which he means that the individual is obliged to acquire a one-sided, coherent and exclusive identity that is adapted to the identities recognized by society.

Conclusion

The core argument of this chapter is that the demand for employees to show flexibility can be analysed as a process of disenfranchisement. On the basis of a focus group study of Danish kindergarten teachers, we have shown that the internalization of flexibility – the ability to constantly bend and shape one's work performances and identity to ever shifting requirements – is both difficult for the kindergarten teachers to handle and putting them under severe mental pressure. That is, the demand for flexibility is not only accompanied by the requirement of breaking down work routines, hence sweeping away the sense of stability and security in work. The demand is also accompanied by a sense of deprivation because they are incapable, without fearing serious reprisals, of criticizing this development. This is severely mentally fatiguing. Moreover, the demand for flexibility seems to have an incessant nature to it: reorganization has become permanent. Under such circumstances the kindergarten teachers never seem to get a firm grip on their working conditions before they have to adapt to new ones. Hence, they never seem to succeed in getting a stable professional foundation upon which they can build their pedagogical endeavour. Subsequently, a feeling of being structurally and institutionally deprived of their professional identity as kindergarten teachers occurs. Or, it leaves them with the feeling of constantly having to renew and adjust their professional identity to the demand for flexibility.

In order to substantiate this analysis, we applied the theoretical framework offered by Honneth. By doing so, we have placed this analysis within the realm of recognition theory. That is, we have shown how the demand for flexibility of the kindergarten teachers brings about insecurity with respect to their performances, skills and abilities, and hence insecurity as to what can lay claim to recognition. This aids us to elucidate why the kindergarten teachers feel mentally pressured by the constant requirement to demonstrate flexibility – to constantly adopt their identity to the flexible regime – in order to strive for recognition. In addition to that, the analysis is supported by using Boltanski and Chiapello's analysis of project work as the principal organizational motif of our time. The analytical grid provided by Boltanski and Chiapello is illustrative as to why many kindergarten teachers have lost their sense of enfranchisement. Project work demands flexibility: projects are formulated consecutively – with a new project always overlapping previous ones, the kindergarten teachers are forced into being sufficiently malleable in order to acclimatize themselves to ever-shifting work situations. As we have shown, such conditions undermine the possibility of putting any form of substantial critique forward, something that is otherwise central to one's sense of enfranchisement.

Notes

1 The Danish term, which is difficult to translate, is pædagog, often translated as 'pedagogue', 'educator' or 'kindergarten teacher'. We have chosen the latter of these terms as that which is most likely to be communicative to an English-speaking audience, but again the reader should be aware that the term is used here in a special sense. A kindergarten teacher, in Denmark, is a public-sector employee who possesses a professional training and qualification in child education. The vast majority of children in the Scandinavian nations attend such state kindergartens between the ages of around three to seven, and it has been speculated that this may be part of the secret behind the stability, high level of social equality, democratic traditions and relative lack of social conflict found in this part of the world. The function of a pædagog thus extends far beyond mere child-minding, a Danish kindergarten teacher is a trained, respected professional doing what is regarded as an important job in society.

2 The demand for increased flexibility can naturally also be viewed from the opposite perspective; namely as the process of replacing powerful, entrenched hierarchies with a more flexible form of organization that is more inclusive and less routine-bound. For several reasons, however, the focus of this chapter is confined to the negative aspects of the increasing demands for flexibility. Firstly, this is because the results of the focus group interviews were overwhelmingly negative in relation to the demand for flexibility. There may be several explanations for this. Many of the respondents emphasized, for example, that much pedagogy rests upon the idea of stability in a child's early upbringing. Although there are obviously differences between pedagogy as such and organizational forms, the kindergarten teachers were of the view that flexible working practices placed pressure on this fundamental pedagogical precept. In addition, several of them were of the opinion that it was difficult to organize themselves more flexibly, as there had been both minor and major rounds of cutbacks at their respective institutions. The predominantly negative experiences with the increasing demands for flexibility should be seen in the context in which the focus group interviews took place; several younger kindergarten teachers, for example, supported the idea of increased flexibility in several respects, but were also critical because they experienced the demand for flexibility in conjunction with demands for savings. In some respects, therefore, this came to be regarded as a form of Newspeak (see also Willig and Korsbæk Sørensen 2010).

3 The original Danish term for 'disenfranchisement' is umyndiggørelse, which means the act of depriving a person of the rights and responsibilities of an adult citizen. This relates directly to Kant's concept of *Unmündigkeit*, as expounded in *Was ist Aufklärung?* (What is Enlightenment?). The concept is straightforward enough in German, and indeed in Danish, but difficult to convey accurately and concisely in English. In English translations of Kant, *Unmündigkeit* has been variously rendered as 'immaturity', 'tutelage' and 'nonage', none of which seemed appropriate to use in the context of the study. We have therefore chosen to translate *umyndiggørelse* as 'disenfranchisement'. It should,

however, be borne in mind that the word is used here in a special sense; meaning not to be deprived of the right to vote, but to be robbed of adult dignity and the right to a say in determining the conditions of one's own life in general.

4 This article deals, as already mentioned, with the negative consequences of flexibility. That is not to say, however, that there are no positive aspects linked to flexibility. It is simply beyond the scope of this chapter to deal with them.

5 Each group consisted of six to eight persons. Since the focus groups were conducted with people recruited form a rather limited number of sources, our main objective was to minimize sample bias rather than achieving generalizability (Morgan 1997: 35). That is, the groups were constituted of kindergarten teachers, some of whom knew each other before the interviews were conducted, while some did not. Some worked in the same town, some had never heard of each other before. None of the focus groups, however, consisted of people who had an asymmetrical power relation; that is, no kindergarten teacher was in the same group as her/his superior. In that respect, no direct power relation influenced the focus group discussion.

6 Including Silkeborg, Skanderborg, Odder and Aarhus, which vary in population size from 35,000 to 250,000 inhabitants.

7 For an account of the oral presentations, see Willig (2009).

8 That being said, we are under the clear impression that our study is merited by the fact that it does not try to conceal its critical endeavour. By applying Sennett's definition and partly normative perception of flexibility, and later using the concept of recognition and work put forward by Honneth and Boltanski and Chiapello's ideas on project life in the new spirit of capitalism, our analysis is thoroughly critical. The way in which critique is presented here could, of course, have been entirely different had we used important perspectives from the poststructuralist tradition, such as Michel Foucault (2002) and Judith Butler (2002). The poststructuralist perspective could have shed analytic light on the dogmatic character of some of the views that were expressed by the respondents of what disenfranchisement entails. Luc Boltanski's (2011) latest work and the Kantian inspired work by Ian Mackenzie's (2004) discussions on the concept of critique could also contribute to a more elaborated definition of the concept of disenfranchisement. This has not, however, been the topical focus of this chapter.

9 All names are pseudonyms.

10 It is obvious that a thorough investigation into the sociological literature on professions would have nuanced our discussion on this particular point. We are aware of the fact that particularly the works of Andrew Abbott (1988) would have enabled us to develop an interesting analytical prism through which the kindergarten teacher's feelings of denigration towards their profession could have been constructed. We feel, however, that this is not the place to develop such an approach.

11 The term Boltanski and Chiapello use to describe recent management literature.

References

Abbott, A (1988) *The system of professions: An essay on the division of expert labor.* Chicago, IL: University of Chicago Press.

Anell, BI and Wilson, TL (2000) The flexible firm and the flexible co-worker. *Journal of Workplace Learning* 4: 165–170.

Appelbaum, E and Batt, R (1994) *The new American workplace: Transforming work systems in the United States.* New York: ILR Press.

Atkinson, J (1984) Flexibility, uncertainty and manpower management. *IMS Report* 89: 1–32.

Boltanski, L (2002) The left after May 1968 and the longing for total revolution. *Thesis Eleven* 69: 1–20.

Boltanski, L (2011) *On critique. A sociology of emancipation.* Cambridge: Polity Press.

Boltanski, L and Chiapello, E (2005) *The new spirit of capitalism*. London: Verso Books.
Braverman, H (1974) *Labor and monopoly capital*. New York: Monthly Review Press.
Budgen, S (2000) A new spirit of capitalism. *New Left Review* 1: 149–156.
Butler, J (2002) What is critique? An essay on Foucault's virtue. In: Ingram, D (ed) *The political*, 212–229. Molden, MA: Blackwell Publishers.
Castells, M (1996) *The rise of the network society*. Oxford: Blackwell.
Chiapello, E and Fairclough, N (2002) Understanding the new management ideology: A transdisciplinary contribution from critical discourse analysis and new sociology of capitalism. *Discourse and Society* 13, no. 2: 185–208.
Child, J (2005) *Organization: Contemporary principles and practice*. Oxford: Blackwell Publishing.
Cook, S, Macaulay, S and Coldicott, H (2004) *Change management excellence*. London: Kogan Page.
Dejours, C (1980) *Travail, usure mentale*. Paris: Le Centurion.
Deleuze, G and Guattari, F (1988) *A thousand plateaus. Capitalism and schizophrenia*. London: Athlone Press.
Edlund, J and Grönlund, A (2010) Class and work autonomy in 21 countries: A question of production regime or power resources? *Acta Sociologica* 53, no. 3: 213–228.
Folch-Lyon, E and Trost, JF (1981) Conducting focus group sessions. *Studies in Family Planning* 12: 443–449.
Foucault, M (2002) What is critique? In: Ingram, D (ed) *The political*, 191–212. Molden, MA: Blackwell Publishers.
Greenbaum, TL (1990) Focus groups spurt predicted for the 90s. *Marketing News* 24, no. 1: 21–22.
Hochschild, AR (1997) *The time bind: When work becomes home and home becomes work*. New York: Metropolitan Books.
Honneth, A (1995) Pluralization and recognition. On the self-misunderstanding of postmodern social theories. In: Wright, CW (ed) *The fragmented world of the social. Essays in social and political philosophy*, 220–231. New York: Suny Press.
Honneth, A and Hartmann, M (2006) Paradoxes of capitalism. *Constellations* 13: 41–58.
Kalleberg, AL (2001) Organizing flexibility: The flexible firm in a new century. *British Journal of Industrial Relations* 39, no. 4: 479–504.
Kitzinger, J (1995) Introducing focus groups. *British Medical Journal* 311: 299–302.
Krause-Jensen, J (2010) *Flexible firm: The design of culture at Bang and Olufsen*. Oxford: Berghahn Books.
Kocyba, H (2000) Der Preis der Anerkennung: Von der tayloristischen Missachtung zur strategischen Instrumentalisierung der Subjektivität der Arbeitenden. In: Holtgrewe, U, Voswinkel, S and Wagner, G (eds) *Anerkennung und Arbeit*, 127–141. Konstanz: Universitätsverlag.
Mackenzie, I (2004) *The idea of pure critique*. London: Continuum.
Mariampolski, H (1989) Focus groups on sensitive topics: How to get subjects to open up and feel good about telling the truth. *Applied Marketing Research* 29, no. 1: 6–11.
Morgan, DL (1996) Focus groups. *Annual Review of Sociology* 22: 129–152.
Morgan, DL (1997) *Focus groups as qualitative research*. London: Sage.
Neckel, S (2000) Identität als Ware: Die Marktwirtschaft im Sozialen. In: Neckel, S (ed) *Die Macht der Unterscheidung: Essays zur Kultursoziologie der modernen Gesellschaft*, 37–47. Frankfurt am Main: Campus Verlag.
Peters, M (1992) *Liberation management*. London: Macmillan.
Petersen, A and Willig, R (2002) An interview with Axel Honneth: On the role of sociology in the theory of recognition. *The European Journal of Social Theory* 5: 265–277.

Piore, MJ and Sabel, CF (1984) *The second industrial divide. Possibilities for prosperity*. New York: Basic Books.

Pollert, A (1988) The 'flexible firm': Fixation or fact? *Work Employment and Society* 2, no. 3: 281–316.

Renault, E (2000) *Mépris social – éthique et politique de la reconnaissance: Ethique et politique de la reconnaissance*. Paris: Editions du Passant.

Sennett, R (1998) *The corrosion of character*. New York: W.W. Norton.

Sennett, R (2006) *The culture of the new capitalism*. New Haven, CT: Yale University Press.

Smith, MW (1995) Ethics in focus groups: A few concerns. *Qualitative Health Research* 5: 478–486.

Taylor, FW (1972) *Scientific management*. Westport, CT: Greenwood Press.

Voswinkel, S, Holtgrewe, U and Wagner, G (eds) (2000) *Anerkennung und Arbeit*. Konstanz: Universitätsverlag Konstanz.

Watts, M and Ebbutt, D (1987) More than the sum of the parts: Research methods in group interviewing. *British Educational Research Journal* 13: 25–34.

Willig, R (2007) *Til forsvar for kritikken [In Defence of Critique]*. Copenhagen: Hans Reitzels Forlag.

Willig, R (2009) *Umyndiggørelse [Disenfranchisement]*. Copenhagen: Hans Reitzels Forlag.

Willig, R and Korsbæk Sørensen, P (2010) *Kritik som etik. Neoliberalt nysprog som Umyndiggørelseproces*. In: Aabro, C (ed) *Pædagogers etik*, 192–204. Copenhagen: Forlaget.

9 Evaluations as a process of disenfranchisement

Anders Petersen and Rasmus Willig

It is hardly provocative to claim that we find ourselves in a culture of evaluation, in which evaluations are perceived as indispensable tools of government that pave the way for a positive, valuable and accumulative learning process (Salamon, 2007). Alas, under certain circumstances, the exact opposite holds to be true. Evaluations can actually possess the function of de-skilling that which may already be functioning well by placing critical questions. For each criticism, a well-functioning working routine may be rejected. When asked to fill out evaluation forms, the underlying assumption is that it will help us to learn something new. But the reverse is also the case. As we intend to show, people filling out evaluation forms are sometimes left with the feeling that their skills are being 'unlearned' because of the evaluation per se. In fact, the hypothesis we wish to advance is that some people suffer mentally as a result of these evaluation exercises, which result in harm to both their professional and personal integrity. The evaluation forms often begin innocently enough, from an informative point of view. 'It takes just 15 minutes' – but in some cases, the critical issues get under the skin of the employee and become a permanent mode of self-criticism that damages professional and personal integrity. These innocent 15 minutes can thus turn out to be anything but innocent. This is not something to which the conventional and established evaluation literature appears to pay much attention (see for example Green and South, 2006; Rossi et al., 2004).

Nonetheless, as the American professor of management Hendrie Weisinger so concisely puts it, evaluations are in fact criticism (Weisinger, 2000). This should not be taken lightly. The evaluation forms consist of a series of questions, and are critical in the sense that they help to point out what the recipient could and ought to do differently. It is the relationship between what you do, and how you should or could do it that forms the basis for the criticism. Typically, the questions relate to organisational goals, and deviations from the formulated goals represent the specific field of critical tension. The questions quite literally question the way things are done: Are things being done correctly? Couldn't they be done a little bit better? Could you be a little bit more efficient? Etc.

In this chapter, we will begin by briefly summarising the results of a qualitative empirical study conducted in Denmark in which several respondents expressed criticism of the prevailing culture of evaluation. This empirical study was intended to trace processes of disenfranchisement, which we might briefly define as processes

DOI: 10.4324/9781032714356-11

which deprive contemporary employees of the ability to express criticism of their working conditions without fear of reprisal. In continuation of the study's main focus, several respondents felt that the evaluations per se led to detrimental self-criticism and feelings of inadequacy. In order to approach a theoretical understanding of the respondents' negative experiences with this prevailing culture of evaluation, we turn to Jean-Pierre Le Goff's study of the significance of management strategies in the perception of work. Le Goff's study helps to explain why some people feel that the evaluation forms place them in a permanent examination situation, in which they are tested to see whether they exhibit the correct degree of flexibility and adaptability. We then draw upon the work of Christophe Dejours, who describes how evaluations can be seen as tools that place so much pressure on the modern employee that they help to create an actual culture of fear. These theoretical considerations are then related to the idea of evaluation as a powerful process of disenfranchisement. On the basis of these strong critiques of the culture of evaluation, it becomes possible to formulate a new research hypothesis.

The empirical study – focus group interviews

Over the past 10–15 years, an ideological wave has washed across the public sector in Demark, demanding better services for less money. This ideological wave goes under many different designations, such as 'new public management', 'neoliberalism' or 'strong leadership' (e.g. see Campbell and Pedersen, 2001; Horton, 2006; Lane, 2001) but common to them all is that they place financial/economic rationality above other kinds of rationality. As a consequence, even some of the most fundamental ideas, such as that of the autonomy of the public sector professions and the knowledge base upon which they rely, have been wholly or partly set aside. It is as though each of the public sector professions has become the object of political consumerism and hence forced to measure themselves with standards of efficiency, effectiveness, productivity etc. – all logics we normally associate with the spheres of economy. Soon, no year will pass in Denmark without new reforms being proposed and implemented, in the name of ensuring the greatest possible efficiency and service – such as the recent reforms in the elementary schools, upper secondary schools and universities have shown (Auken, 2010). No area or professional grouping has escaped. The consequences of each of these reforms have been colossal. The human and institutional catastrophes are hard to overlook, but the criticism has barely had time to reach the public arena before a new and improved reform promises a remedy. On the basis of these developmental tendencies, which appear to characterise the entire Western labour market (Bourdieu, 2000: 30–31), the study which was later given the title *Disenfranchisement* (Willig, 2012) investigated the qualitative consequences of the prevailing neoliberal organisation of work. Specifically, the study sought to demonstrate the consequences of this neoliberal form of organisation for one the most basic reproductive stages of society; it demonstrated how criticism by kindergarten teachers of deteriorating working conditions was ignored and dismantled, and how these processes of disenfranchisement were reproduced towards the children. For example, more use was made of comforters to curb the children's noise, since, as a result of the many cutbacks, there were not enough teachers to meet the children's primary needs (Willig, 2012).

The empirical examples presented here derive from a series of focus group interviews conducted in the years 2008 and 2009. In the first series of interviews, 20 focus group interviews were held over four days, with a total of 110 participants. In the second series, 28 focus group interviews were held over seven days, with a total of 138 participants. The first series of focus group interviews encompassed kindergarten teachers, kindergarten managers, staff representatives and day care centre managers, while the second series involved staff representatives and joint staff representatives. The interviewed persons all live in medium-sized towns in Denmark,[1] and the group of joint staff representatives was drawn from the whole country (Willig, 2012). The focus group interview was chosen because this method is particularly good at mapping and identifying the common interpretations and understandings that different groups generate towards a given subject. A much referred-to definition of focus groups is that it is "a research technique that collects data through group interaction on a topic determined by the researcher" (Morgan, 1996: 130). This very broad definition implies three things:

1 Focus group interviews are used to collect data, as opposed to in marketing, where the method is applied as a mean to selling ideas, products, political content etc.
2 Group interaction is the main source of data.
3 The researcher/moderator plays a significant role in creating the group discussion that generates the data (Kitzinger, 1995).

In our study, only oral group interaction was accounted for, that is, we paid no analytical attention to body postures, gesticulations etc. Due to this fact, we invited all the participants in the focus groups to talk to each other, ask questions to each other, comment on each other's experiences and to be critical towards each other about the topic in question. The point is that the researcher via focus groups is interested in more than just the sum of individual utterances but in the accumulated interpretations of the group (Kitzinger, 1995: 299). The moderator/researcher plays a vital part in trying to encourage this interaction. In our particular case, where the topic we wanted to study was the processes of disenfranchisement taking place within the working area of a specific professional group, the moderator was definitely significant. As this theme may be perceived as being relatively delicate and sensitive by the participants, we took a gentle approach to initiating the focus group interviews regarding the kindergarten staff's perception of which processes of disenfranchisement were most prevalent. Two ethical strategies were utilised for this purpose. Firstly, it was emphasised that all statements would be anonymous, and secondly, the serious nature of the topic was defused via a series of oral presentations by the researchers (see also Mariampolski, 1989: 7; Greenbaum, 1990).

Processes of disenfranchisement

In the aforementioned study, enfranchised individuals are defined as people who are able to make their own choices, i.e. people who can exert an influence over their own lives. To have a say in your own life, you must be able to speak freely and thereby influence your surroundings. You must also be able to actively contradict 'the regulations', so to speak, in order to assert such an influence, which means being able to voice critique. The enfranchised person may thus be defined as one who is able to voice criticism, as it is through criticism that such a person asserts his or her influence and choices (Willig, 2012: 26). Individuals may be said to be able to voice critique when they are able to express their opinions without the threat of reprisals, i.e. without fear. However, it is difficult to determine the nature of such fear, which depends upon the environment of the person concerned and the person or group that is the object of the critique. A person's level of fear or lack of same may for example depend on whether the society in which the criticism is presented guarantees freedom of speech, a free press and the right to assembly and on whether this society possesses a protective layer of norms in which the existence of criticism is regarded as a positive phenomenon, rather than one that is condemned. Fear exists when there is the possibility of reprisals, i.e. more or less specific sanctions. In the legal area, such sanctions might for example involve the imposition of punishment on people for their statements, while in the normative area, the sanctions might consist of a person being punished by being bypassed, ignored or overlooked.

Enfranchised individuals who are able to voice critique may thus be defined as persons who can express themselves freely without fear of reprisals, whether in the form of normative or legal sanctions, and who can thereby, via their critique, create autonomous scope for influence over their own lives (Willig, 2012: 27). Conversely, processes of disenfranchisement may be described as processes which cause one or more individuals to fear reprisals in the form of sanctions. A process of disenfranchisement may furthermore be defined as a series of acts or changes which alters the sense of enfranchisement of a person or group. This process is negative inasmuch as it deprives the individuals concerned of the ability to criticise, and is manifested as a loss of the sense of identity and a feeling of powerlessness and paralysis. On the moral–psychological level, being deprived of enfranchisement can lead to a loss of personality; the individuals concerned lose the ability to construe their biographies – i.e. their life stories– in a meaningful way. Their sense of meaning diminishes in parallel with the growing pressure exerted on their ability to criticise, which robs them of the ability to influence their lives. Processes of disenfranchisement often take place without the conscious knowledge of the disenfranchising or the disenfranchised party, or with the tacit acceptance of both parties. Sometimes, individuals who are subjected to such processes may even perceive them as liberating, even when they are actually repressive.

Evaluations lead to detrimental self-criticism

The promotion of freedom via evaluations seems to be a predominant norm in our culture of evaluation. In that respect, evaluations are presented as contributing to the development of professional skills and competences (Green and South, 2006), which aids the evaluated at accomplishing autonomy at work. But questions which are supposed to take just 15 minutes to answer may also possess a punitive function: they may involve a process of disenfranchisement. Insofar as the questions in the evaluations are internalised they punish the sense of self of the individual, who continually asks 'Could I do things a little better?', 'Could I become a bit more efficient?', again and again – until the next evaluation form needs to be filled in. But which kinds of evaluations are we more specifically talking about?

First of all, in the context of our study, evaluations are to be seen through the analytical prism of what Stephen J. Ball calls the performative society. As Ball states:

> Performativity is a technology, a culture and a mode of regulation, or even a system of 'terror' in Lyotard's words, that employs judgements, comparisons and displays as means of control, attrition and change.
>
> (Ball, 2004: 143)

From this perspective, evaluations are, something which became vividly clear in our empirical study, highly corroding. To further clarify this point, a distinction may be drawn between two different kinds of evaluation, namely external and internal. External evaluation is implemented by outsiders, such as local authorities who undertake an assessment and general inspection of the institution in question. This kind of assessment often consists of a number of concrete questions, which systematically tries to evaluate the daily work of the kindergarten teachers with one thing in mind – to optimise their performativity and make their work more effective. Some of the questions kindergarten teachers are met with are:

1 Which social competences are you trying to pass on to the children and how?
2 What are you focusing on when you asses the children's overall development?
3 Which values and ways of communicating these are you trying to pass on to the children?

Now, these sorts of questions are not – in themselves – troublesome. But they become so because of the fact that each evaluation is always concluded by a section of self-reflection. The questions asked here are often few, but they tend to leave a mark:

1 How are you able to do your job better?
2 How are you able to optimise your performativity at work?

A very odd thing is that such external evaluation, in practice, is administered by the employees themselves, which leads to confusion between internal and external evaluations. That is, it is actually a member of staff that hands out the evaluation forms to his/her colleagues. This sometimes leads to confusion between external and internal evaluations and makes it difficult to see who bears the responsibility of the evaluations, and who is actually criticising whom. To make matters worse, internal evaluations are often sent to an external control organ, but according to the participating kindergarten teachers, they then seem to disappear without trace. None of the participating kindergarten teachers actually knew where these evaluation forms went. Nonetheless, they often felt that such evaluations could be located and used against them if the initiators of the evaluations were to find this convenient.

These internal evaluations are interesting inasmuch as they reflect new forms of control in which responsibility can only be located among the staff, since it is they who have established the current standards and procedures which form the basis for their own evaluation. Ownership of the procedures, standards and evaluations thus lies with the institutions themselves, since they have helped to formulate them – in theory, at any rate. But that is often altered. As soon as, for example, an alarmingly high level of noise in a kindergarten is discovered by an outsider – let's say an alert journalist – it turns out that the critique coming from the internal evaluations does not belong to the institution itself after all, but to the public sphere. The ownership is thus only genuine as long as the critique does not reach the ears of the management or the municipal politicians. At the moment it does so, ownership passes to the broader public. This has the effect of placing the professional standards of the kindergarten teachers under extreme pressure. Karen, who has worked as a kindergarten teacher for 24 years, says for example:

> Now, for instance, we have to work out a new institutional policy, and while that's going on, we can't do our proper work and see happy children around us. This retards the children's development. The pressure that is being brought to bear on us is ruining our pedagogical work. You just can't live up to your own professional standards.

According to Karen, it will not take much to cause her workplace to break down entirely, especially now that they have to tick boxes to register and evaluate the development of each individual child. They spend their time documenting the very developmental processes that they do not have sufficient time to promote. Karen continues:

> We spend a lot of time on evaluations, setting up plans for the kids etc. in a very rigid way. And in order to survive we just tick off the question boxes in the seemingly most appropriate places. In that way we get the job done. The most troublesome part of this practice is that we don't do it correctly and the evaluations themselves are not done correctly.

Bente, who has worked as a kindergarten teacher for 11 years, continues along this line:

> Deadlines for the different evaluation forms are often confusing, which leads to the fact that we fill them in without looking at the content.

But even though the evaluations are not done properly, they still leave a mark on the kindergarten teachers. That is, the evaluations support the prevailing norm in our contemporary performative society, namely that 'you can always do things a little better'. The logic entailed is almost a common consensus. The question that arises in this context, however, is not so much whether you really always can do things a little better, as whether you ought to do so, from a pedagogical perspective. Logic dictates that we can always do things better, so the answer would appear to be yes – but in reality, it is no, because 'better' means more efficient child care; and the more efficient the care, the less staff are required, since efficiency in this context is synonymous with child care for fewer resources. In that sense, the kindergarten teachers are actually performing what John MacBeath and Archie McGlynn (2002) call self-evaluation. In their perspective:

> Self-evaluation takes place whenever teachers consider more effective layouts for their classroom, when a school considers the need to change a reading scheme or seeks to improve the style and tone of its letters and reports to parents. Whenever existing provision is examined with a view to its improvement internal evaluation is at work, often informally but increasingly in a self-conscious and systematic way.
>
> (MacBeath and McGlynn, 2002: 25)

In that way, the evaluation forms contribute to the internalisation of self- evaluation and hence to the ideology of efficiency. As Bjarne, one of the few male participants, stated:

> We never seem to get the required time we need to take care of the kids properly. We have to make different educational plans, fill in evaluations forms of different kinds etc. and that hinders us. But even though the conditions for securing good quality work are poor, we still seem to blame ourselves.

Structurally imposed predicaments are being personalised. As Louise, a kind and very obliging nursery teacher, said right after one focus group interview, she and her colleagues always gave the children top marks for everything in the evaluation forms, while they tended to undervalue their own professional performance. She concluded by saying, 'After all, you can always do things better'. That which functions well can in other words always be improved; this is the logic that you hear, again and again. As a consequence of this thinking, practices which work well are being scrapped for no reason. The idea that things can always be done 'a little bit more efficiently' is destroying well-functioning working routines. In the worst cases, this can result in a sense of enfranchisement being replaced by a process of disenfranchisement under the beguiling heading of 'improved efficiency'.

In this respect, the evaluations represent a political critique of public sector employees, the responses to which provide the yardstick by which acceptable performance is judged. In reality, therefore, their function is not to improve the conditions of the children nor the kindergarten teachers but to protect the managerial layers (municipal politicians etc.) whenever external critique reveals that things are not as they should be. Kindergarten teachers can gain the impression that earlier evaluation forms can be brought up from the town hall cellar as evidence to show that they have 'voluntarily' expressed the wish 'to do things a little better'. In this sense, there is always a critical field of tension between the kindergarten, the staff and the child concerning the issue of how they can 'do things a little better'. Seen from this perspective, evaluations comprise one of contemporary society's most refined means of holding critique in check. Instead of critique being directed at poor working conditions, it becomes an internal matter as soon as the evaluation forms are submitted. The evaluations absorb whatever remnants of critique that remain and transform it from outwardly directed critique into critique which is inwardly directed. The critical questions are no longer structurally directed at, for example, municipal politicians, but at the kindergarten, teachers themselves. Apparently then, the evaluation forms create a U-turn for the critical traffic. The consequence of this is an ongoing self-evaluation, or more correctly a continual legal proceeding of the self that judges the self to being more and more effective.

Kindergarten managers often say that filling out the evaluation forms takes very little time. In fact, the focus group interviews revealed that while the kindergarten staff members had not received an abundance of evaluation forms, they nonetheless tended to worry about them a great deal, apparently because such evaluations are so symbolically significant that they have a psychological effect. That is, the criticism exposed in the evaluation forms becomes internalised in the inner consciousness of the individual kindergarten teachers. The result is a permanent alteration in ethics and norms, as the critical questions are now repeated within the boundaries of the self, rather than within the framework of the State or the municipality. The critique goes from being extrovert – 'There's something wrong with our working conditions' – to introvert – 'There's something wrong with me', and the central question becomes: 'How can I become more efficient?' The remarkable result is that the kindergarten teachers lose their sense of enfranchisement when they turn their critique inwards instead of outwards. Each time kindergarten teachers criticise themselves, the profession loses a little more of its vital sense of enfranchisement – and each time they turn their critique inwards, they increase their own risk of suffering stress, depression and burnout (Ehrenberg, 2010; Petersen and Willig, 2004; Willig 2009; Willig, 2012). The criticism thus not only holds dissatisfied staff members in check but also punishes them.

Evaluations as barbarism

Into which theoretical framework can we place these negative experiences? Over the past decade, the French philosopher and sociologist Jean-Pierre Le Goff has attracted attention with analyses of the growth of management strategies in working life (1992; 2000), and what he describes as the blind process of modernisation in businesses and the public sector (1999). Le Goff's fundamental assumption is that adaptation to a constant process of modernisation has been articulated as a social imperative, the legitimacy of which must not be challenged. The negative consequences of such processes of modernisation can thereby be neglected, in spite of their strong propensity to erode social and societal communities.

In the wake of this blind modernisation comes that which Le Goff terms 'gentle barbarism' (Le Goff, 1999). It is gentle because it is supported by modern normative demands, such as for increased autonomy, transparency and accountability; and it is barbarism, because these normative demands pave the way for the introduction of new methods of manipulation and repression. What is new about these normative demands is that they appear to be impermeable to and reject any form of resistance. As a result, the normative demands are practically totalitarian, in the sense that any attempt to reject them is doomed to failure. Briefly put, Le Goff regards the endless demands for change produced by blind modernisation as a destabilising factor, because the mental capacity of the individual has trouble keeping up with the permanent development shifts. This gentle barbarism thus promotes a kind of continuous cultural revolution, which transforms the individual's ways of living, acting and thinking, without allowing him or her sufficient breathing space to adapt (Le Goff, 1999: 8). The concept of blind modernisation is accompanied by a professionalisation of life itself, in which individuals are exhorted to live out their autonomy and accountability, and to be constantly able to motivate themselves and invest their optimum performance and skills in their work. In Western societies, in particular, this has been fostered by the parallel growth of management strategies, the normative demands of which have exerted an extremely powerful influence on the nature of the work.

A common feature of these management strategies is that they have helped to break down the hierarchical organisation principles which previously characterised the Taylorist form of organisation. This process has amongst other things contributed to the incorporation of the "'whole person' into the work, focusing on the so-called 'human factor'" (Le Goff, 2000: 16; see also Cohen, 1999). This means, firstly, that the competencies individuals are likely to internalise include such qualities as mobility, flexibility and polyvalence (see also Bauman, 2001). These skills are presented as aspects of self-realisation, and thus as tools for securing the employability of the individual (see also Boltanski and Chiapello, 2005). Secondly, a moral dictum, in which working individuals must always be able to motivate themselves and optimise their performance on the basis of a vision of the appropriateness of incorporating their entire knowledgeability in the work, has prevailed (Le Goff, 1999: 32). In order to demonstrate that they have invested their knowledgeability in the work, individuals must live up to and realise the normative demands towards flexibility, mobility and polyvalence. According to Le Goff, the individual's flexibility and mobility skills are determined by his or her mental pliancy and elasticity (Le Goff, 1999: 26; see also Sennett, 1998). These two terms refer to the individual's mental ability to display continuous adaptability, flexibility and elasticity, in the sense that the individual does not return to any fixed point. There are thus no limits to the amount of pliability and elasticity required, which is why the polyvalence of the individual acquires such great significance.

Le Goff perceives the idea of autonomy as one of the most important dynamics of modernisation, in that it is inextricably bound up with the extensive responsibility that has been assigned to individuals. The state of autonomy is not, however, something that can be assigned, but must rather be achieved. Autonomy is something to be strived for (Le Goff, 1992: 276), and any quest for further autonomy takes place in the form of individual, active liberation from fixed, meaning-giving frameworks. Autonomy is therefore something that must be developed by oneself, not by society's institutions. From this perspective, the goal of work becomes the conquest of autonomy, which implies that work must provide the structural and psychological conditions for this conquest to take place. Paternalistic and hierarchical organisational structures thus harmonise poorly with this new form of conquest, whereas accommodating the flexible, mobile and polyvalent requirements of work precisely enables such a conquest to take place. In relation to the psychological conditions of work, individuals are reminded that they must attend the management-inspired self-development courses, where they are inculcated with the link between work and personal fulfilment. In addition, individuals must meet the efficiency and productivity requirements that are constantly being laid down by the enterprise.

It is in the light of the demand for continuous improvements in efficiency that the use of evaluation forms becomes particularly trenchant, since in both private companies and public institutions, an increasing number of evaluation processes are being initiated in which individuals are tested on their ability to exhibit flexible, mobile and polyvalent behaviour at work (Le Goff, 1999: 30). From Le Goff's perspective, the expectation of individual autonomy thus also depends on whether the individual follows the path of efficiency and productivity, and the individual must also always expect to be subjected to continuous proficiency tests. This places individuals in an extremely contradictory and destabilising situation, in which they are simultaneously obliged to realise their own autonomy and adhere to specific normative codes for increased efficiency and productivity. This paradoxical situation, in which the individual experiences a kind of quasi- autonomy and quasi-accountability, does not meet the individual's expectations of being able to see his or her own influence in the workplace. The increasing focus on accountability and autonomy thus becomes a burden, as it backfires on individuals in their attempts to live up to the normative demands. Whereas the dissolution of the Taylorist workplace model ought to secure the increased humanisation of work, it is Le Goff's argument that the post-Taylorist focus on individual performance and obligatory autonomy in work has led to a new dehumanisation of work.

The point is that the pressure on an individual's mental capacities is simply increased to such an extent that the individual's relationship with work becomes characterised by insecurity/uncertainty, further exacerbated by the fact that individuals are not given the necessary time and space to stabilise their skills in relation to their work (Le Goff, 2000: 79). In the pervasive zeal for transformation, work is reduced to a continuous process of adaptation to evaluations, which present themselves as the means to make everything more efficient. However, when the expectations of adaptation and change are illusory in relation to the possibility of compliance, what happens is that the individual is separated out and abandoned to his or her own uncertainties. This also erodes the core of collective practices, which is why "gentle barbarism thus manifests itself as a machinery of meaninglessness that destabilises both individuals and collectivities" (Le Goff, 1999: 112, our translation).

The essence of this gentle barbarism is meaninglessness, which Le Goff associates with the gradual siphoning off of substance by virtue of the normative demands. By this, he means that the normative expectations towards mobility, flexibility and polyvalence are practically devoid of any specific content which individuals might otherwise be able to use to guide them in their attempts to adhere to them. The only thing you can be sure of with respect to these normative demands is that you can never be sufficiently mobile, flexible, polyvalent etc. The demands are therefore continually pursued, which creates a breeding ground for the emergence of new control mechanisms, exemplified by ongoing internal evaluations, for which the external evaluation procedures act as accelerators.

Evaluations create a culture of fear

Where, with Le Goff, we can understand evaluation as a form of barbarism, the French psychiatrist and psychologist Christophe Dejours give us the analytical tools to view them as fear-generating. Over the past three decades, Dejours has analysed the psychological influence of working life on the individual. In his first book, *Travail. Usure Mentale* (1980), Dejours describes how the development of the social and organisational division of labour has demanded not only the corporal subjugation of employees but also the suppression of their personalities. For Dejours, 'suffering' is a key term which he unfolds in his analysis of work. What makes him an interesting thinker in this context is that in the later work *Souffrance en France. La Banalisation de l'Injustice Sociale* (1998, hereafter: *Souffrance*), he specifically examines suffering in the light of the increased social internalisation of neoliberal, economically based values and norms. In order to understand Dejours's perspective, it is essential to clarify his concept of work. He defines work as follows:

> In our view, from a clinical standpoint, work is what is implied, in human terms, by the fact of working: gestures, know-how, the involvement of the body and the intelligence, the ability to analyse, interpret and react to situations. It is the power to feel, to think and to invent. In other words, for the clinician, work is not above all the wage relation or employment, but 'working', which is to say, the way the personality is involved in confronting a task that is subject to constraints (material and social).
>
> (Dejours, 2007: 72)

Dejours's view implies that no work is purely mechanical. Even the most Taylorist form of work involves a certain degree of involvement of the personality. Therefore Dejours – in contrast to, for example, those postmodernists who proclaimed the demise of the vitality of work (see Rifkin, 1995) – views work as a key aspect of individual identity (see also Sennett, 1998). In other words: work is an intellectual act of exploration which is associated with personality formation for the individual (Dejours, 1998: 2). Work is thereby ascribed an emancipatory effect, but according to Dejours, it also generates suffering (Dejours, 1998: 49). As we shall see, Dejours believes that suffering has taken over in the neoliberal-oriented work organisation, which focuses to a large degree on continuous competition. In *Souffrance*, he thus diagnoses competition as the primary cause of suffering (Dejours, 1998: 9–10). In spite of the fact that competition is by definition asymmetrical and intended to optimise and combat inefficient economic entities without reference to social exclusion, it operates, according to Dejours, as a self-explanatory aspect of contemporary human life. It is in this context of suffering that Dejours concludes that the integration and production skills of work operate as the fundamental pivot for the reproduction of the neoliberal economy (Dejours, 1998: 175–176). In relation to this, the organisation of work, in the neoliberal context, has come to rely on individual rather than collective premises. Continuing this reasoning, Dejours has observed the existence of three types of fear which abound in modern business and organisational culture.

Firstly, there is the constant fear of being found incompetent (Dejours, 1998: 30), accompanied by the fear of dismissal, and thereby the fear of being "weighed and found wanting". This leads to a fatiguing internal evaluation of the employee's own abilities and skills. Secondly, there is the fear of underperforming (Dejours, 1998: 33). This involves the fear of not being profitable, which results in a debilitating external evaluation of individual performance. The individual thus participates in a perpetual examination, and due to fear, is forced to constantly perform at the 'top of his game' without being given the necessary time for recuperation. As a consequence, he or she has no opportunity to become at one with the work, or in the words of Richard Sennett, the individual is constantly "in recovery" (Sennett, 1998: 135). Thirdly, there is the fear of not achieving recognition for your work (Dejours, 1998: 36). Dejours's point is that the latent fear of not being able to live up to the neoliberal expectations of competitiveness and profitability has an extreme effect on the mental state of the individual. Fear of incompetence and of permanent exclusion leads to an imbalance in the individual's perception of his or her actual capabilities. Dejours regards this latent, destructive contradiction as a kind of default state, in that the dominance and fear of competition has become so ubiquitous and general that suffering has become the normal state of affairs (Dejours, 1998: 39). Consequently, individuals, in an attempt to protect their vulnerable mental fragility, accept the demands of competition towards efficiency, flexibility and mobility.

The immediate consequence of a division of labour that operates with the normality of suffering is that individuals become unsure of their own abilities and skills, since the expectations are distorted, and they are thus obliged to constantly strive to achieve recognition for their accomplishments. In other words, Dejours regards reciprocal recognition as a determining factor in the subject's personal development. As he puts it:

> When the quality of my work is recognised, then my efforts, my anxiety, my doubts, my disappointments, my despondency also make sense [...]

> In the recognition of work, indeed, even in the work itself, the subject can then apply this in the construction of his or her identity [...] But when recognition is lacking in work [...] the subject is condemned to suffering, and only that.
>
> (Dejours, 1998: 37, our translation)

Dejours distinguishes here between two kinds of achieved recognition. Firstly, there is the hierarchical and vertical recognition provided by your superiors with respect to the usability and value of your work, and secondly, the horizontal recognition of peers and colleagues of your work's quality. Both forms of recognition serve as a kind of symbolic payment, which must be made if the individual is to maintain the necessary balance under which to develop his or her personal potential (Dejours, 1998: 121). Recognition is thus a vital element in alleviating suffering, but according to Dejours, the problem is simply that both modes of recognition are becoming increasingly subverted by the fear-based organisational principle upon which competitive work is based. Thus, while the individual is constantly seeking recognition, the conditions for attaining such recognition are changing faster than the individual can benefit from it. The individual is thereby trapped in a wearying 'almost there' hunt for recognition.[2] Seen from this perspective, neoliberalism's embedded forms of fear contribute to the breaking down of the individual by two different types of evaluation.

While the fear of incompetence results in a continuous and ever more intensive evaluation of one's own abilities and skills, the fear of underperforming contributes to the flourishing of external forms of evaluation which focus on the individual's profitability. The point is that these forms of evaluation are mutually reinforcing, and thereby create the basis for a spiral of evaluation that undermines the ability of the individual to maintain a coherent or cohesive personality. This is further underlined by the fact that neoliberalism undermines the very conditions for achieving adequate recognition of one's work, thereby intensifying the third form of fear.

Evaluation as a process of disenfranchisement

We have so far attempted to place the empirically-identified processes of disenfranchisement in a theoretical context. With the help of the theoretical perspectives of Le Goff and Dejours, it has become possible to describe various forms of evaluation as disenfranchising. Common to these two perspectives is that they regard evaluation as the outcome of the development of a new way of organising work. In this new organisation of work – whether the result of blind modernisation or of a neoliberal process of development – evaluation can be seen to act as an apparently powerful process of disenfranchisement. It is in this perspective that we place Le Goff's analysis of the demand for continuous individual efficiency, for in as much as individuals are confronted with the persistent expectation to optimise and operationalise themselves, they are also forced to internalise the idea of 'becoming more efficient'. This has the effect of creating an externally-appointed internal review tribunal, via which individuals submit themselves to constant self-scrutiny.

This internal action, which draws nourishment from external evaluations, functions, from this point of view, as a control measure within the individuals themselves.

The control evaluation directs the critical questions inwards: the question of whether you are complying sufficiently with the demand for permanent flexibility, polyvalence and mobility thus becomes one which individuals must in general answer for themselves. The internal control also ensures that individuals are constantly optimising their employability, since failure to continually fine-tune and adjust will result in prompt punishment in the form of being excluded or overlooked. Through Dejours's perspective, we can analyse the three types of fear as separate processes of disenfranchisement. The first form of fear, the fear of incompetence, entails an internal (debilitating) evaluation of the individual's abilities and skills. In this mode the fear manifests itself internally in the individual, thereby affecting the ability to generate a stable personality. The individual is placed in a situation in which there is a requirement to constantly prove your own worth, whether in relation to your colleagues or superiors. This leaves the kindergarten teachers with insufficient possibility to stabilise their psychological well-being.

The fear of under-performing, and thereby the fear of not being profitable, is however accompanied by an external form of evaluation, which evaluates the individual's actual performance and hence his or her performance capabilities. Seen from this point of view, this form of evaluation functions like a kind of examination which continuously grades the individual's abilities and awards proficiency marks. In order to avoid receiving a poor evaluation (or grade), individuals must therefore train themselves to constantly perform at their best. The performance curve must always be rising, as a declining curve cannot be tolerated. Fear of failing to achieve recognition for your work constitutes the third form of fear, and consequently, the third process of disenfranchisement. From Dejours's perspective, adequate recognition forms the foundation for the development and identity of the individual and appears to be the only real counterbalance to suffering. It is therefore devastating for the individual if the possibilities for achieving recognition are eroded. The problem is that the conditions for obtaining recognition are somewhat obscure, and the compliance requirements are constantly changing – as ensured by, amongst other things, evaluations. This supports a development in the direction of premises for recognition that can never be completely defined and made comprehensible: evaluations constantly alter what may be considered the object of recognition.

With Le Goff and Dejours, we can therefore observe a development that supports the empirical statements from the kindergarten teachers, namely that the critical questions are directed at them, and not at the structural factors that are the cause of their deteriorating conditions. Or to put it another way: the critique is turned away from society and towards the individual. The demands for improvements, flexibility, mobility etc. are imposed on the individual, not on the structural conditions. Consequently, it is increasingly a question of how to exceed the individual's skills and abilities, not about the structural prerequisites which require this. Evaluations are the means and the method for this change. This does not mean that actual causal relationships may be inferred between the prevailing culture of evaluation and the ability to speak out critically. What we did however find among the kindergarten teachers was that they tried to meet the demands for greater efficiency. As in Le Goff's description, they attempted to become more flexible, but some of them also found that this destabilised their sense of professional skill as well as their own mental stability. The fear of not being regarded as sufficiently flexible, mobile and efficient brings about a situation in which evaluations can be characterised as a process of disenfranchisement, as they are not subject to criticism from any party. No one dares to criticise the evaluations, as this would signal that you are one of those who cannot meet the demand for greater efficiency.

This perspective is reinforced by Dejours's argument that evaluations help to establish an actual culture of fear. Evaluations internalise the fear of being found to be incompetent or under-performing, or failing to achieve recognition for your work. The process of disenfranchisement now becomes explicit, as the reprisal takes a concrete form.

New research hypothesis

In his famous essay 'What is Critique?', the French philosopher Michel Foucault states that critique is the ability to pose questions (Foucault, 1997). There is, however, a marked difference between the kind of questions that Foucault describes and those that appear on many contemporary evaluation forms. In Foucault's text, the questions are directed at the state or at the theocracy of the early 1500s. In these cases, it was the people who put the questions to their respective rulers, not the authorities who asked questions of the people, as is the case today. Today, sophisticated evaluation forms bombard staff with questions. As the criticism of the growing culture of evaluation points out, it is beginning to take more time to evaluate services than to provide the services that are evaluated (Salamon, 2007). However, as we have just described, there is apparently also another reason why many people feel uncomfortable about filling out evaluation forms. The question is whether evaluations are in fact perceived as sophisticated management tools, which convey a minor but not inconsiderable criticism of the individual employee. Am I doing things well enough? Could I be a little bit more efficient?

In his famous dystopian novel *1984*, George Orwell provided, with the Ministry of Love, an almost too appropriate illustration of this pervasive culture of evaluation (Orwell, 1991). For those who do not remember Orwell's book, the Ministry of Love arrested those who failed to obey the marching orders of the future and subjected them to torture in the ministry's cellars. Their treatment was deemed to be 'complete' when they once again thought 'correctly'. Today, no one needs to be arrested – why arrest those who fail to toe the contemporary line when the interrogation can simply be posted in a stamped, addressed envelope, or filled in online? It saves both time and resources. Evaluations have rationalised away Orwell's interrogation rooms. Take any evaluation form and think about the structure of an interrogation. First come the factual questions: age, sex, residence and workplace. Then a series of questions which begin to approach the desired information: What could you do better? Finally, there is a small box in which you can add a personal comment, which is consanguine to: 'Do you have anything to add before we conclude the interrogation?'

If we permit ourselves to regard evaluation as a management tool that promotes the partial internalisation of the idea of greater efficiency and creates a culture of fear, this goes a long way towards explaining why many of the interviewed kindergarten teachers perceived evaluation forms to be an expression of control. The new research hypothesis we wish to advance is based on the idea that evaluations can even in some specific empirical cases be interpreted as instruments which help to reverse critique, so that the originators of the critique are no longer the employees, but the employers. Evaluations can thereby be considered instruments to control critique.

Notes

1 Including Silkeborg, Skanderborg, Odder and Aarhus, which vary in population size from 35,000 to 250,000 inhabitants.
2 Perret and Roustang (1993) make a similar point when they state that the post-industrial organisation of work has not produced adequate recognition structures to accommodate the recognition expectations of employees, as a result of which lack of recognition of the value of one's work has become a social and cultural problem (Perret and Roustang, 1993: 138–9).

References

Auken, S (2010) *Hjernedød: Til forsvar for det borgerlige universitet* [Brain-dead: In defense of the respectable university]. Copenhagen: Informations Forlag.
Ball, SJ (2004) Performativities and fabrications in the education economy. In: Ball, SJ (ed) *The Routledge Falmer Reader in Sociology of Education*, 143–156. London: Routledge.
Bauman, Z (2001) *The Individualized Society*. Cambridge: Polity Press.
Boltanski, L and Chiapello, E (2005 [1999]) *The New Spirit of Capitalism*. London: Verso Books.
Bourdieu, P (2000 [1998]) *Acts of Resistance. Against the New Myths of Our Time*. Cambridge: Polity Press.
Campbell, JL and Pedersen, OK (eds) (2001) *The Rise of Neoliberalism and Institutional Analysis*. Princeton, NJ: Princeton University Press.
Cohen, D (1999) *Nos Temps Modernes*. Paris: Flammarion.
Dejours, C (1980) Travail. Usure Mental. Paris: Le Centurion.
Dejours, C (1998) *Souffrance en France. La Banalisation de l'Injustice Sociale*. Paris: Éditions du Seuil.
Dejours, C (2007) Subjectivity, work, and action. In: Deranty, J-P, Petherbridge, D, Rundell, J, Sinnerbrink, R (eds) *Recognition, Work, Politics. New Directions in French Critical Theory*, 71–87. Leiden: Brill
Ehrenberg, A (2010) *The Weariness of the Self: Diagnosing the History of Depression in the Contemporary Age*. Montreal and Kingston: McGill-Queen's University Press.
Foucault, M (1997) What is critique? In: Lotringer, S and Hochroth, L (eds) *The Politics of Truth*, 41–81. New York: Semiotexte.
Green, J and South, J.(2006) *Evaluation*. Maidenhead: Open University Press.
Greenbaum, TL (1990) Focus Groups Spurt Predicted for the 90s. *Marketing News*, 24(1), 21–22.

Horton, S. (ed.) (2006) *New Public Management, its Impact on Public Servants' Identity*. Bradford: Emerald Group Publishing.
Kitzinger, J (1995) Introducing Focus Groups. *British Medical Journal*, 311: 299–302.
Lane, JE (2001). *New Public Management*. London: Routledge.
Le Goff, JP (1992) *Le Mythe de l'Entreprise. Critique de l'Idéologie Managériale*. Paris: Éditions La Découverte.
Le Goff, JP (1999) *La Barbarie Douce. La Modernisation Aveugle des Entreprises et de l'École*. Paris: Éditions La Découverte.
Le Goff, JP (2000) *Les Illusions du Management. Pour le Retour du Bons Sens*. Paris: Éditions La Découverte.
MacBeath, J and McGlynn, A (2002) *Self-evaluation: What's in it for Schools*? London: Routledge Falmer.
Mariampolski, H. (1989). Focus groups on sensitive topics: How to get subjects to open up and feel good about telling the truth. *Applied Marketing Research*, 29(1), 6–11.
Morgan, DL (1996) *Focus Groups as Qualitative Research*. London: Sage Publications.
Orwell, G (1991) 1984 [Danish Translation]. Copenhagen: Gyldendal.
Perret, B and Roustang, G (1993) *L'Économie contre la Société. Affronter la Crise de l'Intégration Sociale et Culturelle*. Paris: Éditions du Seuil.
Petersen, A and Willig, R (2004) Work and Recognition. Reviewing New Forms of Pathological Developments. *ACTA Sociologica*, 47(4): 338–350.
Rifkin, J (1995) *The End of Work. The Decline of the Global Labour Force and the Dawn of the Post-market Era*. New York: Putnam Books.
Rossi, PH, Lipsey, MW and Freeman, HE (eds) (2004) *Evaluation, a Systematic Approach*. Thousand Oaks, CA: Sage.
Salamon, KL (2007) *Selvmål – det Evaluerede Liv* [Own goal – the evaluated life]. Copenhagen: Gyldendal.
Sennett, R (1998) *The Corrosion of Character*. New York: W.W. Norton.
Weisinger, H (2000) *The Power of Positive Criticism*. New York: AMACOM.
Willig, R (2009) Self-Realization Options: Contemporary Marching Order in the Pursuit of Recognition. *Acta Sociologica*, 52(4): 350–364.
Willig, R (2012) *Disenfranchisement. An Essay on the Infrastructure of Critique*. London: Peter Lang.

Part 3

Grief and diagnostic culture

10 Introduction to Part 3

Svend Brinkmann

I had the great privilege to work with Anders Petersen on two major research projects during the last ten years of his life. From 2013 to 2016, we studied the impact of psychiatric diagnoses such as depression and ADHD on individuals and society in a project called Diagnostic Culture. And from 2017 for the next five years, we worked on a joint project called The Culture of Grief, which was originally conceived as an attempt to understand the ongoing pathologization of bereavement and the inclusion of psychiatric diagnoses of grief into the reigning clinical manuals. As I write these words, it becomes clear to me how much of a difference there is between understanding grief analytically and scientifically on the one hand, which was what we attempted to do together, and experiencing all of its existential aspects on the other hand, which I am now left to do alone without my colleague and friend.

Our friendship began in 2009, when I was employed at Aalborg University, where Anders already worked. I had read some of Anders' illuminating work on social pathologies and depression, and I was grateful when he invited me to join an ongoing series of seminars, which he organized, under the heading of Psychiatry and Society. I met a group of sociologists, philosophers, and psychologists who shared an interest in how social processes shape our experiences of suffering and the ways in which we categorize human deviance and discontent. Anders was the friendliest colleague one could think of, always willing to help, taking care of practical issues, and providing insightful comments in discussions and when giving feedback to academic papers of others. There was always something to learn from Anders, just as he was always open to input from others.

Collegiality developed into friendship, and when we managed to obtain a research grant to study diagnostic cultures, we had what I think of as probably the best years of our academic careers. Although the topics of psychiatric diagnoses – and depression specifically – were serious and heavy, our meetings were full of energy and discussions that enabled us to understand the complexities of diagnoses and human experiences. Anders always managed to sympathize with everyone who suffered from some kind of problem and at the same time direct his critical sociological eye at the social forces that affect the ways in which people live. This balance is otherwise hard to strike: For in diagnostic cultures, people are often seeking diagnostic understandings of the problems they experience, so being critical of diagnoses – and perhaps outright anti-psychiatric – is quickly perceived as

DOI: 10.4324/9781032714356-13

wanting to take a framework away that provides suffering with some kind of meaning. Anders did not want to take anything away from people, but rather to add understandings of difficult phenomena that would help people develop solidarity and cope better together, as witnessed in the chapters in this volume.

In our final project 'The Culture of Grief', Anders continued his sensitive investigations of human suffering in contemporary culture. Often invoking a metaphor of the seismograph, Anders argued that we can use the current explosion in psychiatric diagnoses as an indicator that basic societal structures and social life are shaking. This also applies to the emerging diagnoses of complicated grief reactions.

The two chapters that comprise this section 'Grief: The Painfulness of Permanent Human Absence' and 'Grief in an Individualized Society: A Critical Corrective to the Advancement of Diagnostic Culture' (both written together with Michael Hviid Jacobsen) illustrate the penetrating and integrative mind of Anders Petersen. These texts emit a sense of humanism with a deep understanding of the existential aspects of grief. The grief arises from an experience of painful absence is likely a human universal that tells us something important about the relationality of existence. At the same time, readers are provided with concrete cultural and historical detail that demonstrate how social processes affect the fundamental human emotion of grief. Today, we live in an individualized society, where grief has been colonized by psychology and psychiatry, paving the way for a medicalization and pathologization of grief responses. Anders was critical of how this development leads to a neglect of the social dimensions of grief, with the risk of perpetuating the loneliness one may feel in bereavement, leading to a further need for psychological and psychiatric interventions.

The antidote is to understand grief as social and relational. Anders practised the craft of sociology in a way that always built on respect for the individual person, who was never reduced to social forces, but who was also not elevated to some kind of self-contained atom. In his life and in his research, Anders Petersen was keenly aware of human relations. Our relations to Anders continue after his death – in our memories, in the ways in which he inspired us, and in the many perceptive papers and books that he wrote.

11 Grief

The painfulness of permanent human absence

Anders Petersen and Michael Hviid Jacobsen

Introduction

Throughout our lives, many things and people come and go. Things and lives sometimes come to an end, at times, because we decide to end them ourselves, at other times, because external agencies or forces beyond our reach terminate them. For example, we may lose money, friends, jobs, prestige, self-respect, dreams and so on. Life is full of such momentary or more lasting losses. As a consequence, we may feel sad, empty and even depressed. In everyday language, we sometimes say that we 'grieve' such losses. Most often, however, we will eventually come to replace the missing thing or person: we make new money, have news friends, find new jobs and regain our prestige, self-respect and dreams. Grief, it seems, comes in many different guises. Sometimes we grieve for something that is not going to be as we have hoped for. For instance, imagine that you are the parents of a multi-handicapped child, then it is indeed possible to grieve that the life opportunities for this child already from the outset seem severely diminished, we may also grieve that the family business built up through many generations went bankrupt, or we may grieve a romantic relationship that never turned out to last.

Seen through this lens, life may be defined as a shorter or longer wait for the experience of grief. Only very few people, if any, are allowed to pass through life without ever experiencing some kind of loss, be it expected or unexpected, natural or tragic, accepted or unbearable. If not a certainty, then at least grief is something that must be calculated as part and parcel of what lies ahead. In general, 'grief' is an emotion triggered by the sense or experience of loss, and grief is thus an 'emotion of absence' that arises from the realization that we have lost something or are missing someone who was somehow important or dear to us (Jacobsen and Kofod, 2015). Such is our everyday usage of the notion of 'grief' – it is used indiscriminately for many different types of loss and forms of absence. However, if the concept of 'grief' should be meaningfully separated from 'loss' in general terms or from other types of 'absence', then it would be worth reserving the notion of 'grief' for experiences of irretrievable loss of human life and thus to link it to the experience of death. Life is so full of what clergyman Granger E. Westberg once called "little griefs" that may in

DOI: 10.4324/9781032714356-14

themselves feel disturbing and painful but which in time will most often be mitigated and pass by. At times, however, we encounter "large griefs" such as irretrievable loss and especially death (Westberg, 1961: 11). Such large griefs may call the world into question and challenge the very meaning of life. The concept of 'grief' as a human emotion is therefore often associated with permanent and absolute absence – that is death. Unavoidably, death triggers the experience of what Jean-Paul Sartre (1956 [1943]) once called a 'concrete nothingness' – the existential realization of someone or something missing – and for good. Pierre, in Sartre's famous example, is simply not here right now – he will, in fact, never return again. Experiencing such permanent and absolute absence is and remains an integral part of human life. Throughout life, we are thus constant spectators, as Sigmund Freud once insisted, to the deaths of others (family, friends, acquaintances and complete strangers), and not until we ourselves eventually die and perish do we stop being spectators, and others are then left to witness and grieve our disappearance. In this way, grief is safely and silently passed down through generations.

Even though grief is such an integral part of human existence, it seems to be a rather invisible emotion in everyday life. It is, after all, not very often we come into contact with people who are openly grieving. For all practical intents and purposes, grief nowadays most often takes place behind closed doors. In contemporary Western society, there is apparently something negative about grief (Charmaz and Milligan, 2007: 518). This is not simply because grief phenomenologically is associated with negation and absence, but more so because grief painfully reminds us that a happy life is always until further notice and is threatened by the eventual loss of exactly those people who make life happy. Grief is an assault on happiness (Ariès, 1974: 94). Grief is a difficult emotion in a society that celebrates openings and which finds it difficult to face or to accept endings. Grief becomes problematic in a society that regards death as a problem. And grief, as we shall see later in this chapter, becomes particularly problematic in a society that thinks of grief as an illness that requires diagnosis and treatment.

In this chapter, we will examine grief as an everyday emotion from many different perspectives: definitional, philosophical, sociological, psychological, historical and literary. First, we will look into how we may define grief as an emotion. Then we will present some of the many different faces of grief, before moving into a short historical overview of our changed attitude towards and ways of grieving in which we will also deal with how grieving in public in contemporary society can be seen as a case of so-called spectacular grief. Finally, we will deal with grief as an illness and look at how it is diagnosed and treated within contemporary psychological and psychiatric practice. It is important already initially to stress that this is not a chapter on grief theories, but a discussion of grief as an 'emotion of absence', or an emotion associated with death, that is deeply embedded in everyday life. This chapter does not aspire to present a systematic or comprehensive review of the vast research literature on grief, but it draws on, discusses and engages with parts of that literature which is found particularly useful for understanding grief as an everyday emotion.

Defining 'grief'

In his famous study *The Concept of Anxiety*, Søren Kierkegaard once argued that anxiety is to be perceived as a basic human condition. Anxiety, according to Kierkegaard, is to be understood as an existentially and religiously embedded condition (strongly connected with hereditary sin) that individuals have to address when making free choices. Thus, according to Kierkegaard, anxiety is intrinsically linked with the ongoing formation of individual freedom (Kierkegaard, 1980 [1844]). Could we, perhaps, think of grief in a similar vein? Well, in *A Treatise on Human Nature*, David Hume considered grief (alongside fear, hope and joy) to be one of the basic human emotions – what he referred to as the 'direct passions' (Hume, 1978 [1740]). Although Kierkegaard's and Hume's reflections on anxiety and grief, in several respects, are dissimilar, one common denominator unites them: they are both intrinsically human emotions. For our purposes here, what is important is, of course, Hume's proclamation that grief is human emotion 'writ large', in all its overwhelming effects. Whether grief also qualifies as what emotion researchers call a 'basic emotion' is debatable, but it is nevertheless, as we have already stated, almost certainly inescapable.

Positioning grief within the realm of human emotion does not, however, relieve us from the difficulties involved in attempting to define grief in a more specific sense of the term. There are many different definitions and theories of grief, and grief is often discussed and debated in relation – and sometimes in juxtaposition – to rather similar concepts such as 'sorrow', 'bereavement', 'mourning' and 'loss' (see Sprang and McNeil, 1995) or 'sadness' (see Bonanno, Goorin and Coifman, 2008). It is beyond the scope of this chapter to discuss these definitional and theoretical distinctions here, but rather to focus on approaching grief as a human emotion by asking the following question: What then, triggers this emotion? As we have touched upon in the introduction, we consider grief an 'emotion of absence'. Hence, grief occurs when we have lost someone or something important in our lives, though grief might also occur even before the actual loss has taken place. This is what Erich Lindemann (1944) once referred to with his concept of 'anticipatory grief': the mere anticipation of a loss to come is enough to generate the reactions of grief. Here the concept and understanding of loss is of great importance. As Nina R. Jacoby has recently shown, one is able to classify losses along two dimensions – personhood/artefact and materiality/immateriality – and thus to sort loss experiences into three general categories: (a) relationship loss (person, animal), (b) status loss (way of being, such as health or job), and (c) (im)material object loss (e.g., artefacts, places, ideals) (Jakoby, 2015: 112). In relation to grief, all of these categories are generously covered in the existing literature. For example, it is sometimes suggested that loss due to divorce (e.g., Weiss, 1975) or geographical separation (e.g. Price, 1998) can trigger grief-like responses. And in contemporary society, it is by no means considered peculiar that some researchers have included the loss of pets into the grief vernacular. In fact, it has even been argued that 'the death of a pet induces grief responses of comparable severity to the loss of human relationships' and that 'people often describe being more emotionally attached to their pets than to humans in their lives' (Carmack and Packman, 2011: 273). Moreover, the discussion, which we will not enter here, on whether animals themselves (such as elephants or dolphins) are capable of eliciting grief responses similar to those of humans is still ongoing (see, e.g., McGrath et al., 2013).

Neither do we want to challenge these statements nor this line of research as such – in fact, we are appreciative of the theories that seek to understand grief within a broader context of loss. Here we simply wish to limit ourselves – and hence the definition with which we work – to discussing grief in relation to the human emotions generated by the loss of human life. But not just any human life. In our perspective, a qualification and sensitzation of the concept requires that grief relates to the strong and deep emotions involved in the involuntary loss through death of another human being who are perceived to be of significant importance by the grieving actor in question. Thus, the spontaneous grief response that sometimes occurs in relation to the death of a music celebrity (as we saw when Michael Jackson or more recently Prince and David Bowie passed away) or a member of a royal family (as we saw when Princess Diana died), and to which we return later, is beyond this relatively narrow definition. Vital to us – as the title of this chapter strongly indicates – is also the connection between grief and (how it is displayed in) everyday life. The experience of absence of a significant other reverberates as a powerful and difficult feeling in one's everyday life, exacerbated by the lack of conversation, bodily contact and overall interaction that one shared with the human being who passed away.

At display, hence, is the grief experienced in everyday life. In this respect, grief is mostly associated with negative experiences. In fact, neurologically and physiologically, grief experiences can be quite similar to the intense withdrawal symptoms experienced by somebody who is quitting drugs. Craving, desperation and longing are among the symptoms frequently involved in grief. More specifically, empirical studies have shown that grief's 'symptomatology' (varying somewhat from individual to individual and within individuals from time to time) includes such diverse physical and mental feelings and activities as: sleeplessness, restlessness, loss of appetite, frustration, hallucinations, 'irrational' behaviour, shortness of breath, heaviness, in the chest, nausea, headaches, uncontrolled weeping, sadness, despair, hopelessness, apathy and irritability (Lofland, 1985: 172).

As some note, however, grief reactions can also oscillate between negative and positive experiences – such as laughter and joy – hence emphasizing that 'grief reactions are not uniform or static. Rather, as many bereavement investigators have noted, grief seems to occur in waves' that each brings something new to the shore of the experience of loss (Bonanno, Goorin and Coifman, 2008: 803). This entails that grief is not, in and by itself, bad, and that good aspects of grief can actually be explored – even to an extent that one can (and perhaps should) talk about a so-called 'good grief' (Westberg, 1961) or 'good mourning' (Meyer, 2015).

But whether one situates the analysis of everyday grief experiences within the realms of the good or the bad, it is our contention that grief as an emotion of absence should be concerned with social relations. As phenomenological scholar Thomas Fuchs has recently stated: "Like hardly any other psychic phenomenon, grief discloses the fact that as human beings we are fundamentally related to and in need of others, that indeed our self is permeable and open to them" (Fuchs, 2017: 6). Thus, grief cannot – as we shall expand on later – only be understood as an 'individual' emotion. Although grief is always manifested in a person, the experiences of grief are nonetheless socially shaped and reshaped (Jakoby, 2012). It is also seldom that only one single person is grieving the absence of a significant other and this grief is most often shared with others who also mourn the loss. One could thus say that grief is deeply interwoven in historically changing socio-structural contexts, rules and norms and (also) takes place – and changes form, content and structure – in actual face-to-face interactions with other people in everyday life situations.

The many faces of grief

Having framed grief in this manner is obviously not to say that it is easily captured. Grief has, indeed, many faces: it is a multi-facetted, multi-dimensional and multi-layered emotion that can be connected to a multitude of different emotional and physical experiences (Jackson, 1972; Sprang and McNeil, 1995). By frequently invoking the facial metaphor in the literature on grief, it becomes obvious that grief, besides being a deep-seated and mostly invisible emotion within the individual, apparently also has a certain observable physiognomy evident, for example, in frowning, a sullen or sad look and not least tears (in Voltaire's memorable words 'the silent language of grief'). Add to this other bodily sensations felt by the grieving person such as fatigue, forgetfulness, aches and pains, shortage of breath, headaches and loss of appetite just to mention a few, and it becomes obvious that grief also has a physical dimension, as times even referred to as a 'broken heart syndrome'.

As we have already touched upon, grief can itself trigger a number of other emotions. As explicated by George A. Bonanno and colleagues: "In addition to sadness, grief has been associated with a wide range of negative emotions, such as anger, contempt, hostility, fear, and guilt … and … genuinely positive emotional experiences related to amusement, affection, happiness and pride" (Bonanno, Goorin and Coifman, 2008: 798). Moreover, as the authors just quoted discuss in great detail, grief can also be triggered by other emotions such as particularly by sadness, which the authors believe shares considerable features with grief but at the same time is quite different from it. Any attempt to blur the distinction between the emotions in question would hence be misleading and analytically unproductive. Rather, one should separate them form each other in order to pave the way for finer grained analysis of sadness as well as grief experiences. That is not to say, however, that the concepts are not closely intertwined. What the authors argue is rather that the phenomenology of sadness is somewhat mirrored "by the ways in which sadness appears to give way to more complicated grief reactions during bereavement" (Bonanno, Goorin and Coifman, 2008: 801). In sum, sadness can be supportive of so-called complicated grief, a terminology that more than indicates a distinction from 'normal' – or non-pathological – grief. We shall return to some of the implications of this later in this chapter.

A pursuit of the many faces of grief cannot, of course, restrict itself to mentioning the interconnectedness with other emotions or looking at the physical aspects of grief. It has to explicate how the permanent absence of someone significant is actually experienced and expressed in everyday life. As mentioned, grief is a social emotion unfolding in concrete social and historical circumstances. Knowing that we are not able to exhaust this area of research here, we have selected some areas that show the great variety of different experiences and expressions of grief. For example, the relation between social class and the experiences and expressions of grief has been analysed, among others, by Julie-Marie Strange (2002). Strange, taking her point of departure in literature written in and discussing late Victorian and Edwardian Britain, makes a nuanced analysis of the complexities involved in working-class grief during the time in question. According to Strange, there is no doubt about the fact that materiality played a vital part in the possibilities of expressing grief. As she writes: "Grief was, undoubtedly, inextricable from material circumstance: bereavement provoked concerns about the costs of burial, while the death of a wage earner depressed a family's finances" (Strange, 2002: 149). Some researchers have argued that this crated a somewhat blasé attitude towards grief from the working-class – that their material insecurity encouraged a containment of grief, thereby showing a lack of sensibility towards grieving (see also Vincent, 1980). But as Strange shows, one can also claim that grief was managed by the working-class. That is, working-class individuals developed specific strategies for confronting both death and grief that allowed them to handle their grief in a pragmatic way. She states:

> In managing grief, working-class families did not negate loss but, rather, they formulated positive, constructive and, crucially, malleable means for its expression … Grief was articulated, first, through the social rites of mourning and, second, via personal and abstract symbols and signs.
>
> (Strange, 2002: 160–161)

These ways might not have been shared (or societally sanctioned) definitions of grief by the ruling class of society, but nonetheless important manifestations of grief expressions that bear witness to the socially variable nature of grief and how it is dealt with in everyday life.

In a similar vein, albeit in relation to contemporary society, Kenneth J. Doka has written extensively about what he calls "disenfranchised grief" (Doka, 1989). As he has written in a short piece:

> the concept of disenfranchised grief recognizes that societies have sets of norms – in effect, 'grieving rules' – that attempt to specify who, when, where, how long and for whom people should grieve. These grieving rules may be codified as personal policies.
>
> (Doka, 1999: 37)

Disenfranchised grief, then, is the grief of those who incur a loss but a loss that cannot be publically acknowledged or socially accepted. Indeed, certain types of grief (for example following an AIDS-related death) may even be stigmatized or delegitimized. According to Doka, disenfranchised grief can be identified in three primary forms: (1) lack of recognition of the grieved relationship, (2) lack of recognition of the bereavement experience itself and (3) lack of recognition of the individual griever (Doka, 2002). The notion of disenfranchised grief bridges sociological and psychological understandings of grief. It not only conceptualizes issues of societal legitimization of grief but also delivers a prism through which one is able to understand the personal consequences of disenfranchised grief. Needless to say, a lack of recognition in any of these realms can have devastating personal outcomes.

This analytical framework has paved the way for concepts such as 'gagged grief' – the socially sanctioned 'shushing' of grief experiences – mostly effecting marginalized groups such as homosexuals, who would like to publically grieve the loss of a partner but is socially prevented from doing so (Green and Grant, 2008). Another interesting concept that owes its theoretical scaffolding to disenfranchised grief is 'suffocated grief' (Bordere, 2010). This concept is particularly applicable to the predicament of young African American males who, according to Tashel C. Bordere, find their grief disenfranchised in multiple ways: by stereotypical gender messages that emasculate instrumental grieving; by the often violent circumstances surrounding death and by society's devaluation of African American lives. Thus, in the face of these circumstances, these males are denied the opportunity to express their grief in a functional or purposeful way to them, which is why

> they must 'suffocate' and silence their grief. Young African American males are often faced with powerfully negative societal responses to their natural outpourings of grief and coping strategies. Certain expressions of mourning (e.g., rap music, tattoos, graffiti, and mourning T-shirts) may be actively rejected, and even condemned as inappropriate or 'dysfunctional' to the mourner or 'offensive' to others.
>
> (Molaison, Bordere and Fowler, 2011: 383)

Suffocating and silencing ones grief – and being socially scorned for the ways in which one attempts to grieve – is potentially devastating. What is being suffocated is, in fact, large and pivotal aspects of one's self. The denial of functional ways of grieving is, in many respects, an undermining – perhaps even a ridicule – of identity. Moreover, it might provoke undesirable psychological reactions when the grief is being contained and restricted: suppressed emotions can contain the ingredients of an explosive cocktail.

From glorious grief through obscene grief to 'spectacular grief'

Grief not only has a history within each and every human being experiencing it but also has a social history. According to GWF Hegel, history is about what man does with death. Throughout history, from the Stone Age and ancient Greek and Roman empires, there have been many historical shifts and transitions in our mourning practices and understandings of grief, some knowledge of which has been preserved for posterity (see, e.g. Davey, 2013 [1890]). However, most historians who have worked with death and mourning cultures – such as Philippe Ariès, Johan Huizinga or Michel Vovelle – have taken the dark Middle Ages as their analytical starting-point. Perhaps the most cited piece of work documenting and systematizing our changing attitudes towards death and grief was proposed by Ariès, who in his magisterial *The Hour of Our Death* (1981) from the myriad of historical detail carved out four different 'death mentalities' in the West from medieval times to contemporary society. Without going into detail with these four epochs – 'tame death' in the Middle Ages, 'death of the self' in the Late Middle Ages and Renaissance period, 'death of the other' in the 19th century, and 'forbidden death' in the 20th century – Ariès told a story of an increasing alienation towards death and grief throughout the past 1,000 years. Death and grief, previously such familiar and visible phenomena in everyday life, gradually disappeared and were replaced by distance, embarrassment and taboo.

Before grief was a feeling that one would unavoidably be confronted with many times in life in the shape of magnificent mourning clothes, slow funeral processions, the grand architecture of the graveyard and in the elaborate mourning rituals and customs following the event of death. Especially during the time of 'death of the other' in the 19th century was the culture of grief nothing less than a glorious public celebration of loss (Stearns, 2007). Recollecting even the period of World War I and his own adolescence, Geoffrey Gorer, whose father drowned when the Lusitania sank, remembered how "in the summer of 1915, and thereafter, widows in mourning became increasingly frequent in the streets" (Gorer, 1965: xx). However, with the coming of the 20th century, with its secularization and celebration of science, death was increasingly privatized, surrounded by a strange scent of obscenity, and was in the middle of the century described by Gorer (1955) as 'pornographic'. When death became pornographic, grief became something akin to emotional masturbation that should, for the sake of all, be reserved solely for the grieving person. Mourning had to a large degree been removed from public space, the days of the funeral procession moving at a leisurely pace were now over, mourning clothing went out of fashion and comprehensive mourning rituals were gradually replaced by silence and denial (Bedikian, 2008). According to Ariès, death became institutionalized, professionalized and medicalized – a technical phenomenon that the 'doctors of death' began to control and manage. With this privatization and professionalization of death also followed the privatization and professionalization of grief, and increasingly grief was seen as a 'morbid state which must be treated, shortened, erased by the 'doctors of grief' (Ariès, 1974: 99–100). We return to this topic again later.

Previously in this chapter, we stated that in our definition of grief as the experience of the permanent loss of a loved one we would not include those expressions of mourning that are associated with public grief over non-significant others. However, it is important to stress that besides its 'feeling side', grief – like so many other emotions – also contain a 'display side' (Lofland, 1985: 173) that is perhaps particularly evident in the dramaturgy and manifestation of public grief. Grief therefore not only is an individual emotion experienced by an individual human being but also can be, and most often is, a shared feeling of loss that is somehow performed or put on display. In recent decades there have been signs of the gradual return of grief as a public event, not least relating to grieving the return of soldiers in coffins from international conflicts or mourning the victims of terrorist attacks. Anthony Giddens (1991) once repeated Freud's notion of 'the return of the repressed' as a signifier of late-modern society, and others have claimed that the death taboo is apparently dissolving (see Berridge, 2002; Walter, 1994). Yet others have spoken of a new phase in death mentality substituting Ariès's 'forbidden death' and have claimed that this fifth phase of 'spectacular death' also leads to manifestations of 'spectacular grief' (Jacobsen, 2016).

In times of peace, public mourning and collective expressions of grief are however still mostly held at a minimum, whereas during times of war, unrest or insecurity, public mourning rituals and ceremonials serve the important purpose of igniting the national spirit. So whenever there have been recent terrorist attacks – in France, Belgium, Germany, Denmark, England, Sweden, Spain or elsewhere – people seem to feel the need to gather to express their solidarity with the victims, to confirm the social bond and to state that they are not afraid. We have seen similar kinds of manifestations when crowds gather to mourn the often tragic, dramatic or unexpected death of celebrities. Just think of the mourning of Princess Diana, Michael Jackson or Prince. Before them, and well before the age of 'internet mourning rituals', the assassinations of John F. Kennedy, John Lennon and Olof Palme were mourned in quite similar ways. However, not just the deaths of national heroes or celebrities receive this special kind of public attention. Often when someone dies in public under tragic circumstances such as from violent attacks or violent accidents, we will see what is variously called 'roadside rituals', 'spontaneous altars' or 'makeshift memorials' at the site of death marking the public's anger, compassion and grief. Haney, Leimer and Lowery (1997) have listed several characteristics of this so-called spontaneous memorialization and its expressions of grief in public at the site of a dramatic or tragic death. For example, that they are open to participation and that nobody is in principle excluded from the circle of grief, that the items and mementos left at the small shrines marking the site of death are personally meaningful to the mourners, that they often constitute a bricolage of religious and secular symbolism, that they breach with normal conventions for the form and duration of grief, and that mourners often in small notes or on cardboard signs communicate messages (moral or political) that go beyond the actual death that is being mourned. In this way, we may say that such 'spectacular grief' today seems to serve as an important vehicle for expressing a grief that is perhaps in many ways still silenced and tabooed. So we now live in times of what Erika Doss (2010) has called 'memorial mania' or we might also call it 'mourning mania' in which we want to make a public spectacle of the losses we experience. Obviously, it is debatable if this kind of 'spontaneous mourning' expression, in fact, qualifies as 'grief' at all, and if so if this kind of grieving for celebrities or complete strangers is comparable to the one experienced when a significant other passes away.

Diagnosing grief – from 'normal grief' to 'complicated grief'

"There isn't any need for a civilized man to bear anything that's seriously unpleasant", says Mustapha Mond, the fictitious 'Resident World Controller of Western Europe' in Aldous Huxley's dystopian novel *Brave New World* published in 1932. The answer to the question of human suffering in Huxley's book was 'Soma': not a drug taken by the citizens as a reaction to any specific illness, but in order to prevent unpleasant things to occur (Huxley, 2006[1932]). Now, we cannot put the perspective of suffering explicated in Huxley's novel on the same footing as the situation in contemporary society. Still, it seems worthwhile to discuss it in relation to a situation, in which so-called prolonged grief disorder will become a separate diagnosis in the *ICD-11* to be published in 2018. How can we understand the transformation from normal (or uncomplicated) grief to complicated grief – and hence grief becoming a distinct diagnostic category?

In order for grief to become a diagnostic category, it has to be perceived not only as an emotion but also as a disease. The disciplines of psychology and psychiatry have been instrumental in this line of thought, which is by no means new. Already in 1961, George L. Engel asked the pertinent question: 'Is Grief a Disease?'. He began his paper by acknowledging that this might be an odd question, since most people would not think of grief along such lines. But still, he argued – as the medical scholar he was – that it is worthwhile contemplating the question in light of the new medical research that developed in the historical epoch in which he lived (Engel, 1961). Had Engel, however, been a devout Freudian, he would have answered the question quite quickly with a pretty definitive 'no'. In Freud's famous essay 'Mourning and Melancholia', written during World War I, he stipulated that grief was not to be understood as a pathology and that "although mourning involve great departures from the normal attitude to life, it never occurs to us to regard it as a pathological condition and refer it to medical treatment" (Freud, 1957 [1917]: 252). In contemporary society, however, Freud's standpoint is being increasingly challenged. Or, one might even say that it has already been surpassed by the exact opposite point of view. Perhaps we can explain this by pointing out that Freud – and his psychological theories – was only a hiatus in the history of psychiatry (Shorter, 1997: 145). Psychiatry is predominantly a medical discipline that – particularly since the launch of the DSM-*III* in 1980 – is best understood as 'diagnostic psychiatry'. According to Allan V. Horwitz, who coined this term, "diagnostic psychiatry defines diseases through the presence of overt symptoms, regardless of the causes of these symptoms. It regards diseases as natural entities that exist in the body and that generate the particular symptoms a person displays" (Horwitz, 2002: 56). Within the realm of diagnostic psychiatry, then, the primary causes of mental diseases are not sought in childhood disturbances – or in difficult socio-economic living conditions for that matter – but instead in disturbed brains and neurochemical activities, all of which manifest themselves in various symptoms that can be monitored, measured and communicated. In that respect, the main focus is on symptoms that can be classified and collected into a given diagnosis.

Now, grief was not included in the *DSM-III* – neither in the *DSM-5* (2013) for that matter. But as mentioned, 'prolonged grief disorder' will occur in the *ICD-11*. The proponents of the diagnosis (such as, e.g., Priegerson, et al. 2009) claim that it will help to distinguish pathological grief from the diagnosis of depression and from normal grief, thereby enabling the right kind of treatment to those who suffer from pathological grief and avoiding unnecessary treatment of normal grief responses. Of course, this is not an easy task. The symptomatology of normal and prolonged/complicated grief is not that straightforward to separate from each other. But it is, according to those in favour of the diagnosis, worthwhile. As it is stated in a review article about whether complicated grief meets the criteria for a mental disease or not: 'the potential benefit of creating a new diagnosis in order to identify individuals who require clinical attention appears to outweigh the potential harm as long as the diagnosis is applied properly' (Shear et al., 2011: 107). We will have to wait and see whether the diagnosis will be applied properly or not. Meanwhile, the debate about – and the critique of – the transformation of grief into a diagnostic category will most likely continue to intensify.

Quite a few scholars have argued that grief should not be understood as a disease (e.g. Averill and Nunley, 1998). Instead it should be addressed as a prototype of intense but normal sadness that society 'writ large' does not perceive as pathological. As Horwitz and colleague Jerome C. Wakefield claim, it is common sense not to consider intense grief reactions to be symptoms of a psychiatric disorder. Instead, most people would define grief as a normal reaction to severely constraining circumstances (Horwitz and Wakefield, 2007: 31). The problem arises when grief reactions are thought of as medical signs of a disease. The coming diagnosis of prolonged grief disorder can be seen as an example of the pathologization of normal grief that Horwitz and Wakefield also detect in relation to the diagnosis of depression. The consequences of this, according to Horwitz and Wakefield, dubious diagnostic approach to considering what is respectively "normal" and "pathological" is not only a potential rise in the numbers of false-positive diagnoses (Horwitz and Wakefield, 2007: 38) but also that this understanding buttresses the medicalization of grief. Peter Conrad's (2007) influential analysis of the medicalization of society – in which he stipulates how normal human distress, suffering and personal troubles is increasingly transformed into medicalized objects and mental disorders – has been applied by Julia Bandini (2015) specifically in relation to grief. She points to three potential consequences of the medicalization of grief: (1) a potential for overdiagnosis and overtreatment, (2) a potential for expanded market shares for pharmaceutical companies (some years ago, John Abraham (2010) discussed the possibilities of a regular pharmaceuticalization of society as a situation in which an expansion of treatment with pharmaceuticals denotes how society perceives the normal way of treating human suffering, so why not a pill for grief, one could ask?), and (3) a loss of traditional and cultural methods of adapting to the loss of a loved one (Bandini, 2015: 351). The risk of diagnostic thinking colonizing other forms and ways of relating to grief is indeed present. As Svend Brinkmann has argued, this is not only the case in relation what we normally construe as traditional or cultural modes of coping with issues such as grief. It is also shown in the languages we use to articulate issues of human suffering as such. He claims that alternative understandings of human suffering "have been somewhat depreciated by the status of the diagnostic language" (Brinkmann, 2016: 52). That is not to say that other languages – social, existential, political etc. – have disappeared from our vocabulary. They have, though, less status than the diagnostic ditto when it comes to articulating – and thus to organizing – our suffering. Why should grief be an exception?

Both the protagonists and the critics of the grief diagnoses may have valid and convincing arguments. What is often ignored in this debate, however, is the individualization of grief that the diagnoses can lead too. By allowing the logic of diagnostic psychiatry to absorb grief, there is a severe risk that grief is being turned into an individual problem to be dealt with individually. Hence, one loses sight of the social dimensions and expressions of grief – which also takes place in everyday life – and thereby of the fact that grief has been triggered by the loss of a significant other who is now absent in the griever's life. The diagnoses then risks individualizing a difficult life experience and thus casting a shadow on the vital social aspects of grief, thereby echoing an overall transformation in contemporary society in which 'the social' is being marginalized, perhaps even neutralized.

Treating and relieving grief

From giving a diagnosis usually follows attempts at curing, treating, relieving or healing. We have, until now, touched upon many different components and understandings of grief reactions and experiences. In the previous paragraphs it has become clear that a wide array of academic developments and societal transformations have been influential in relation to the multiple spheres of grief. Some of the same (historical) dynamism is also found in the ways in which grief is treated and relieved.

As we have seen, for psychology and medical science, it was simply too tempting not to leave grief alone. Previously, grief was primarily the domain of pastoral and communal care. With the rise of modern society and modern science, it was no longer an emotion that could not remain outside the advancing regime of cure and treatment for long. For a long time during the 20th century, the experience of grief was shrouded in almost mythological theories and iron-clad models that insisted that it should be seen as a series of consecutive stages that would eventually end in resolution and acceptance of the loss. Until the late 1990s, the theoretical hypothesis of 'grief work' was central within clinical lore and hence was incorporated in most intervention programs. Grief work, in the simplest understanding of the term, suggests that grief has to be worked on (and coped with) in order for the grieving person to let go and move on in life. As Tony Walter has hinted at, the embedding of this idea in clinical lore is perhaps due to William Worden's hugely popular book from 1983 *Grief Counseling and Grief Therapy* (Walter, 1999: 161). In Worden's book, he suggested four tasks that bereaved people should accomplish for the process of mourning to be completed: (1) accepting the reality of the loss, (2) working through the pain of grief, (3) adjusting to the environment in which the deceased is missing and (4) finding an enduring connection with the deceased whilst embarking on a new life. Now, grief work is not – as the last of the four tasks indicate – entirely incompatible with continuing the bond with the deceased. Nevertheless, the core idea that grief can be governed by tasks and eventually be 'accomplished' and 'completed' has in recent decades been met by severe criticism. In fact, as Walter quotes Margaret Stroebe and colleagues for stating: "Not only is there very little scientific evidence on the grief work hypothesis, but studies that bear on the issue yield contradictory results" (Stroebe et al. in Walter, 1999: 160). Following these types of questions concerning the efficacy of the grief work hypothesis, other theoretical models have been developed in order to deal with grief. One of these models is the 'two-track model', which is defined in the following way:

> The Two-Track Model of Bereavement advocates for the assessment of both functioning and the nature of the continuing attachment to the deceased when significant others die – and this is across the entire course of the bereaved person's lifetime. The clinical focus of the model derives directly from its binocular focus.
>
> (Rubin, Malkinson and Witztum, 2011: 49–50)

The theoretical scaffolding presented in the two-track model is not new. One of the authors just quoted, Simon S. Rubin, embarked on this theoretical endeavour back in 1981 (Rubin, 1981). Since then, Rubin and co-workers have elaborated on the model making it applicable in the areas of research and practice. The first of the tracks in the model addresses the question of biopsychosocial functioning and examines whether intervention is needed in these realms. The second track addresses the type of relationship the griever has to the deceased, which adaptive strengths and weaknesses there exist and examines if intervention in the relationship domain is required. Thus, the two-track model serves to organize a reality – that might be more complicated in real life than in the model – in order to conceptualize some specific points to pay attention to and on which prepare intervention with the bereaved. It rests on letting go of and staying connected to the deceased as a dual process in which the interplay is not unilinear or predictable as in the conventional stage models. So the 'two-track model', ideas about 'continuing bonds' and other more recent inventions in grief theory and grief therapy insist that instead of rigid stages, tasks to be performed or equally one-dimensional scenarios, we should rather focus on the constantly changing and complex dynamics of the grieving process. The danger obviously lurks that even models and theories that on the surface seem to open up for the multifarious dimensions of grief (looking at 'tracks' instead of 'tasks') can be taken too literally or ideologically by being transformed into regulations and proscriptions for practice.

There is doubtlessly a lot to be learned from the many theories of grief that continue to be developed within and proposed for clinical practice. Without recourse to any abstract theorizing or empirical findings, however, we suggest that the best way to learn to live with grief is by reconciling ourselves to the fact that everything human must die. This is and continues to be the way of all flesh. Any notion about a 'good grief' must therefore necessarily be seen as an extension of the notion of 'good death' that has been suggested within palliative care practice. Of course, there are many formal definitions and criteria of such a 'good death', but perhaps the most important thing, after all, is to avoid a 'bad death' (Jacobsen, 2017) and with it also a 'bad grief'. Scientific theories, clinical models and therapeutic or medical treatments might perhaps not be the most appropriate sources to consult if one wants to avoid such a bad grief, because they usually end up reducing the multi-facetted, multi-dimensional and multi-layered dynamics of grief to 'stages', 'tasks', 'interventions' and similar ideas. As C.S. Lewis, who after experiencing the loss of his beloved wife Joy Davidson, wrote a small and wonderful book titled *A Grief Observed* containing his 'mad midnight moments' of contemplating grief, once importantly suggested: "I thought I could describe a state; make a map of sorrow. Sorrow, however, turns out to be not a state but a process. It needs not a map but a history" (Lewis, 1984 [1961]: 55).

Conclusion

In this chapter, we have introduced to some general ideas and more specialized insights about grief as an everyday emotion. We have drawn generously and admittedly also unsystematically on various definitional, philosophical, sociological, psychological, historical and literary sources of inspiration in order to try and capture the multi-facetted, multi-dimensional and multi-layered and always changing nature of human grief. Throughout this chapter, we have revisited and discussed different aspects of the grief experience and in the process have aspired to show how it makes sense to reserve the notion of 'grief' for those losses in human life that are indeed irrevocable and definitive. Other experiences of absence or loss in everyday life may also contain certain germs or glimpses of grief, but if the notion of grief is to retain any analytical value and avoid dilution, it should be related to the death of significant others.

This chapter started out by stating that grief is hard to come to terms with – not merely as a theme for research (not least due to the heaps of work now published on the topic) but also as a fundamental human experience. Sociology, psychology, history, theology, medical science, literature, poetry and other branches of human knowledge and insight can take us some way in understanding grief. However, in order to be fully appreciated, grief needs to be experienced first-hand. As Edgar N. Jackson once proposed: "It may well be easier to confront the dynamics of grief in theory than in the form of the baffling and often contradictory behavior of a person in the midst of a grief experience" (Jackson, 1972: 9). Scientific theories, conceptual apparatuses, research methods, psychiatric diagnoses and treatment regimes one way or the other always end up objectifying grief. However, grief is first and foremost a lived experience – a human response to the experience of the permanent and irretrievable absence of a loved one. Let us therefore end this grand tour of grief as an everyday emotion (but also as a scientific construct) with an apt observation by C.S. Lewis who in his aforementioned 'diary of grief' reminded his readers of the following – not only something that concerns us all as human beings but also something that each and every researcher of grief and bereavement should carefully remember:

> We were even promised sufferings. They were part of the programme. We were even told 'Blessed are they that mourn' and I accepted it. I've got nothing that I hadn't bargained for. Of course, it is different when the thing happens to oneself, not to others, and in reality, not in imagination.
>
> (Lewis, 1984 [1961]: 33)

References

Abraham, J (2010) Pharmaceuticalization of Society in Context: Theoretical, Empirical and Health Dimensions. *Sociology*, 44 (4): 603–622.

Ariès, P (1974) *Western Attitudes Toward Death from the Middle Ages to the Present*. Baltimore, MD: Johns Hopkins University Press.

Ariès, P (1981) *The Hour of Our Death*. London: Allen Lane.

Averill, JR and Nunley, EP (1988) Grief as an Emotion and as a Disease: A Social-Constructionist Perspective. *Journal of Social Issues*, 44 (3): 79–95.

Bandini, J (2015) The Medicalization of Bereavement: (Ab)normal Grief in the DSM-5. *Death Studies*, 39 (6): 347–352.

Bedikian, SA (2008) The Death of Mourning: From Victorian Crepe to the Little Black Dress. *Omega: Journal of Death and Dying*, 57 (1): 35–52.

Berridge, K (2002) *Vigor Mortis: The End of the Death Taboo*. London: Profile Books.

Bonanno, GA, Goorin, L and Coifman, KG (2008) Sadness and Grief. In: Lewis, M, Haviland-Jones, JM and Feldman Barrett, L (eds.) *Handbook of Emotions* (3rd Edition), 797–810. New York: Guildford Press.

Bordere, TC (2010) *Violent Death and Culturally Sensitive Strategies for Outreach and Practice with Youth*. Minneapolis, MN: Association for Death Education and Counseling.

Brinkmann, S (2016) *Diagnostic Cultures: A Cultural Approach to the Pathologization of Modern Life*. London: Routledge.

Carmack, BJ and Packman, W (2011) Pet Loss: The Interface of Continuing Bonds Research and Practice. In: Neimeyer, RA, Harris, DL, Winokuer, HR and Thornton, GF. (eds) *Grief and Bereavement in Contemporary Society: Bridging Research and* Practice, 273–284. London: Routledge.

Charmaz, K and Milligan, MJ (2007) *Grief*. In: Stets, JE and Turner, JH (eds.) *Handbook of the Sociology of Emotions*, 516–543. New York: Springer.

Conrad, P (2007) *The Medicalization of Society*. Baltimore, MD: Johns Hopkins University Press.

Davey, R (2013 [1890]) *A History of Mourning*. London: Jay's.

Doka, KJ (1989) *Disenfranchised Grief: Recognizing Hidden Sorrow*. Lexington, MA: Lexington Books/D. C. Heath and Co.

Doka, KJ (1999) Disenfranchised Grief. *Bereavement Care*, 18 (3): 37–39.

Doka, KJ (ed.) (2002) *Disenfranchised Grief: New Directions, Challenges and Strategies for Practice*. Champaign, IL: Research Press.

Doss, E (2010) *Memorial Mania: Public Feeling in America*. Chicago, IL: University of Chicago Press.

Engel, GL (1961) Is Grief a Disease? – A Challenge for Medical Research. *Psychosomatic Medicine*, 23 (1): 18–22.

Freud, S (1957 [1917]) Mourning and Melancholia. In: Strachey, J (ed.) *The Standard Edition of the Complete Psychological Works of Sigmund Freud*, Volume XIV, 243–258. London: Hogarth Press.
Fuchs, T (2017) Presence in Absence: The Ambiguous Phenomenology of Grief. *Phenomenology and the Cognitive Sciences*, 17: 1–16.
Giddens, A (1991) *Modernity and Self-identity: Self and Society in the Late Modern Age*. Cambridge: Polity Press.
Gorer, G (1955) The Pornography of Death. *Encounter*, October, pp. 49–52.
Gorer, G (1965) *Death, Grief and Mourning*. New York: Doubleday.
Green, L and Grant, V (2008) Gagged Grief and Beleaguered Bereavements? – An Analysis of Multidisciplinary Theory and Research Relating to Same Sex Partnership Bereavement. *Sexualities*, 11 (3): 275–300.
Haney, CA, Leimer, C and Lowery, L (1997) Spontaneous Memorialization: Violent Death and Emerging Mourning Ritual. *Omega: Journal of Death and Dying*, 35 (2): 159–171.
Horwitz, AV (2002) *Creating Mental Illness*. Chicago, IL: Chicago University Press.
Horwitz, AV and Wakefield, JC (2007) *The Loss of Sadness: How Psychiatry Transformed Normal Sorrow into Depressive Disorder*. New York: Oxford University Press.
Hume, D (1978 [1740]) *A Treatise of Human Nature*. Oxford: Oxford University Press.
Huxley, A (2006 [1932]) *Brave New World*. New York: Harper.
Jackson, EN (1972) *The Many Faces of Grief*. London: SCM Press Ltd.
Jacobsen, MH (2016) 'Spectacular Death' – Proposing a New Fifth Phase to Philippe Ariès's Admirable History of Death. *Humanities*, 5 (19): 1–20.
Jacobsen, MH (2017) 'The Bad Death' – Deciphering and Developing the Dominant Discourse on 'The Good Death'. In: Parvaresh, V and Capone, A (eds.) *The Pragmeme of Accommodation: The Case of Interaction around the Event of* Death, 351–373. New York: Springer.
Jacobsen, MH and Kofod, EH (2015): Sorg – en fraværsfølelse under forandring ['Grief – Changes in an Emotion of Absence']. In: Glavind Bo, I and Hviid Jacobsen, M (eds.) *Hverdagslivets følelser – tilstande, relationer, kulturer* [Emotions of Everyday Life – States, Relations, Cultures], 245–280. Copenhagen: Hans Reitzels Forlag.
Jakoby, NR (2012) Grief as a Social Emotion: Theoretical Perspectives. *Death Studies*, 36 (8): 679–711.
Jakoby, NR (2015) The Self and Significant Others: Toward a Sociology of Loss. *Illness, Crisis and Loss*, 23 (2): 129–174.
Kierkegaard, S (1980 [1844]) *The Concept of Anxiety*. Princeton, NJ: Princeton University Press.
Lewis, CS (1984 [1961) *A Grief Observed*. New York: Walker and Company.
Lindemann, E (1944): Symptomatology and Management of Acute Grief. *American Journal of Psychiatry*, 101(2): 141–148.
Lofland, LH (1985) The Social Shaping of Emotion: The Case of Grief. *Symbolic Interaction*, 8 (2): 171–190.
McGrath, N, Walker, J, Nilsson, D and Phillips, C. (2013) Public Attitudes Towards Grief in Animals. *Animal Welfare*, 22: 33–47.
Meyer, E (2015) *Good Mourning*. New York: Gallery Books.
Molaison, V, Bordere, TC and Fowler, K (2011) 'The Remedy is Not Working': Seeking Socially Just and Culturally Conscientious Practices in Bereavement. In: Neimeyer, RA et al (eds) *Grief and Bereavement in Contemporary Society: Bridging Research and Practice*, 375–387. London: Routledge.

Price, DM (1998) Deciding What is Right When We are So Different. In Doka, KJ and Davidson, JD (eds.) *Living with Grief: Who We Are, How We Grieve*, 239–248. New York: Routledge.

Prigerson, HG., Horowitz, MJ, Jacobs, SC, Parkes, CM, Aslan, M, Goodkin, K and Maciejewski, PK. (2009) Prolonged Grief Disorder: Psychometric Validation for Criteria Proposed for DSM-V and *ICD-11*. *PLoS Med*, 6 (8): 1–12.

Rubin, SS (1981) A Two-Track Model of Bereavement: Theory and Research. *American Journal of Orthopsychiatry*, 51 (1): 101–109.

Rubin, SS, Malkinson, R and Witztum, E (2011) The Two-Track Model of Bereavement: The Double Helix of Research and Clinical Practice. In: Neimeyer, RA, Harris, DL, Winokuer, HR and Thornton, GF (eds) *Grief and Bereavement in Contemporary Society: Bridging Research and* Practice, 47–56. London: Routledge.

Sartre, JP (1956 [1943]) *Being and Nothingness*. London: Philosophical Library.

Shear, MK, Simon, N, Wall, M, Zisook, S, Neimeyer, R, Duan, N and Keshaviah, A. (2011) Complicated Grief and Related Bereavement Issues for DSM-5. *Depression and Anxiety*, 28: 103–117.

Shorter, E (1997) *A History of Psychiatry: From the Era of the Asylum to the Age of Prozac*. New York: John Wiley and Sons.

Sprang, G and McNeil, J (1995) *The Many Faces of Bereavement: The Nature and Treatment of Natural, Traumatic and Stigmatized Grief*. New York: Brunner/Mazel Publishers.

Stearns, PN (2007) *Revolutions in Sorrow: The American Experience of Death in a Global Perspective*. Boulder, CO: Paradigm Publishers.

Strange, JM (2002) She Cried Very Little: Death, Grief and Mourning in Working-Class Culture, c. 1880-1914. *Social History*, 27 (2): 143–161.

Vincent, D (1980) Love and Death and the Nineteenth Century Working-Class. *Social History*, 5 (2): 223–247.

Walter, T (1994) *The Revival of Death*. London: Routledge.

Walter, T (1999) *On Bereavement: The Culture of Grief*. Buckingham: Open University Press.

Weiss, RS (1975) *Marital Separation*. New York: Basic Books.

Westberg, GE (1961) *Good Grief*. Philadelphia, PA: Fortress Press.

12 Grief in an individualized society

A critical corrective to the advancement of diagnostic culture

Michael Hviid Jacobsen and Anders Petersen

Introduction

We hold it to be neither provocative nor suggestive to claim the following: it is by now a truism that we live in an individualized society in which individuals are held accountable and responsible for seeking answers to a vast array of societal challenges and problems. Although the perspectives vary slightly – and the addressed consequences of the development differ – prominent sociological scholars have pinpointed this situation for some decades now (Giddens, 1991; Beck and Beck-Gernsheim, 2002; Bauman, 2001). The overall rationale of individualization is that individuals, in several historical tempos, have become emancipated from societally sanctioned and supported types of collective life-forms and (traditional) communities in which they were previously embedded. Nowadays, instead, society is supportive of – and even demands – individuals who are responsible for creating and realizing their own lives, competences and potentials vis-a-vis institutions such as education, work and family. As Ulrich Beck and Elisabeth Beck-Gernsheim famously formulated it: "The individual is becoming the basic unit of social reproduction for the first time in history" (Beck and Beck-Gernsheim, 2002: xxii).

This does not, however, entail the complete dismantling of societally enforced norms and rules but rather the emergence of a situation in which individualization has become the structurally imposed norm that individuals have to strive for and live by. Individuals living in contemporary society cannot choose individualization; they are forced to choose it. One cannot escape individualization; it has now, for all practical intents and purposes, become a task, as Zygmunt Bauman (2000) so poignantly puts it. Perhaps we can clarify this a bit more by pointing to a fundamental concept that captures the central component of individualization – namely, autonomy. In our historical epoch of enhanced individualization, we cannot escape autonomy – rather we are forced to being autonomous. French sociologist Alain Ehrenberg explains this interconnection by claiming the following. The realization of one's personal autonomy in contemporary society has become a specific form of societal discipline (Ehrenberg, 1991). That is, individualization is an overall societal demand, formulated as an ideal that each individual ought to follow. Hence, in an individualized society, the autonomous person is heralded as the most precious

DOI: 10.4324/9781032714356-15

ideal and value that we should strive for and ultimately be successful in achieving. As this logic operates as the overarching premise of contemporary society, it also encapsulates our most intimate features and feelings in life: identity, love, sexuality and so on. We have to choose our identity – it is not chosen for us. As Anthony Giddens almost programmatically stated: "We are not what we are, but what we make of ourselves" (Giddens, 1991: 75), and we cannot avoid (trying) to make something of ourselves. The same applies in relation to love, sexuality, friendship and so on (see, e.g., Bauman, 2003).[1]

It is the contention of this chapter that one of our most principal emotions, or what has been referred to as a 'foundational human emotion' (Brinkmann, 2018) – namely, grief – is also increasingly permeated by the central tenet of individualization. As we have written elsewhere, we perceive grief as 'an emotion of absence'. That is, grief refers to the human emotion generated by the involuntary loss through death of another human being who is perceived to be of significant importance by the grieving person in question (Petersen and Jacobsen, 2018: 194). In contemporary society, these emotions are predominantly understood as 'individual' emotions that manifest themselves inside those who grieve. In that respect, grief has become – and is increasingly becoming – an individual undertaking and even a privatized pathology that we are individually responsible for and hence individually have to cope with according to specific societal standards and norms. This understanding of grief not only influences lay perceptions and personal manoeuvrings of grief but also resonates well with contemporary research into the phenomenon we call grief and with institutional practices. As we will show in this chapter, this development is partly due to an intensified psychologization and psychitrization of grief that has taken place during the last few decades, meaning that even the more obvious social dimensions of grief seem to become more and more marginalized. This causes, we argue, some serious problems. These problems have been supported, we argue, by the emergence of the diagnosis of 'prolonged grief disorder' that occurs in the diagnostic manual *ICD-11* from 2018. In the wake of addressing grief in a diagnostic language – and hence understanding the suffering of grief within the realm of medicine – not only the individualized perspective of grief is supported but risks of overdiagnosis, pharmaceuticalization and overtreatment are also immediate. Thus, we will start this chapter by addressing the increasing psychological and psychiatric colonization of grief, including the coming diagnosis of grief. In the second section, we shall focus on some of the most apparent consequences of this development. In the third section, we will argue in favour of a revitalization of some of the most significant social dimensions and contexts of grief that are – we will show – so important. We conclude this chapter by formulating new pathways and trajectories that we believe research into grief should take.

The psychological and psychiatric colonization of grief

Let us start by making one thing clear: there is not one rather but a lot of answers to the question what grief is or even to what it has been. Historically speaking, the phenomenon of grief, as Peter N. Stearns (2007) has pointed out, two is extremely dynamic and interwoven with historically changing socio-structural contexts and societal fluctuations, as well as economic, cultural and normative transformations, and it is interpreted, experienced and enacted within a plethora of religious frameworks and rituals. When it comes to academic research into grief, we often find – even within the same disciplines – discrepancies in how grief should be understood and interpreted. Hence, a uniform definition of grief is a difficult task as is also the charting of its many different faces (Jacobsen and Petersen, 2018). This is by no means odd or undesirable. Quite the contrary, we would argue. Academic vigour and 'difference of opinion' is always called for and grief need not be one-dimensionally categorized. In fact, particularly when it comes to the phenomenon of grief, English author C. S. Lewis reminds us all that perhaps we do not need a fleshed-out map but rather an unpredictable narrative when it comes to understanding it. As he poetically wrote:

> Sorrow, however, turns out to be not a state but a process. It needs not a map but a history, and if I don't stop writing that history at some quite arbitrary point, there's no reason why I should ever stop. There is something new to be chronicled every day. Grief is like a long valley, a winding valley where any bend may reveal a totally new landscape.
>
> (Lewis, 1988 [1961]: 50)

However, the logic of the map – to stay within the realm of this metaphor – has colonized the understanding of grief. This map, as we will show, is in modern society largely constructed by relying on psychological and psychiatric theories and clinical insights.

Our usage of the notion of 'colonization' is far from coincidental. We are inspired by Jürgen Habermas, who in his seminal work, *The Theory of Communicative Action*, shows how the lifeworld has been colonized by the logics and rationalities of what he refers to as the system (Habermas, 1987). According to Habermas, the lifeworld is to be perceived as the 'background' environment of practices, competences and attitudes representable in terms of people's cognitive horizons. Habermas grounds his social theory in communication and thus focuses on the lifeworld as consisting of socially and culturally sedimented linguistic meanings. The lifeworld is, shortly speaking then, the everyday lives of informal (linguistic) interactions, culturally grounded understandings and mutual accommodations. The system, on the other hand, strictly refers to mutual patterns of strategic action that only serve the interests of institutions and organizations. The main characteristics of strategic actions are, crudely speaking, that they are essentially driven by the means of money and power. The thesis Habermas defends is that the rationality of the system – under the auspice of modern society and late capitalism – forces itself upon the lifeworld, thereby colonizing it. He writes:

> When stripped of their ideological veils, the imperatives of autonomous sub-systems make their way into the lifeworld from the outside – like colonial

> masters coming into a tribal society – and force a process of assimilation upon it. The diffused perspectives of the local culture cannot be sufficiently coordinated to permit the play of the metropolis and the world market to be grasped from the periphery.
>
> (Habermas, 1987: 355)

According to Habermas, colonization is largely the same as assimilation. The social logics of the lifeworld are being replaced or pushed aside by those of the system, whereby the lifeworld fully attunes its operational (linguistic, social, cultural, etc.) modus vivendi to that of the system. Now, how can we apply this concept in relation to grief? Well, by showing how the phenomenon of grief has increasingly been colonized – in various tempos – by psychological and psychiatric understandings, we illustrate how other perspectives have lost ground. We are not claiming, however, that we are witnessing a wholesale collapse of other perspectives of grief, but rather that a significant downplaying of these has taken place. This is a development that, as we will show later, has been amplified by the emergence of the diagnosis of grief and the focus on treatment that follows in its wake.

In order to address this process of colonization in a proper manner, we have to divide the following section into two parts. While the first part begins with Sigmund Freud – and thus the psychologization of grief – the second dives into the psychiatrization of the phenomenon in question.

The colonization of grief

It all begins with Freud.

Sigmund Freud's groundbreaking essay 'Mourning and Melancholia' (1957; originally published in 1917) is rightly considered the first rigorous academic journey into the phenomenon of grief (Archer, 1999) and the "first to introduce the concept of grief into the psychological lexicon" (Granek, 2010: 49). That is not to say, of course, that prior to Freud, grief was not religiously, anthropologically or philosophically reflected upon (Walter, 1999). But Freud's systematic effort to separate mourning from melancholia, the coining of concepts such as 'grief work' and his understanding that grief should not be considered a pathological condition in need of medical treatment, is to be seen as (one of) the most important foundation upon which academic research into grief rests. Freud, so to speak, set a course for the academic study of grief – a course paved with psychological and psychoanalytical concepts – that is to be perceived as "a watershed in the history of the conceptualization of grief within the discipline and was crucial to the development of grief as a psychological kind" (Granek, 2010: 52). According to Leeat Granek, Freud not only secured a place for grief in the psychological domain but also established the foundation for identifying grief as a psychological entity as such.

Although Freud's conceptualization of grief was quickly scrutinized by other psychologists, Granek persuasively argues that the overall perspective of grief as a strictly psychological phenomenon was never really in jeopardy. In fact, its psychological status was only strengthened (Granek, 2010: 53). The reason why that is the case can be explained in the following manner: as Freud's understanding of grief was the exemplary point of departure, other researchers had to address their critique against his original conceptualization, the primary one being 'grief work'. By 'grief work' Freud expresses his conviction that the grieving person is able to (and ought to) work with, and eventually work herself out of, her grief. Ultimately, the griever should distance herself from her grief, hereby liberating herself from the person she has lost. This is not, and Freud is very clear about this, something one can do instantly. It is a process (Freud, 1957 [1917]: 243). The first part of the process is to obey the 'command of reality' – that is, convince oneself that the person lost really is dead. The next part is to severing the ties – that is, breaking the bonds – with the deceased. Only by doing so, Freud emphasizes, one is able to emancipate oneself from the grief and thus enable an unrestrained connection with oneself and the social world again. Freud formulates this in the following manner:

Why this compromise by which the command of reality is carried out piecemeal should be so extraordinarily painful is not at all easy to explain in terms of economics. It is remarkable that this painful unpleasure is taken as a matter of course by us. The fact is, however, that when the work of mourning is completed the ego becomes free and uninhibited again (Freud, 1957 [1917]: 244). Now, Freud knew that this emancipation is perhaps never fully accomplished. Although the griever should extricate time and resources to other spheres of life than those associated with the deceased, Freud is painfully aware of the fact that this is a slow and strenuous endeavour that might never come to a full stop (Granek, 2010: 52).

Freud's many heirs, epigones and successors, explicitly as well as implicitly, incorporated the central premise of the grief work hypothesis – namely, that working with grief is an individual venture that only the grieving individual can embark upon. Amongst some of the most important and influential scholars who followed in the footsteps of Freud – but also diverged significantly from his approach – we find Elisabeth Kübler-Ross (1969). In her five-stage model of grief, the individual component of grief is clearly emphasized. Kübler-Ross stipulates (1) denial and isolation, (2) anger, (3) bargaining, (4) depression and (5) acceptance as the distinct phases grievers have to deal with in order to emotionally manage loss and move on in their personal lives. The same overall logic applies to Collin Murray Parkes' (1972; 2001) theory of grieving. In a similar vein to the attachment theory of John Bowlby (1973), Parkes identified four particular phases of bereavement that people go through. These are: (1) shock or numbness, (2) yearning and pining, (3) disorganization and despair and (4) recovery. According to Parkes, grief is best understood as a process of transition of the bereaved individual – a transition that is permeated by a burdensome workload that the grieving individual has to accept in order to steer his/her way through the phases and finally reach the final destination – namely, recovery. Although William Worden's (1991) perspective on grief differs from the others – in terms of vocabulary and by formulating specific tasks people more actively have to work through instead of phases they have to go through – he still perceived these as individual tasks. More specifically, Worden suggested, there are four tasks one should accomplish in order to complete the process of grieving and hence re-establish the lost equilibrium. These are: (1) accept the reality of the loss, (2) work through the pain of grief, (3) adjust to the environment in which the deceased is missing and (4) find an enduring connection with the deceased while embarking on a new life. According to Worden, these phases need not to be approached in a linear fashion[2] and some grievers should even return to the same task many times. For that same reason, Worden acknowledged the fact that it is extremely difficult to settle on a specific timeline for the completion of the different tasks. Grief takes time, so to speak. Finally, Margaret S. Stroebe and Henk Shut's (1999) 'dual process model' of coping with bereavement is worth mentioning. As opposed to the grief work thesis – or to Worden's task-oriented theory for that matter – they focus on two particular stressors (loss and restoration oriented) and the oscillation between them in coping with grief (Stroebe and Shut, 1999: 197). Thus, they do not concentrate on the emotional management of loss but rather on the process of successfully coping with grief and how that sometimes entails avoiding some of the difficult aspects of grief. Avoidance is not, they argue, negative as such but can actually be seen as part of an extended adaptive coping strategy. Excessive avoidance, however, can be perceived as maladaptive coping and hence detrimental to a positive outcome. Moreover, their model "emphasizes the equally strenuous tasks of attending to life changes brought about by bereavement, doing new things, managing new roles and identities etc." (Kofod, 2017: 34), something which the previously mentioned perspectives did not deal with. Stroebe and Shut make clear that while adaptive coping is necessary in order to achieve restoration – what they refer to as healthy or functional grief – maladaptive coping will lead to the opposite: dysfunctional/ unhealthy grief.

It is evident that these mentioned perspectives and theories have come a long way since Freud. They have challenged some of his central doctrines and clinically shown that some of his pivotal ideas needed correction. Indeed, their perspectives have developed alternatives to the shortcomings of Freud's theory but also to each other. It is equally evident that these perspectives have not moved beyond an individualized focus on grief. The point we wish to establish is that these perspectives pay attention to, and thereby support, an individualized perspective on grief that fits nicely within the confines of an individualized society. That is, to use the vocabulary we presented in the introduction, they – as an over-arching premise – perceive grief as a hindrance to realizing one's personal autonomy, which is why the final acceptance, recovery, altering roles and identities and so on entails the reorientation of one's possibilities of realizing autonomy. Per definition, at least under the auspice of these understandings, this is an individual endeavour, a personal achievement or, in Bauman's words, a task to be performed.

What we furthermore want to direct attention to is the fact that theories of grief, within the recent decades, have maintained their individualized foci but altered the grounds on which they do it. The gist of the matter is not that the aforementioned perspectives on grief phases, tasks or processes have withered away and disappeared into oblivion. This is certainly not the case. Both researchers and clinicians working within the field of grief – but also laypeople – are often confronted with them and their specific modelling of grief. Our contention is rather that we have been witnessing a transformation of perspectives. This transformation is not to be understood as a clear-cut paradigmatic shift. In fact, it has been argued that all of the mentioned understandings have "shaped and informed the recent suggestions to conceptualize grief as a mental disorder" (Kofod, 2017: 36) and hereby, albeit indirectly and involuntarily, contributed to paving the way for the psychiatric colonization of grief.

The contemporary dominance of psychiatry

Sigmund Freud never made a direct distinction between normal and pathological grief. That is not to say, however, that he thought grief was a normal state to be in. In his account, grief departed greatly form normal undertakings of life as such. But and this is pivotal, it never occurred to him 'to regard it as a pathological condition and refer it to medical treatment' (Freud, 1957 [1917]: 252). Hence, no distinction between normal and pathological grief is needed. However, as historian of psychiatry Edward Shorter has stated, Freud is to be considered a hiatus in the overall history of psychiatry (Shorter, 1997: 145). This does not entail, though, that Freud left no mark in psychiatric thinking. He did indeed. It is to say that his psychoanalytical approach within the realm of psychiatry has been replaced by a biomedical understanding. By entitling one of the chapters in his history of psychiatry 'From Freud to Prozac' (Shorter, 1997: 288), Shorter addresses this development in a clear-cut manner. Perhaps the same is the case when it comes to grief? The complete disregard of Freud's perspective, and the increased focus on the pathological dimensions of grief, has led to a situation in which the victorious implementation of a specific form of psychiatric rationality is taking place.

It is obviously the case that this development did not happen overnight. Without claiming that it took its point of departure in 1961, when George L. Engel asked the famous question, "Is grief a Disease?" (Engel, 1961), it is nonetheless a good place to start. What Engel did in this text was to question the assumption that grief was a normal endeavour when mourning the death of a loved one. Could it be the case, Engel asked, that grief sometimes is to be perceived as a disease? His answer to that question was yes. Some grief reactions were indeed to be perceived as causing illness and hence, under certain circumstances, grief was to be perceived as a disease. Engel's stance has been interpreted as if he stated that grief per se is a disorder and that it hence should be perceived as such (see Wilkinson, 2000). In fact, Stephen Wilkinson, whom we are referring to here, uses Engel as a stepping-stone to claim that all grief (even normal grief) is to be understood as a mental disorder (Wilkinson, 2000: 289). This is, of course, a rather radical claim and something that is not commonplace in grief research. Perhaps Wilkinson is stretching his argument a bit too wide? Or perhaps he misinterprets Engel in order to substantiate his own argument. Margaret S. Stroebe seems to think so. As she has shown, Engel's text cannot be used for the purpose of pathologizing all grief. As she writes, Engel rather

> took grief as an illustrative example to explore the very nature of the concept of disease, his intention was to encourage debate about the categorization of

> disease, to urge readers to reflect on what constitutes a disease. Engels did not claim that grief is a disease.
>
> (Stroebe, 2015: 277)

What is of interest here, however, is really not whether specific interpretations of Engel do him justice or not. It is rather the fact that his article paved a significant part of the way in framing normal grief as opposed to grief that could (should?) be perceived as a disease and hence as something pathological. The premise of this discussion differentiates itself from the ones taken by the psychological theories we referred to above by ingraining pathological grief firmly within the realm of psychiatric thinking, thereby also opening the doors wide open for the biomedical approach to disease. As noted by Granek in her convincing article about the increasing psychiatrization (and pathologization) of grief, this development materialized itself in the late 1980s – something which has continued to influence a great deal (if not the majority) of grief research ever since. As she writes:

> By this point, grief theory had become decontextualized from experience and had been psychologized completely. The focus was entirely on symptoms, and the ability to measure, diagnose, and manage grief… By the early 1990s, the focus on grief was almost entirely on its dysfunctional nature.
>
> (Granek, 2010: 64)

Obviously, the intense focus on complicated grief (e.g., Shear et al., 2011), complicated grief disorder (e.g., Horowitz, 2005) and disordered grief (e.g., Prigerson and Maciejewski, 2017) that has settled in grief research over the last couple of decades supports Granek's overall claim. Particularly, the implementation of the grief diagnosis Prolonged Grief Disorder in the *ICD-11* is a manifestation of the power of psychiatry when it comes to understanding grief as a (potential) pathological disorder. By implementing grief in this diagnostic manual, there is no doubt about the fact that this perspective on grief got its most vital stamp of approval. The description of Prolonged Grief Disorder in the *ICD-11* manual is as follows:

> Prolonged grief disorder is a disturbance in which, following the death of a partner, parent, child, or other person close to the bereaved, there is persistent and pervasive grief response characterized by longing for the deceased or persistent preoccupation with the deceased accompanied by intense emotional pain (e.g. sadness, guilt, anger, denial, blame, difficulty accepting the death, feeling one has lost a part of one's self, an inability to experience positive mood, emotional numbness, difficulty in engaging with social or other activities). The grief response has persisted for an atypically long period of time following the loss (more than 6 months at a minimum) and clearly exceeds expected social, cultural or religious norms for the individual's culture and context. Grief reactions that have persisted for longer periods that are within a normative period of grieving given the person's cultural and religious context are viewed as normal bereavement responses and are

> not assigned a diagnosis. The disturbance causes significant impairment in personal, family, social, educational, occupational or other important areas of functioning.
>
> (*ICD-11*, 2018)

It is beyond the scope of this chapter to deal more specifically with the entire content of the diagnosis – all its symptoms, the specific criteria and so on – but we will shortly dwell on the most important arguments of why the diagnosis is perceived to be justifiable. One of the recurring arguments in favour of the diagnosis is that it is the only valid way of distinguishing pathological grief from PTSD, anxiety and depression (e.g., Shear et al., 2011). The main point in this argument is that too many people for too long have received a diagnosis of PTSD, anxiety disorder or especially depression when they in fact were suffering from complicated grief. The mix up of these types of suffering is understandable. The various symptoms of these diseases are quite similar. The treatment, on the contrary, is said to be very different. Lately, a great deal of effort has been put into establishing psychological treatment, where Katherine M. Shear's programme, Complicated Grief Treatment – which is scaffolded around Bowlby's (1973) attachment theory, which we referred to earlier – is amongst the most well-known and recognized (Shear, 2010). As the name indicates, this treatment programme is concerned with targeting 'grief-specific' treatment to those who suffer in a debilitating way from their loss. The programme does not cover other mental disorders, and neither should it. The focus is solely on grief because, as the argument goes, the "suffering of bereaved people often confuses clinicians" (Shear, 2010: 10). This confusion is first and foremost detrimental to the bereaved because it hinders the right treatment of their anguish, often by placing them in the same category as those who are depressed. Second, as Shear states, it is inhumane not to treat people who suffer from their loss (Shear, 2010: 10), when we in fact have the right tools to do so. So, offering the right and effective kind of treatment is not only the right thing to do practically speaking but also the only moral right thing to do. In that respect, Shear's treatment programme reminds us of a very important thing that describes the realm of psychiatry – namely, that it is "a unique medical domain that, unlike other branches of medicine, is necessarily confronted with moral issues. Indeed, without confronting these issues it would never be able to treat those forms of suffering that are themselves moral" (Ehrenberg, 1998; 2010: 23). Suffering from grief is indeed a moral concern as such. Another thing is the severity of the suffering. In order to objectify the scale of the suffering, one relies on the successful endeavour of clearly differentiating between 'normal grief' and 'pathological grief'. In fact, the possibility of this demarcation is another argument in favour of the diagnosis.

Several grief researchers – and practitioners for that matter – conceive the diagnosis as the most concise sharpening tool; it enables the carving out of this distinction (e.g., Prigerson et al., 2009). But what qualifies as 'normal grief' then? In fact, there is no easy way to describe what normal grief consists of because it varies immensely. It is dependent on a vast array of personal, theoretical, cultural and societal dimensions. Some grief researchers, in order to reduce the complexities of normal grief, use vignettes. One of those who does so is Shear, who, together with quite a few colleagues, has used this method to describe what 'normal grief' is. In such a vignette they write a story about Patricia, who lost her husband, Paul, at the age of 50. At the beginning, Patricia was devastated, felt an intense yearning and as if her mind was in a fog that she could not control. Her emotions were running wild; she cried a lot and felt unable to function in her life. But, after seeing a grief counsellor, things started to get better. The counsellor helped, as they explain, Patricia to understand

> that her symptoms were normal… After a few months, Patricia noticed that there were hours, then days, were the fog lifted. She started to laugh again. She accepted an invitation to go out with friends even though she did not really want to, and she had a good time. A vision of her life without Paul began to emerge and the intensity of yearning for him subsided.
>
> (Shear et al., 2011: 113)

Three years after the death of her husband, so the vignette ends, Patricia meets another man whom she ends up marrying a couple of years later. Paul is still on her mind, but she has managed to continue her life in a fruitful manner without him.

Now, prior to this vignette, Shear and her co-authors have thoroughly described the research and evidence that in their perspective legitimizes a grief diagnosis, and hence the drawing of a distinction between 'normal grief' and 'pathological grief'. Thus, the vignette is a testimony to all that which is not considered pathological grief and thereby does not have the relevant criteria of a disorder. As we saw in the description of prolonged grief disorder, Patricia's story accounts for the exact opposite of the symptoms and the severity of the grief eligible to the label of pathological. This line of research, however, has been scrutinized. Jerome Wakefield, one of the foremost critiques of the label of pathological grief, and hence of implementing prolonged grief disorder in the *ICD-11*, states very clearly that "several arguments presented to support the claim that intense grief lasting 6–12 months is more pathological, rather than a severe normal variant" (Wakefield, 2013: 111) are conceptually flawed and do not hold water in respect to the testing of the research evidence. He thus states that the diagnostic proposals "are thus scientifically unwarranted" (Wakefield, 2013: 111). In his perspective, the scientific requirements for the diagnosis of grief are simply not satisfactorily met and thus, no clear-cut distinction between normal and pathological grief can be instated. But it has been, as we have already mentioned above, and this leads us to the third argument in favour of the diagnosis – namely, what one might call the 'argument-by-numbers'.

When taking the diagnostic criteria into consideration, it is often estimated that somewhere between 7% and 10% of grievers are in fact suffering from complicated grief or prolonged grief disorder (Kersting et al., 2011; Lundorff et al., 2017). Some researchers even suggest that as many as 12% of all bereaved individuals meet the criteria of suffering from prolonged grief disorder (Maciejewski and Prigerson, 2017). Once a part of this statistic, it goes without saying that treatment is needed.

And then we return to the moral issue of psychiatric disorders again: it would be morally wrong not to categorize them rightfully and thereby enable them to be offered the right kind of treatment, the arguments go. By the power of the knowledge that as many as up to 10% of grievers suffer – and hence have the symptoms categorizing the diagnosis – follows a moral obligation to react.

It is, to a large degree, by the force of the arguments presented here that we have witnessed the increasing psychiatrization of grief. For us, it is not a question of the validity of these arguments in themselves – albeit they have been questioned and scrutinized – but it is more the significant impact of this development that is of interest. In that respect, we find it obvious that the psychiatrization of grief, in which the diagnosis can be called the crown jewel of the development, has strengthened the individualization of grief. By making grief into a diagnostic and potentially pathological category, psychiatry has expanded its territory and hence its area of expertise, a significant narrowing of the phenomenon of grief has simultaneously taken place. That is, a diagnosed grief can only be located inside the head (and to a certain extent the body) of the grieving person. It is he/ she who is being labelled mentally ill when receiving the diagnosis. It is hence also he/she who has to take care of the pathological grief, which is where the specific grief treatment comes into the picture. It is his/her functionality that is at stake when diagnosed. All the arrows of grief thereby point in the direction of the person in grief, thereby potentially downplaying the multitude of social dimensions of grief and largely neglecting the negative aspects of this development.

Some consequences of this development

What we have shown in the previous sections of this chapter is the latest colonization of grief that the profession of psychiatry has brought about. Grief now belongs to a long list of psychiatric phenomena that have become so proliferated in contemporary society – more and more people are being diagnosed with mental disorders – that some commentators have even begun to speak of a necessary softening of the way in which we understand the distinction between normal and pathological. In his latest book, *Our Psychiatric Future*, British sociologist Nicholas Rose plays with words in the title. The psychiatric future is not in the future – the future is already here. One way of addressing this fact is by stating that "when it comes to the scope of psychiatry today, can we still hold the idea that in some fundamental way, to be diagnosed with a mental disorder is to be classified 'pathological'?" (Rose, 2018: 8). His answer to this question is no, and that this labelling is way too pejorative when it comes to diagnoses of depression, anxiety, panic disorders and the like. So many people suffer from these diseases that it has become normal to do so, the argument goes. His idea is thus that we should alter the meaning of normality (and pathological) and think of it as a performative term that is best understood in its uses and in relation to its consequences. If we pause for a minute and begin to think of the diagnosis of grief in this manner, one might say that grief belongs to the same group of sufferings that Rose mentions and hence cannot be considered pathological, especially not if as many as up to 10% of grievers have sufficient symptoms to meet the diagnostic criteria. In this respect, those diagnosed with prolonged grief disorder should not be perceived as pathological.

Although Rose's argumentation is somewhat convincing – and potentially very influential – it nevertheless leaves a great deal of confusion when it comes to grief. First of all, one of the main intentions of the diagnosis is – as we have mentioned – precisely to distinguish between normal and pathological grief in a very substantive way. The protagonists of the diagnosis make this claim again and again: normal grief is not in need of treatment; pathological grief is. Hence, a clear-cut distinction is needed. But what if that distinction is blurred by stating that it is normal to suffer from pathological grief? What is normal grief then? Is normal grief then also pathological because the 'condition' contains distress, suffering, impairment, pain and so on, and hence meets all the necessary criteria of a disorder, as Wilkinson seem to suggest (Wilkinson, 2000)? A relativization of normal grief, which seems to be the logical consequence of Rose's argumentation, causes problems.

The same applies to the 'medicalization', to use Peter Conrad's (2007) influential term, of the phenomenon in question. Conrad's analysis of the overall medicalization of society, in which he clearly stipulates how normal human distress, suffering and personal troubles are increasingly being transformed into medicalized objects and mental disorders, is obviously applicable when it comes to grief. And so it has been by Julia Bandini (2015). In her analysis, three potential consequences of the medicalization of grief stand out. First, she directs attention to the potential for overdiagnosis and overtreatment. In some respects, one could make the bold claim that the mere fact that the diagnosis is being introduced will lead to overdiagnosis. A slightly less bold statement is that overdiagnosis will occur because the definition of grief as a disease has been broadened so much that people who just meet the criteria will be given the diagnosis and the offered treatment. Of course, this could potentially open an avenue of overtreatment. Second, Bandini addresses the potential for expanded market shares for pharmaceutical companies. Whereas Bandini is cautious in her conclusions, Granek is more straightforward in her analysis of the medicalization of grief and the possibilities of pharmaceutical intervention. According to her, there is no doubt about the fact that the usage of antidepressant medication in the treatment of complicated grief is widespread already and that the future will witness even more medicinal treatment (Granek, 2016: 117). This reminds us of John Abraham's (2010) analysis, in which he discusses the possibilities of a regular pharmaceuticalization of society. This entails, according to him, a situation in which an expansion of treatment with pharmaceuticals denotes how society perceives that as the normal way of treating almost any kind of human suffering. Following the line of this argument: Why not a specific pill for grief? Third, Bandini mentions a loss of traditional and cultural methods of adapting to the loss of a loved one (Bandini, 2015: 351). Perhaps Nancy Berns' (2011) analysis is of help here. The contemporary focus on achieving closure (which of course is a myth) as a way to end the painfulness of grief bypasses the often lengthy and 'difficult' methods of adopting to the loss that are offered by tradition and community or that are ingrained in longstanding cultural practices. Or we might turn our attention to Danish psychologist Svend Brinkmann, who has argued that this development is not only the case in relation to the suffering of grief. It is also shown in the languages we use to articulate issues of human suffering in general. In his view, alternative understandings of human suffering "have been somewhat depreciated by the status of the diagnostic language" (Brinkmann, 2016: 52). Other languages – social, existential, political and so on – have not evaporated from our vocabulary. They have, however, less status today than the diagnostic ditto when it comes to articulating – and thus to organizing – our suffering. Would it be that difficult to imagine that the same thing will happen when it comes to grief (for more on this, see Petersen and Jacobsen, 2018)?

Addressing the social dimensions of grief in an individualized society

It should be rather obvious by now that the psychiatric colonization of grief has led to an increasing individualization of the phenomenon and to a serious of (potential) consequences that deeply influences the ways in which we handle grief in contemporary society. In that respect, the installing of the grief diagnosis signifies a landmark. This development is, at the same time, easily comprehended and odd. The former, because this development fits so nicely with the overall tendencies of individualization in contemporary society as such. The latter, because the social dimensions of grief are so obvious and important that any element of their neglect seems almost outrageous (see Vera, 2003). After all, as Nina R. Jakoby so poignantly has stated, grief is a social emotion (Jakoby, 2012). It is so because our emotions of grief are socially shared, shaped (reshaped), distributed and sanctioned. Moreover, only one person seldom grieves the absence of a significant other. Most often, the reality and experience of loss are shared with others who also mourn the loss. As summarized by Liz Stanley and Sue Wise: "People respond to dying and death, not as decorticated individualized nomads, but as members of networks of interpersonal relationships" (Stanley and Wise, 2011: 960). In this way, grief is indeed an interpersonal and relational phenomenon existing between the dead and the bereaved as well as among the bereaved. Besides this, grief is deeply interwoven in historically changing socio-structural contexts, rules and norms and (also) takes place – and changes form, content and structure – in actual face-to-face interactions with other people in everyday life situations (Jacobsen and Petersen, 2018).

Of course, it is beyond the scope of this chapter to deal exhaustively with all the many different social dimensions of grief that are in danger of being trivialized if we continue to follow this individualized path. We will, thus, here merely pick out three aspects in order to support and highlight our argumentation. The first concerns the component of identity-formation. Phenomenologist Thomas Fuchs, in a recent article, stated the following:

> This expansion and mutual overlaps of selves may be regarded as the most essential presupposition of grief. For it means that the other is present for me both as other, as the real person, and as the 'other-of-myself', as part of my self experience. This renders me totally vulnerable, for in losing the

> other, I lose 'half of my self', as it were – the potentialities of experience and self-realization that were bound to the other, and the part of my self and identity that were represented by him.
>
> (Fuchs, 2017: 50)

We are, also in grief, interconnected with others. When a significant person in our lives dies, this alters our sensation of self and hence the continuation of our identity-formation. Or, as Fuchs writes – echoing George Herbert Mead's (1934) social-psychological truism – parts of our identity are necessarily bound to and dependent on (the recognition of) the significant others. In grief, then, one not only mourns the other as a specific entity – father, friend, husband and so on but also grieves the loss of the part of the other that was intrinsically connected to one's own further realization in life. In grief, one is thus afflicted by the absence here and now and the absence of some parts of one's future. That goes, of course, for others as well. The loss of future potentialities that were connected with the deceased is a loss most commonly felt by more than just one individual person. In that sense, the deceased has an impact on a wide variety of identities and self-realizations. On a more fundamental level, this implies that identity-formation hardly can be reduced to an individualized endeavour. We cannot just make ourselves up as we wish. As human beings, we are entangled in a web of connections with others that influences and in significant ways steers our formation of identity. Not controlling it but having important impacts on it. In grief, this becomes blatantly obvious.

The second social dimension we wish to direct the attention to is the social stratification of grief. As German-British sociologist Norbert Elias stated many years ago, death is a problem of the living (Elias, 2001 [1983]). Elias is utterly correct, but he also knew that the dead came in many guises. That is, while living, the dead held various social positions that in many ways were transgressed into the way in which people died and into how people were grieved afterwards. All lives matter, but some lives matter more and are more grieveable one could say. How does that show? Well, as many have witnessed when visiting graveyards across the globe, the political, social and economic elite as well as what we nowadays call 'celebrities' have been honoured with more pompous tombstones, mausoleums and luxurious gravesites than the 'common man'. It is only rarely that those at the lower end of the social scale – those with less social status and power – have been offered the same gesture, both due to economic circumstances and because of the fact that their lives were not perceived to be as valuable to the common public or society as such. Hence, in the greater scheme of things, some lives have historically been deemed – in quite an obvious way – to be more grieveable than others. In contemporary society this element is visible in numerous ways. Just think about the millions of immigrants, who, in a desperate attempt to seek living conditions that are worthy of human beings, drown while crossing the Mediterranean in dilapidated boats. Or what about the millions of people on the African continent who die each year from AIDS or other diseases that are in fact treatable? The lack of public grief or mourning over these millions of people is more than thought-provoking, especially when contemplating who else is mourned in the public sphere. In order to describe what it is one grieves about and who is worthy of grief, American philosopher and sociologist Judith Butler (2016) has coined the term 'grievability'. In her account of the phenomenon, what becomes so obvious is the fact that it is the societally differentiated valuation of life that decides what we mourn about and who is worthy of grieving. Some lives are simply so quickly forgotten – or dumped on the historic scrapheap to rot – that there is no incitement to mourn them. Here, however, we need not forget that the social stratification of whom we mourn relates not only to economy and status but also to gender, geography, cause of death etc., in such a way that we, as a society, almost automatically mourn some much more than others (see also Morse, 2018).

As the social stratification of grief is related to whom we mourn, it is also linked to how we grieve. Although this aspect has not captured a lot of attention within grief research (Allen, 2007), it nevertheless deserves more academic interest. Why? Because although we (at least in the Western hemisphere) have witnessed the dismantling of many status hierarchies, the existence of different social classes is still evident and different classes tend to grieve differently. British historian Julie-Marie Strange (2002; 2005) has continuously documented how the care of the dead, the character of the tombstones (private vs. public graves), testaments and so on bear witness to a significant social stratification between the poor and those who were prosperous in the 18th century. What is more, the same differentiation can be made in relation to grief. Whereas the upper classes had the time, social space and economy to mourn their dead, the poor had to develop a much more pragmatic culture of grief that balanced their need to commemorate the deceased and take care of the family's economy at the same time. The simple equation is: if grief keeps you away from work for too long, you don't get food on the table (see also Vincent, 1980). The relevant question to ask is whether this is significantly different in contemporary society, not least if we look at it on a global scale.

The third and final social dimension we wish to address here is the stigmatization of grief. Where the social stratification of grief is mainly concerned with status and economy, the stigmatization of grief concerns the acceptability, appropriateness and normative legitimacy of grieving the death of a particular person or even the question of whom is 'allowed' to grieve. The concept of 'stigmatized grief' is indebted to Canadian sociologist Erving Goffman's work on stigma (Goffman, 1963). In his work, the concept revolves around how certain identities or actions result in discrediting identities or stigmatization of actions due to their deviance from prevailing societal norms. More specifically, Goffman outlined three types of stigma that were related to behaviour, looks/appearance or affiliation with specific societal groups. It is American gerontologist Kenneth J. Doka (1989) who – by coining the term 'disenfranchised grief' – has most poignantly stipulated the connection between stigma and grief. More specifically Doka defines the concept in the following manner:

> The concept of disenfranchised grief recognizes that societies have sets of norms – in effect 'grieving rules' – that attempt to specify who, when, where, how, how long, and for whom people should grieve. These grieving rules

> may be codified as personal policies... Such policies reflect the fact that each society defines who has a legitimate right to grieve, and these rights correspond to relationships, primarily familial, that are socially recognised and sanctioned.
>
> (Doka, 1999: 37)

An important empirical basis, that Doka based his concept of 'disenfranchised grief' on, was the many AIDS-related deaths in the United States in the 1980s. These were, to a large extent, surrounded by widespread cultural homophobia, a fear of getting HIV/AIDS and thus a considerable stigma that was often specifically targeted at homosexuals – something that has been portrayed by Matthew McConaughey in the 2013 movie by Jean-Marc Vallée, Dallas Buyers Club. In the movie, McConaughey's real-life character, Ron Woodroof, is not only heavily stigmatized for getting AIDS by his friends and relatives (who think it is a 'gay disease') but also for helping – and mourning – the people who are dying from AIDS. The legitimacy of mourning the people who by the majority of the population were to blame for their own misfortune due to their 'deviance' was put into question, scrutinized, socially sanctioned and even violently opposed. The grief of 'such' persons is, in itself, deviant and must therefore be combatted. Where do we find disenfranchised grief in contemporary society? Well, there are plenty of examples. One could be the following from our own local community: in 2006, an 18-year-old girl who attended high school in the Northern part of Denmark was brutally killed by her ex-boyfriend at a school dance. Just after the murder, the 23-year-old young man committed suicide. In the Danish media coverage of the events, the tragic loss of the 18-year-old girl was publicly and spontaneously mourned. The grief of her family members was displayed. But there was no mentioning of the grief that affected the parents, friends and relatives of the 23-year-old man. Could this be because the grieving of such a murderer was perceived to be illegitimate? Was it inappropriate to mourn the loss of a brutal killer? Without denigrating the emotional distress of the family of the girl who was killed, one can only speculate about how it must have felt for those who mourned this young man!

Now, one might question whether grief is either disenfranchised or enfranchised, and also problematize that grief 'works' in these binary codes. It nevertheless seems obvious that every society has certain specific "grief hierarchies" that order which kinds of grief are more legitimate than others (Robson and Walter, 2012). These hierarchies are in no way static. They are attuned to the normative structure and development in society, and hence to political, social, cultural and economic currents that alter the overall texture of society.

Conclusion

In this chapter, we have introduced a line of thought that shows not only how grief has become increasingly colonized by psychological and psychiatric thinking but also a line of thought that criticizes this development. Our aim has not been to go about this in any methodically stringent way, but rather to address some of the social dimensions of grief that are at risk of being trivialized – or be less in focus – in the wake of this development. The individualization of grief is, as we have intended to show, by no means independent of significant currents in contemporary society. That is, we are not able to understand the individualization of grief only by addressing the psychological or psychiatric vernaculars, perspectives and theories that have shaped grief historically. A considerable part of the analysis has to take the societal development into consideration that supports this development. The (continuous) adjustment to an individualized identification with grief is deeply embedded in prevailing norms of continuing individualization – and hence autonomous self-realization – as the overarching societal ideal. Perhaps then, we can highlight this – in a rather provocative manner – by stating that grief, in contemporary society, is best understood as an all-out assault on our happiness (Ariès, 1974: 94) because grief entails suffering that puts an end to the ongoing realization of one's personal autonomy. Suffering and happy self-realization do not go well hand-in-hand. Therefore, we need to eliminate the suffering as soon as possible by diagnosing and treating its source(s). In order to do that, we need a conceptualization – an ordering – of grief that matches this perspective. In that respect, the diagnosis of complicated or prolonged grief fits like a glove. However, one of our main reservations about the diagnosis is precisely that this ordering runs the risk of neglecting the more obvious social aspects of grief. Our contention is thus that a sociology of sorrow or grief should address these dimensions that we have touched upon here even more, but also that it needs to investigate the wide variety of crucial social dimensions of grief that we have not had the opportunity to focus on in this chapter: the social disciplining of grief, the socially supported and sanctioned scripts of grief, the social struggle for just the right to grieve – just to mention some areas that we believe are in need of thorough sociological investigation.

Notes

1 We are well aware of the fact that this is not the case across nations or continents. Our claims, broadly speaking, cover societies primarily within the Western hemisphere.
2 The same is true with Elisabeth Kübler-Ross's model.

References

Abraham, J (2010) Pharmaceuticalization of Society in Context: Theoretical, Empirical and Health Dimensions. *Sociology*, 44 (4): 603–622.

Allen, C (2007) The Poverty of Death: Social Class, Urban Deprivation and the Criminological Consequences of the Sequestration of Death. *Mortality*, 12 (1): 79–93.

Archer, J (1999) *The Nature of Grief: The Evolution and Psychology Reactions to Loss*. London: Routledge.

Ariès, P (1974) *Western Attitudes Toward Death from the Middle Ages to the Present*. Baltimore, MD: Johns Hopkins University Press.

Bandini, J (2015) The Medicalization of Bereavement: (Ab)normal Grief in the DSM-5. *Death Studies*, 39 (6): 347–352.

Bauman, Z (2000) *Liquid Modernity*. Cambridge: Polity Press.

Bauman, Z (2001) *The Individualized Society*. Cambridge: Polity Press.

Bauman, Z (2003) *Liquid Love*. Cambridge: Polity Press.

Beck, U and Beck-Gernsheim, E (2002) *Individualisation*. London: Sage Publications.

Berns, N (2011) *Closure: The Rush to End Grief and What It Costs Us*. Philadelphia, PA: Temple University Press.

Bowlby, J (1973) *Attachment and Loss: Separation, Anxiety and Anger* (Volume II). London: Hogarth Press.

Brinkmann, S (2016) *Diagnostic Cultures: A Cultural Approach to the Pathologization of Modern Life*. London: Routledge.

Brinkmann, S (2018) The Grieving Animal: Grief as a Foundational Emotion. *Theory & Psychology*, 2: 193–207.

Butler, J (2016) *Frames of War: When is Life Grieveable*? London: Verso.

Conrad, P (2007) *The Medicalization of Society*. Baltimore: Johns Hopkins University Press.

Doka, KJ (1989) *Disenfranchised Grief: Recognizing Hidden Sorrow*. Lexington, MA: Lexington Books/D. C. Heath & Co.

Doka, KJ (1999) Disenfranchised Grief. *Bereavement Care*, 18 (3): 37–39.

Ehrenberg, A (1991) *Le Culte de la Performance*. Paris: Hachette-Pluriel.

Ehrenberg, A (2010 [1998]) *The Weariness of the Self*. Montreal: McGill-Queen's University Press.

Elias, N (2001 [1983]) *The Loneliness of the Dying*. New York: Continuum.

Engel, GL (1961): 'Is Grief a Disease?' – A Challenge for Medical Research. *Psychosomatic Medicine*, 23 (1): 18–22.

Freud, S (1957 [1917]) Mourning and Melancholia. In: Strachey, J (ed.) *The Standard Edition of the Complete Psychological Works of Sigmund Freud* (Volume XIV), 237–258. London: Hogarth Press.

Fuchs, Th (2017) Presence in Absence: The Ambiguous Phenomenology of Grief. *Phenomenology and the Cognitive Sciences*, 17: 43–63.

Giddens, A (1991) *Modernity and Self-Identity: Self and Society in the Late Modern Age*. Cambridge: Polity Press.

Goffman, E (1963) *Stigma: Notes on the Management of Spoiled Identity*. Chicago, IL: Aldine.

Granek, L (2010) Grief as Pathology: The Evolution of Grief Theory in Psychology from Freud to the Present. *History of Psychology*, 13 (1): 46–73.

Granek, L (2016) Medicalizing Grief. In: Harris, DL and Bordere, TC (eds) *Handbook of Social Justice in Loss and Grief: Exploring Diversity, Equity and* Inclusion, 111–124. London: Routledge.

Habermas, J (1987) *Theory of Communicative Action, Volume One: Reason and the Rationalization of Society*. Boston, MA: Beacon Press.

Horowitz, M (2005) Mediating on Complicated Grief as a Diagnosis. *Omega*, 52 (1): 87–89.

ICD-11 (2018) Prolonged Grief Disorder. Available online at: https://icd.who.int/browse/2024-01/mms/en#1183832314.

Jacobsen, MH and Petersen, A (2018) Sorgens socialitet – en sociologisk kommentar til psykologiseringen og medikaliseringen af menneskelige følelser. *Psyke & Logos*, 39 (1): 55–73.

Jakoby, NR (2012) Grief as a Social Emotion: Theoretical Perspectives. *Death Studies*, 36 (8): 679–711.

Kersting, A et al. (2011) Prevalence of Complicated Grief in a Representative Population-Based Sample. *Journal of Affective Disorders*, 131: 339–343.

Kofod, EH (2017) *Parental Grief After Infant Loss: Grief as a Normative Practice*. PhD thesis in Psychology. Aalborg: Aalborg University.

Kübler-Ross, E (1969) *On Death and Dying*. London: Routledge.

Lewis, CS (1988 [1961]) *A Grief Observed*. New York: Walker & Company.

Lundorff, M et al. (2017) Prevalence of Prolonged Grief Disorder in Adult Bereavement: A Systematic Review and Meta-Analysis. *Journal of Affective Disorders*, 212: 138–149.

Maciejewski, PK and Prigerson, HG (2017) Prolonged, but not Complicated, Grief is a Mental Disorder. *The British Journal of Psychiatry*, 211: 1–2.

Mead, GH (1934) *Mind, Self, and Society*. Chicago, IL: University of Chicago Press.

Morse, T (2018) The Construction of Grievable Death: Toward an Analytical Framework for the Study of Mediatized Death. *European Journal of Cultural Studies*, 21 (2): 242–258.

Parkes, CM (2001 [1972]) *Bereavement: Studies of Grief in Adult Life* (3rd Edition). London: Routledge.

Petersen, A and Jacobsen, MH (2018) Grief – The Painfulness of Permanent Human Absence. In: Hviid Jacobsen, M (ed.) *Emotions, Everyday Life and Sociology*, 191–208. London: Routledge.

Prigerson, HG and Maciejewski, PK (2017) Rebuilding Consensus on Valid Criteria for Disordered Grief. *JAMA Psychiatry*, 74 (5): 435–436.

Prigerson, HG, Horowitz, MJ, Jacobs, S C, Parkes, CM, Aslan, M, Goodkin, K and Maciejewski, PK (2009) Prolonged Grief Disorder: Psychometric Validation for Criteria Proposed for DSM-V and *ICD-11*. *PLoS Med*, 6 (8): 1–12.

Robson, P and Walter, T (2012) Hierarchies of Loss: A Critique of Disenfranchised Grief. *Omega*, 66 (2): 97–119.

Rose, N (2018) *The Future of Psychiatry*. Cambridge: Polity Press.

Shear, KM (2010) Complicated Grief Treatment: The Theory, Practice and Outcomes. *Bereave Care*, 29 (3): 10–14.

Shear, M, Simon, N, Wall, M, Zisook, S, Neimeyer, R, Duan, N and Keshaviah, A (2011) Complicated Grief and Related Bereavement Issues for DSM-5. *Depression and Anxiety*, 28: 103–117.

Shorter, E (1997) *A History of Psychiatry: From the Era of the Asylum to the Age of Prozac*. New York: John Wiley and Sons.

Stanley, L and Wise, S (2011) The Domestication of Death: The Sequestration Thesis and Domestic Figurations. *Sociology*, 45 (6): 947–962.

Stearns, PN (2007) *Revolutions in Sorrow: The American Experience of Death in a Global Perspective*. Boulder, CO: Paradigm Publishers.

Strange, JM (2002) She Cried Very Little: Death, Grief and Mourning in Working-Class Culture, c. 1880–1914. *Social History*, 27 (2): 143–161.

Strange, JM (2005) *Death, Grief and Poverty in Britain, 1870–1914*. Cambridge: Cambridge University Press.

Stroebe, MS (2015): 'Is Grief a Disease?' Why Engel Posed the Question. *Omega*, 71 (3): 272–279.

Stroebe, MS and Schut, H (1999) The Dual Process Model of Coping with Bereavement: Rational and Description. *Death Studies*, 23 (3): 197–224.

Vera, MI (2003) Social Dimensions of Grief. In: Bryant, CD (ed.) *Handbook of Death and Dying* (Volume 2), 838–846. Thousand Oaks, CA: Sage Publications.

Vincent, D (1980) Love and Death and the Nineteenth Century Working-Class. *Social History*, 5 (2): 223–247.

Wakefield, J (2013): Is Complicated/Prolonged Grief a Disorder? – Why the Proposal to Add a Category of Complicated Grief Disorder to the DSM-5 Is Conceptually and Empirically

Unsound. In: Stroebe, MS, Schut, H and Van den Bout, J (eds) *Complicated Grief: Scientific Foundations for Health Care Professionals*, 99–114. London: Routledge.
Walter, T (1999) *On Bereavement: The Culture of Grief*. Buckingham: Open University Press.
Wilkinson, S (2000) Is 'Normal Grief' a Mental Disorder? *The Philosophical Quarterly*, 50: 289–304.
Worden, WJ (1991) *Grief Counselling and Grief Therapy: A Handbook for the Mental Health Practitioner* (2nd Edition). London: Routledge.

13 Outro

Working with Anders Petersen – a dialogue with Michael Hviid Jacobsen, Søren Christian Krogh and Carmen Kuhling

Bert van den Bergh, Sabine Flick, Kieran Keohane and Domonkos Sik

Sabine

To start with: when you think of Anders as an academic researcher, when you think of him as your colleague, what comes first to your mind?

Michael

As a colleague and a collaborator, I have only very few times seen him angry or infuriated or in a negative mood. Every morning when he came to our building, he was almost always in a very good and happy mood, unless he had heard something on the radio that really made him angry, it could be something about the climate, it could be something about the Danish Government and cutbacks to the educational system, or something like that. But if there had been no bad news, he was always in a good mood when he showed up and then we always had to start Monday morning by talking about the weekend's football results and after that we turned to sociology.

Apart from that, I would say that Anders as a colleague and collaborator was a very generous person, always willing to help me and others; never saying no to tasks or assignments. Always had the time to listen to students whenever they wanted to talk to him. Always being willing to go that extra mile when no one else wanted to take on an assignment and everyone else looked out the window or looked down under the table, Anders would say, OK, I'll do it, or I will start. So, in that way, generous with his time and with his ideas.

Carmen

I didn't work as closely in the same kind of capacity as the rest of you, but I really enjoyed the time I spent with Anders when he'd come to Ireland for his various projects, and one thing I really liked about him, one of the many things, is his capacity to deal with contradiction or paradox. As you know, Anders has written so much on evaluation culture and the demand for flexibility and self-actualization in neoliberal societies, but I invited Anders to be on a panel to evaluate my department, and that

DOI: 10.4324/9781032714356-16

must have been a poisoned chalice for Anders in some ways! But the grace with which Anders handled the contradictions required by that role was really amazing. As well as performing the professional role of an objective evaluator, at the same time, Anders was able to be – as well as critical – respectful and generous to us, clear and focussed on getting the job done, and collaborative and engaging with the other international reviewers. Anders did a really lovely job of traversing the various contradictions that are involved in occupying those various subject positions and wearing those different hats. And afterwards, Anders was able to debrief with us and talk reflexively and humorously about the paradox of having to perform roles in the very capacities that he criticizes so robustly and so accurately. I thought it was a really lovely way of showing how he could synthesize the academic and the personal – being kind and generous yet at the same time being critical and efficient, and that's a really difficult balance to find!

Søren

Most of my relationship to Anders as a colleague was with him as my PhD supervisor. And I think he was very aware of the well-being of his PhD students. I know that other PhD students would agree that he was really looking out for each of his PhD students, and I think that's a really nice quality.

Bert

Thinking about his style of writing: sometimes there are these terms in his texts, for instance he writes somewhere, finishing a chapter, 'Perhaps!', with an exclamation mark. And, writing about the individualization of grief as something that 'seems almost outrageous'. Once I typified his style as modestly furious. There is a lot of passion in his writing and at the same time he is so careful. And so, there is so much openness. Would you say this is typically Anders, or is it also maybe something Danish?

Søren

I think it's not necessarily a Danish thing, it's more of an Anders thing. It has a lot to do with Anders' personal writing style, but also with the criticalness and the sort of ways in the field that he is involved in within sociology.

Michael

I certainly do agree with the observation that Anders would often end a text, also in collaboration with me and others, with question marks. And when Anders passed away, Søren and me and another colleague, we would take over most of his teaching. And when I went through his PowerPoint presentations, the same pattern appeared. Many of Anders's PowerPoints would contain information of a theoretical or conceptual nature, but they would always have quite a few lines in which Anders is asking the students about their opinion or their experience. So, there were many sentences that had a question mark afterwards, and I think with my knowledge of Anders that it had to do with his conviction – it's a bit like the Oracle in Delphi – 'think for yourself'. Anders was not someone who was in the business of persuading other people or telling them what to think, but he wanted to raise their level of reflection, by pointing exactly, as Carmen said, to many of the ambivalences and contradictions and paradoxes and dilemmas of modern life. And he didn't want to provide the answer. I think maybe also because Anders didn't have the answer. I mean, he remained curious until the end.

I've never seen Anders say anything for certain. He was not a positivist. So definitely I don't think it's a Danish thing. There are many, many Danish scholars who would do the contrary, but Anders was a very open-minded person who wanted his students and listeners in general to think for themselves. Hopefully based on the knowledge he provided.

Søren

He did the same thing in our book on achievement culture in schools. We have this concept – *præstationsfrigørelse* – it means something like 'emancipation through achievement'. Our idea is that if we broaden our view on what a valid achievement looks like, then achievement in itself can be very liberating. In the book, we ask questions about how we could widen our perception and evaluation of achievements. And then he writes things like: Could the presentation look like this, or could the science experiment be done in that way? So, presenting a lot of questions to schoolteachers.

Sabine

When I remember Anders, it was that he was always very into public debate. And I'm not working in Denmark, so I could never really tell in what sorts of debates he was intervening or what he actually was always pointing the finger at, but he was pretty much engaged. So, what was the most remarkable memory you have when we think about Anders as a public figure, as a person who really tries to engage?

Michael

Back from 2004–2005, there was this big international debate about public sociology, inaugurated very much by Michael Burawoy, talking about different types of public sociologists, and I think Anders was very much a public sociologist in a number of different respects. First of all, he often participated in doing teaching late nights, sometimes in different parts of Denmark, for a very low pay in what is called in Danish the People's University, which is a programme where scholars from the university or elsewhere can offer lectures or courses for ordinary people or people who might just have an interest, and Anders did that very often, almost all over Denmark. He very much enjoyed going to these evenings and talking about many different things. And then he also ventured out to do a lot of lectures for practitioners: schoolteachers, the people working within the pedagogical profession, trying to share his knowledge and his ideas with them. So, he was very much on the road, in that way he was a very public sociologist.

He also was a columnist. He had his own column in the Danish newspaper called *Nordjyske*, in which he wrote a piece on a regular basis, very often inspired by something very every day, like during the COVID-19 pandemic, he wrote a piece about the importance of going out for a walk and clearing your head and the social use of walking as a way of thinking about the world, relating to the world, gaining some kind of resonance, so also in that way he was a very public sociologist.

Anders never became a public sociologist as someone who was preaching to others, what they are supposed to do. Many sociologists may do that. But Anders never told someone by being on the radio or the television what they needed to do. It was always with the question mark. In the end, what do you think? How do you think we can do this better? Can we do this in a different way? This was typical Anders, to ask questions in a critical way and then allow people to have their own thinking.

So, in that way, he was a very public sociologist, in the way he ventured around Denmark and the way he wrote many different pieces for Danish newspapers. I don't think he liked to be called an expert on anything, Anders was not an expert. He was more like someone with theoretical and also sometimes empirical knowledge who wanted to share it with other people in a generous way. He was not the philosopher king who was telling us how to live our lives. That was definitely not his ball game.

Bert

One could call him perhaps a question mark expert.

Michael

Yeah, that's a good expression.

Søren

It's important – at least for me – to underline that he wasn't public in the way as one usually thinks about public academic figures. He was publicly known for instance at schools and in mental health promotion, he helped with different reports, he aided in policies and so on, but he wasn't widely known. I think he was well-known at places that mattered to him and to his sort of crowd. He wasn't someone you would ask about just anything.

Michael

Anders was never in the business of public sociology because he wanted to make money. He didn't have that interest. When he said yes to something, showing up at

7:00 o'clock on a November evening in the middle of nowhere to do a presentation for ten schoolteachers, he did it because he really thought it was valuable in itself and not because it would make him popular, or he would get a lot of money for it. He felt a kind of inner urge to share his perspective with others. And in that way, he was not only a very generous person but also a humble person. He didn't do it for fame or fortune. He did it because he thought it was part of his scientific obligation to share his perspective with others.

Søren

The period after he died, I could really see it in my inbox. So often I was contacted about doing these sorts of things, it rose really quickly. I was really surprised by how many different things Anders was involved in. For instance, I got called up by a person who did theatre, participant theatre, and he was very passionate about that, and he spoke about how Anders was giving notes and advice. There were a lot of these sort of people who rang me and asked me to be involved with all sorts of different stuff that Anders was involved in, and it just really hit me how widespread Anders also engaged with the public. In so many – I wouldn't say strange ways – but in so many varying ways and some of it was very artistic, and some of it was, like Michael said, ten schoolteachers on a cold November evening. He was just very sort of spread out in a fascinating way.

Bert

This book on the performance society is that the last big solo piece he wrote or isn't that the case? Because connected to that question is, I wrote a chapter with Anders in the book you edited, Michael, and I know how difficult it can be to write a text together with somebody, but with Anders it was so easy. So doing a solo piece for him was perhaps less natural than doing a duo piece. Do you agree? He really enjoyed that.

Michael

Anders and I sometimes took some time off and we went to a small hotel in the northern part of Jutland. We went there I think five, six, seven times over the past three or four years of his life. We were up there for two days, and we listened to Pink Floyd while we were sitting in a room, and we listened to it very loudly. And then we would sit writing on our own stuff and also do some collaborative work. We would normally have a book; we were editing or had a piece we were writing together. And I know, towards the end, Anders was working on a book on anxiety. I don't think he finished it. I think it was quite close to turning into being a full book, but I read parts of it when we were sitting in this hotel, and we discussed it and talked about it, and I actually don't know what happened to that manuscript. It must be on a computer somewhere. Perhaps it should just stay there. I'm not sure it's something that Anders necessarily would like us to read, but I know he was working very much on anxiety towards the end.

And I share Bert's experience: Anders was for me very easy to work with. Sometimes we actually wrote a full piece and then we said this is my piece, but it contains our joint ideas. Anders could write a piece and then I was in it without really having written any of it. And the other way around. Because we thought about things in a very similar way. But, on the other hand, Anders and I were extremely different in our approach to the world, in our politics, in many different areas. We had many conversations about the normativity of social science and issues like that. So, although Anders was easy to work with and things almost by magic just wrote itself, we were also very different.

Carmen

Following on from what Michael just said about Anders' relationship to difference, I think it gave him kind of a frisson, a sort of electricity and energy as well, because Anders talked about working with psychologists and other people, some of whom were at times very inscribed within the kind of diagnostic psychiatry model that Anders was critical of, but still he enjoyed that collaboration across the gaps; he had the intellectual curiosity and also personal generosity to be able to engage with differences in a much more flexible way than many intellectuals and academics that I have met.

Kieran

I never met anybody who could handle criticism as gracefully as Anders. I've been at many conferences and symposia with him, and you know how sometimes people take up a position just to be contrarian, but Anders always responded generously and openly, and I've never seen him take offense or give offense in such a situation. Anders had an amazing ability to divest his ego from it. In our highly egotistical academic profession Anders could just suspend that. I remember consciously saying to myself, 'I wish I could do that' and modelling myself after Anders thereafter.

Søren

I recently published an article with Ole Jacob Madsen, a Norwegian professor of psychology, a lot of it is actually somewhat critical of Anders' work on achievement culture, because our argument is, in short, that it's a very sort of class blind perspective when it comes to applying it to youth. When we started it Ole Jacob asked me: Are you sure you want to write this? Anders is your supervisor, and so on. I remember during my supervision Anders and I would discuss these things, and he was very enthusiastic when I criticized his work and engaged with his work like this. So, it was almost like the more I could attack his work the more excited he got.

And then another thing: there was a moment in supervision when I was a bit stuck – and a couple of weeks ago I gave this advice to another PhD supervisor who had a PhD student who was a bit stuck as well – I was really in doubt about at which schools I should do my interviews and how I should approach this, and I thought about it so much and was afraid of contacting the schools and so on, and then he said: 'Søren, sometimes you just gotta do something'. And I did something.

Michael

When I remember Anders and the way he was working he was not a systematic person, he was very open minded. He drew on so many different sources of inspiration: Zygmunt Bauman. Charles Taylor, old critical theory, new critical theory, and literary writings, Michelle Houellebecq, stuff like that. So, in that way, he was very eclectic. It was a qualified eclecticism. He took whatever he could use to build what he needed to build. He was like an intellectual craftsman. He wanted to construct something, and he used the materials that were available.

And Anders was very critical of the contemporary university system. He regarded it as an instrumental machine in which the people who were working there, but also the students, were being put through a big machine. If you remember the video from the song 'The Wall' by Pink Floyd, you have this big meat chopper, and the students fall into the chopper, and they come out as minced meat all of them: that was our critical image of the modern university system. So, in order to live with this system and survive within it, Anders was extremely keen to have international connections, and this is where all of you come in. You were Anders' big escape. You were his exile. He thoroughly loved his Irish connection and his colleagues in Europe elsewhere. For him, this was the life-giving energy in his academic life, because he was so sick and tired of ordinary university life. To Anders, the Irish connection, as I call it, was perhaps one of the most important things to him, but also the SPCC group. For him, without that, I'm not quite sure he would have been here as long as he was.

Bert

Typically Anders is the following as well, I think. In his text on depression, he refers a few times to Ehrenberg and also to Dan Blazer. And he agrees with Ehrenberg's analysis, but partly. Because when Ehrenberg sort of suggests that we are living in a changed situation but not in a worsened situation, Anders says 'No!'. And then Dan Blazer, totally the opposite: we are living in a situation of hopelessness and disintegration. And then he says as well: 'No!'. You know, in between the two. That is very much the way he was thinking. Let's recognize the malaise and at the same time refuse to think that we don't have an exit. That sort of links with his whole appearance, like you once described, Kieran: this tall kind of Viking guy, so full of life and so full of fun, so collaborative, addressing all these complex, dark and serious themes.

Sabine

Did Anders somehow found like a school, or are people working with this stuff?

Søren

I think a lot of students are very interested in engaging with his work. I think especially the achievement society book from 2016 is very popular among students. Both students early in their studies as those writing their master theses. I think Anders also had a sort of a fan club. I think he inspired a lot of students to work with the achievement culture because it struck a nerve with them.

Carmen

I think Anders also has what you might call a virtual legacy here in Ireland, because some years ago, I took over a sociology of mental health module, and at about that time, I was training as a psychotherapist. I had many interesting conversations with Anders about psychotherapy and sociology, which prompted Anders to give me his critique of psychotherapy. When I started teaching the sociology of mental health module, there were 15 students. Using Anders' essays on grief, anxiety, depression as case studies, and Anders' other themes and critiques of diagnostic psychiatry, alternative theoretical, historical, philosophical points of view and so on, the class went from 15 students to 125. I attribute that to how Anders' work resonated with students – they loved his work! It was probably 50/50 in terms of gender and many of the students were international. I was really happy to see the level at which these students, many from Psychology, many from other universities in continental Europe, were engaging with Anders' material in a really enthusiastic way. I love Anders' clarity. His nonjargonistic explanation of complex concepts really resonates.

Søren

I completely agree with Carmen and feel his writing style resonates very well. The few times I've heard him give public lectures, he would always start by saying that his sort of validation was if you could nod along with what he was saying and feel it in your own sort of way. And I think that's also why he was very popular among students because the achievement pressure and so on they related very strongly to that. And this was equally true for both male and female students.

Bert

A question about the book Anders wrote on the performance society. Since we can't read Danish, the question is if it entails a sort of integration of the themes he addressed earlier, like depression and grief and such. Are they integrated in this book, or is it more focused on certain of these themes? For us it is important to know to be able to position that book.

Michael

It is, of course, difficult to know exactly what Anders thought about the chronology of his own work. First of all, for me it's important to say I don't think the translation of the book title to *The Performance Society* is accurate. It should be translated as *The Achievement Society*, because if it's called *The Performance Society*, people will somehow relate it to a dramaturgical or Goffman kind of thinking, which is definitely not what Anders is doing. I think the fact that you need to achieve something with yourself, with your life, is a constant pressure on the shoulders of people and perhaps particularly young people. This is what Anders wants to do with the book. I reread parts of his PhD from 2007 immediately after he passed away. And I hadn't actually read the thesis as such, or in any comprehensive way earlier. But I think there is a connection between what he did in his PhD thesis, which is basically one of his earliest published pieces of work, and *The Achievement Society*. This interest in finding out what it is that actually characterizes contemporary society. His concern with doing a critical diagnosis of society. Anders regarded contemporary society as being almost marinated in problems. There are problems all over the place or at least people would experience the world as full of problems, full of dangers, full of pressures, full of things that they were unable to live up to. And you can see that in his PhD thesis, which deals with depression, but also large chunks of *The Achievement Society* deal with the same issues.

But in the time Anders was writing his PhD thesis some of the reference points in the achievement society book had not been published yet, for example, some of the ideas by Ehrenberg, and Bauman. So, in that way, there is also a new theoretical dimension in *The Achievement Society*. Sometimes we look back upon a person's writings as if it took place within 24 hours, but from Anderson's PhD thesis to *The Achievement Society*, it's actually a decade and a lot of theoretical work was published in that connection. I think if Anders was to write another *Achievement Society*, a second version or a reissue, the inspirational work of Andreas Reckwitz and Hartmut Rosa would most certainly be more present in that revised book.

Søren

I think indeed Rosa in particular would be very present. He's only mentioned briefly in *The Achievement Society*, and I can see the connection between Anders' PhD thesis and the involvement after that and how it ended up in *The Achievement Society*. I agree with Michael that it should be translated as 'achievement' and not 'performance' because I've actually had reviewers who were confused when I said performance because they thought of Goffman and so on in that sort of symbolic interactionist way.

I also think he was very much inspired by Svend Brinkmann's book, two years earlier, *Stå fast*, which is translated as *Stand Firm*. He was very much inspired by combining all these perspectives in a way that appealed to the broader public. The way he wrote *The Achievement Society* was very different from his thesis and his other articles and his work on disenfranchisement, which he did after his thesis with Rasmus Willig. He had an interest in making the achievement society book more publicly available, in a broad sense.

Michael

He wanted to be read also outside the academic community by practitioners, he wanted to reach out and install some kind of critical thinking in these people. And he actually achieved that with *The Achievement Society*. So, he was very, very proud of it.

And I remember when he was writing it – I have to admit – I was rather sceptical whether or not he would be able to finish it, because he talked so much about it, and I never really saw anything apart from some sections. And all of a sudden, then, the book was handed into the publishing house, and it came out pretty quickly after that, which means also that the reviewers from the publishing house had a positive understanding of it. But I also know, and this is perhaps not so well known, that he had a few people in Denmark who were a thorn in the side of Anders, who didn't like the way he was writing. There were also voices out there who strongly disagreed with Anders and who thought he was a kind of a left-wing scholar who had a special agenda of telling us how to live our lives. And I think this is a gross misunderstanding.

Bert

Could one say, Søren, that the book you two did on the achievement society for secondary school kids, or at least a part of it, is sort of a second version of *The Achievement Society*?

Søren

Yes, I think what was added in particular was the idea of achievement as something that can also be liberating. Emancipation through achievement. Within Danish politics, there are a lot of debates where one side would argue that we need to focus less on achievement and the other side will say achievement is a good thing. But what we try to show in this book – and that is more Anders than me – is that achievement needn't be viewed as something either good or bad if we just sort of widen the scope of what a valid achievement is and what achievements are supposed to look like. A lot of these young people struggle to meet a very specific achievement formula every day, all day. In my interviews, for instance, they talk about doing a gap year to heighten their social qualifications, so they will be better in their next education and so on. The idea of achievement emancipation is to help the local schools and the local context widen the scope of what an achievement can look like. It is actually very liberating to achieve in an environment that isn't as strict in focus on achievement in one way. So, in that way, one can inspire curiosity and pursuing of interests. And I think if Anders were to write the book again that part and focus would take up even more space. And I know he just got funding to pursue it further, within a pedagogical sense, but sadly he never got to that.

The phrase 'achievement culture' has become a very integral part of everyday Danish language, and some of it is definitely attributed to Anders' work. But Anders was also a bit sceptical of using the word achievement culture because it sort of indicates that it's a problem among youth. And then we were asked to write this book on achievement culture among youth. So, we started off by saying this is a broader societal issue. So, when we talk about achievement culture, that's what we mean.

Bert

Me being a psychologist and a philosopher, I know about the tensions between, let's say, the empirical angle and the theoretical angle. Was there such a tension in Anders? Is there an empirical Anders and a theoretical Anders, and did they get along together well?

Michael

I don't think there's a split in his work in that way. And the main reason is that Anders did little empirical work. Anders was using existing material, sometimes he also did interviews, focus group interviews, and I think with Søren there was a collaboration that was more empirical, but most people when they talk about Anders and when they remember his work, remember him much more as the theoretical Anders. He was not really that concerned with empirical data as far as I remember him, and as far as I read his work, he was much more concerned with theoretical work, conceptual work, constructing a critical diagnosis of society. And then providing conceptual ideas that other people could test or use in their empirical work.

Søren

But I remember we did all these focus groups interviews together and he was actually really good at it. I was really inspired by how he interviewed. But I agree with Michael, he encouraged others to sort of pursue and also criticize and work with his ideas empirically, me included.

And I also remember – because I think the critique for lack of empirical data also stuck with him in some way – one time when he came into my office, I was sitting with a colleague who was also very quantitative, and he had this grin on his face, and he said: I just came from this conference, and he talked about this scale that measured self-silencing. It's originally constructed for explaining the higher rate of depression in women from a more sort of social, cultural perspective. And I remembered that he said we need to do something with the scale, and we did this translation and then we tested it and so on. I've never published anything on it yet, but then he laughed, and he said, look at me, thinking in quantitative data! It was a really funny conversation.

Sabine

Michael, earlier you mentioned a theme that you wanted to talk about: Anders and the climate change. I remember once, before we had the conference in Frankfurt, he came by train, and we walked through the city and had a long conversation about all this. And this was a long time ago, before it was all over the news. Now we're all pretty aware of what we're doing. So maybe you can share something.

Michael

The climate was very important for him. He also stopped eating meat. In our friendship and in our work relationship he was the green person, and I was the black person, because I didn't take the climate problem as seriously as Anders did, but for him this was, besides the achievement society, the main issue in his last year. The climate situation and how we could create a more sustainable way of living in contemporary society. So, it was a problem for him that he was so principled, but that was typically Anders. He couldn't take the plane. And I would try to persuade him many times. But he wouldn't do it.

He was very principled about this. He didn't want to take the plane to Copenhagen either, although he could fly quite easily from Aalborg to Copenhagen. He could also fly easily from Billund or elsewhere in Denmark, but he wanted to go by car or by train, and that actually made it difficult for him the last few years to go anywhere because it would take up so much of his time. And Anders was a family man, as you know. So, to stay away a whole week because he was going to take the train to go through Europe was not an option.

Domonkos

I was talking recently with a journalist, and she said: if someone starts working with questions like depression, anxiety, there must be some personal motivation in it. I don't know if you are aware what could have been this personal motivation for Anders.

Søren

I think some of it was perhaps – and I know we talked about Anders being political or not- also his interest in critiques of neoliberalism and capitalism. I can see that clearly in his work, so it's political in that sense, but I don't know about his personality traits, or something like that, which would make him pursue that. I think your guess is as good as mine. But for me, I think it's mainly the argument that we can make up a society that causes illness. I think that was his main motivation and understanding, the potential for illness within contemporary society. I don't think it was necessarily depression, or something like that, that he had close contact with. I think it was more the question of how we have ended up with a society that causes specific kinds of illness. I think that was his motivation.

Carmen

And I think he also had a quiet kind of concern for people made vulnerable by neoliberalism and capitalism and that's something that shines through his work, his concern for workers that are misrecognized and mistreated in certain ways and people that are problematically labelled by various aspects of psychiatric culture and so on.

Kieran

I remember two formative moments. One was in Cork a long time ago, when we first started to talk about social pathologies of contemporary civilization, and we had the first conferences, in Aalborg in 2010 and the second one in Cork in 2011. And they really worked. We had come up with 'social pathologies' and 'contemporary civilization', a big picture frame. And I can't say that it was I that coined the terms, or Anders, for in any situation like that, in a conversation, it's very difficult to say: was that your word or was that my word? But it worked!

And a next time we had a conversation like this, I think it was in Rotterdam, and we were talking about the title for the book that later became *Late Modern Subjectivity and Its Discontents*. We were trying to get a title to work. And our conversation was working off Freud's title *Civilization and Its Discontents*, for that's the level at which Anders wanted to conceive of these issues. Not topic by topic, 'depression' or 'anxiety' or something like that. Anders was reaching for a vision that was broader and deeper and more inclusive and synthetic. How can we see all of these problems – depression, anxiety, troubles of identity and anomie, loss of meaningfulness, voicelessness and new modalities of power as a cumulative, recursive thing, very much related to the social forms of late modern, late capitalist society. Anders wanted to find something encompassing, not a 'frame' in any rigid sense, but a kind of paradigm shift away from the diagnostic and individualizing nosology of diseases towards a vision that was more philosophically, sociologically and anthropologically inspired, holistic and critical, broad and deep, addressing the human condition and questions of meaning under conditions of late modern global capitalism and neoliberalism.

Bert

What was also underlined by this conversation – and we needed or shouldn't go deep into that, of course – because it popped into my mind, saying that Anders refused to accept that there is no exit, and of course, that's not what happened to him. What was underlined by this conversation is this is an incomprehensible thing. It's even more incomprehensible now, and I think we should leave it, we should leave it like that. We should leave it a mystery.

Kieran

Indeed. To me, there are kind of two Anders. That Anders, who is like overflowing with life and energy and the joy of it. Being so collaborative and funny and all. But then also there's an Anders we missed somehow in there. You know, all re-search is me-search as they say, and somehow none of us here were quite aware of that. But it doesn't for a minute detract from the other Anders, the Anders who was a life affirming… no, a life force!

Sabine

Maybe the last question we could address is: What should we take from his work and put into sociology? What would be the most striking thing to really take into account, to really think about, which could also coin the thinking?

Michael

Anders had a following, every year there would be three, four or five students who would hang around. That would also relate, I think, to the fact that he took such a keen interest in the climate change debate, which many of our students on the master courses would find interesting. But what Søren is saying about *The Achievement Society*, that is the book most students will associate with Anders' professional work, and I think this is also the book that will live on for a very long time. That is basically his legacy.

Søren

Acknowledging that within Danish, Scandinavian society, broadly speaking, young people are suffering from an achievement culture. I think Anders had a huge part in drawing that debate and qualifying it, and seeing how these achievement demands have spread out among youth and how this has affected the rapid decline in youth mental health. Today the word 'achievement culture' – in Danish it's one word – is very much melded into everyday language. Anders had a huge role in that, without being a public figure in the classical way. But among schoolteachers, among municipal policy making and so on, I think Anders has had a huge influence.

Bert

Including pointers for how to deal with that, because that is what your book for secondary school kids is about?

Søren

Yeah, that's the 'emancipation through achievement' idea. We write in the book that this term is actually somewhat still in the making, and we're very open about that. I've continued to work on it a little bit. I have ideas about taking it into an international audience, but again it's still, like we say in Danish, not fully baked yet, so we can't really take it out of the oven.

Kieran

I would hope that the idea of 'social pathologies of contemporary civilization' would carry Anders' work into the future. We had been discussing together, before Anders death, and afterwards, in the wake of his loss, how we have to find some way of living well or living positively. Besides presenting critique we must also speak to the idea of the Good Life; not in any kind of naive way but helping to make a turn away from the darkness, the darkness that engulfed our friend, and I think we'd be doing justice to the spirit of Anders' life and our friendship to help to make that turn that he himself in the end couldn't quite make.

Index

For Product Safety Concerns and Information please contact our EU representative GPSR@taylorandfrancis.com
Taylor & Francis Verlag GmbH, Kaufingerstraße 24, 80331 München, Germany

www.ingramcontent.com/pod-product-compliance
Ingram Content Group UK Ltd.
Pitfield, Milton Keynes, MK11 3LW, UK
UKHW020004200926
475702UK00015B/2468
* 9 7 8 1 0 3 2 7 1 4 3 8 7 *